W9-BHN-333

THE NEW DEAL
The Critical Issues

Alan Butvinik
155 w 27 st.
BAYONNE. N.I.
07002

201 4360053

CRITICAL ISSUES IN AMERICAN HISTORY SERIES

Barton J. Bernstein, *General Editor*

Robert F. Berkhofer, Jr., *The American Revolution*
* Gordon S. Wood, *The Constitution and the Confederation*
* William W. Freehling, *The Civil War*
Sheldon Hackney, *Populism*
* Marilyn Blatt Young, *American Expansionism*
David M. Kennedy, *Progressivism*
Joan Hoff Wilson, *The Twenties*
Otis L. Graham, Jr., *The New Deal*
* Barton J. Bernstein, *The Origins of the Cold War*

* Books not yet published. Additional titles to be announced.

THE NEW DEAL
The Critical Issues

Edited by

OTIS L. GRAHAM, JR.
University of California, Santa Barbara

 LITTLE, BROWN AND COMPANY   BOSTON

COPYRIGHT © 1971 BY LITTLE, BROWN AND COMPANY (INC.)

ALL RIGHTS RESERVED. NO PART OF THIS BOOK MAY BE REPRODUCED IN ANY FORM OR BY ANY ELECTRONIC OR MECHANICAL MEANS INCLUDING INFORMA- TION STORAGE AND RETRIEVAL SYSTEMS WITHOUT PERMISSION IN WRITING FROM THE PUBLISHER, EXCEPT BY A REVIEWER WHO MAY QUOTE BRIEF PASSAGES IN A REVIEW.

LIBRARY OF CONGRESS CATALOG CARD NUMBER: 72-161420

FOURTH PRINTING

Published simultaneously in Canada by Little, Brown & Company (Canada) Limited

PRINTED IN THE UNITED STATES OF AMERICA

CONTENTS

v

INTRODUCTION

Teachers of history are often asked, usually in a tone of some irritation, "Why can't historians agree?" Such a question reveals a distinct lack of sympathy for our difficulties. We ought to become more militant about them. Each practicing historian is a specialist in these difficulties, but none more so than those of us who try to understand and write about the recent past. The historiography of the New Deal exemplifies the hazards of our discipline, and especially the modernist end of it.

Not long ago I heard myself advising a graduate student against undertaking dissertation research on the New Deal. It is full of traps for the scholar. This is true not simply because of its economic and bureaucratic complexity. Even if its issues had been as relatively simple as those of the 1830s, the 1930s would still be formidable for the historian. Many witnesses are alive to contradict him. Worse, in the center of the controversy is the liberal state, an institution that has shaped the lives of all Americans for thirty years and is yet surrounded by intense emotions. Historians confronting parts or all of the New Deal must work in a setting of the jealous memories of participants and eye-witnesses, amid continual political battles to dismantle or extend the Roosevelt achievement. Live people, live issues — the wary scholar would scout these threats to his calm and objectivity, and do a biography of some nineteenth-century Vice-President.

Fortunately, there are scholars whose desire to understand and clarify the recent past has overruled their natural preference for working in fields where passion has somewhat cooled and most blind alleys have already been discovered. The literature on the New Deal is extensive, and strikingly coherent. But one also finds in this literature chastening reminders of the dangers of moving in so closely behind the journalists.

For at least fifteen years after Roosevelt died the New Deal remained central to American politics. Politics continued to turn upon the questions of the 1930s — whether the government should regulate the economy; whether deficit spending was an acceptable federal policy; whether the government should subsidize special groups (that had not been subsidized before); whether the government should provide the jobless and indigent with minimal economic security; whether the government should support education, scientific research, and the arts; whether the government should occasionally enter the field of production and selling (i.e. electric power); whether the government should be internationalist in foreign policy. The Truman and Eisenhower years reverberated with debate along these familiar lines, and as late as 1964 a Presidential election seemed to turn on whether or not to repeal the New Deal. This election finally ended public debate over the New Deal, and it is now clear that pragmatically the governmental arrangements of the 1930s were permanently established by the end of the first Eisenhower administration. But whether one judges by the tacit acquiescence of Republican administrators or by the end of serious ideological conflict, it took many years both for the nation to firmly authorize the state to remain activist in economic regulation and welfare responsibility and for the debates to shift from essences to details.

As long as the New Deal was under fundamental attack, scholars were unable, with the rarest exceptions, to break free of this political debate. Written history often resembled an academic extension of the political war going on in the country. On the right a group of publicists, ex-politicians, and scholars argued that the New Deal had been a Bad Thing, a threat to our liberties and an unnecessary and dangerous European importation; slightly to their left was a liberal centrist group who described the New Deal as a Good Thing, an improvised solution to economic and political crisis, and one that preserved the essentials of American democracy.

This argument never seemed to be going anywhere. The liberal side attracted better talent, but if it appeared to be gradually winning the argument it was less because the liberals found anything new and irresistible to say than because the actual course of American history was making the conservatives look ludicrous and unreasonable. The dangerous New Deal went unrepealed, but life went on, American capitalism remained robust, and the welfare state somehow never materialized as a police state. The imagined horribles of the corruption of American character and the dissolution of the Constitution never occurred. A generation after the 1930s, the profit system was still unshaken; the rich were very rich, and the poor very poor. One might be forgiven the feeling that in the late 1950s, if not earlier, scholars' disputes about the New Deal were not very interesting: of course Roosevelt and the New Dealers had been attractive, decent men; of course the New Deal was not socialism; of course its improvisations had been in the American tradition; of course it had strengthened rather than weakened the economy and the political system.

The conservative critics of the New Deal, in disputing these issues, attacked along unpromising lines. The conservative point of view virtually disappeared from scholarly discussion, but the liberals, undoubtedly aware that the Taft and Eisenhower Republicans might well try to dismantle the New Deal, continued their arguments that the New Deal had been a great success and ought to be kept. In the late 1950s, in scholarly circles if not in politics, there was a period of near-unanimity. Always timely, the Harvard historian Arthur M. Schlesinger, Jr., administered the coup to the anti–New Deal tradition with the publication (in 1957, 1959, and 1960) of three volumes in his *The Age of Roosevelt* — stylistically brilliant, laudatory, convincing. The opponents were routed. For the excitement of a critical view, one could only turn to those two fine critical portraits of Roosevelt, Richard Hofstadter's sketch in *The American Political Tradition* (1948) and James M. Burns' biography, *Roosevelt: The Lion and the Fox* (1956). In the absence of real controversy, scholars and teachers busied themselves with the question of whether the New Deal was evolutionary or revolutionary. Since friends and enemies lined up on both sides, it was not entirely clear why this issue was so vital. To paraphrase another Roosevelt, it was the only controversy we had.

Then came the 1960s, with their dramatic alteration of American politics. In national politics the right (or most of it) finally absorbed the New Deal. Congressional Republicans during the Democratic administrations of John F. Kennedy and Lyndon Johnson quarreled over appropriations and priorities but did not raise any fundamental challenge to a broad federal role in national life. The Nixon administration, which brought Republicans into office in 1969, adopted New Deal internationalism, made no attack upon labor, trimmed but did not eliminate spending for poverty, agriculture, research, and education, proposed even more economic security through a reform of the welfare system that included a guaranteed annual income, increased social security benefits, and grandly ignored the un-American governmental power and fertilizer business in the Tennessee Valley. Despite the talk of laissez-faire ideologists like Barry Goldwater and William F. Buckley, the Republican party in office accepted the liberal governmental framework. In 1970, one was struck by the lack of important differences between the last five American Presidents. The New Deal was safe.

That is, it was safe from the right, from any substantial possibility that the New Deal regulatory and welfare apparatus would be dismantled.[1*] Men of conservative social outlook gradually accepted the fact that they must and easily could live with the New Deal, and some even became its defenders, with only occasional grumbling about the welfare load. But in these years when the propertied influential classes were putting aside their hostility to a more active government and learning to accept the postwar political economy, the spirit of dissent and criticism, instead of disappear-

* See p. 180 for notes to this article.

ing, shifted over to the left. In the 1960s America was overtaken by a swarm of unsolved social problems for which the New Deal solutions had not yet proven adequate — persistent zones of poverty, racial conflicts and disparities, urban disorder, environmental despoliation. Angry books, illustrated articles, television documentaries, congressional committees, even impeccably establishment presidential commissions discovered malnutrition, peonage, prison brutality, rats in slum apartments, unemployed and unemployable millions. FDR's bottom one-third was still there! And after all those New Deal laws and agencies had been in force for thirty years, after we had been told of the blessings of affluence. John F. Kennedy proposed more federal spending on our social estate and more help for the poor, but intellectuals in the 1960s were divided between enthusiasm for more of the New Deal, and the suspicion that the persistence of these 1930-ish problems suggested the inadequacy of New Deal solutions. The experience of living through the 1960s produced respect for the hidden strengths of the capitalist system and for the impregnability of the "individual freedoms" of businessmen and southern whites. As the 1960s wore on, the government seemed increasingly inept despite its size, too feeble to protect the public from the private forces that were bringing such deadly dislocations to our cities, our economy, our countryside.

In this setting, discussion of the New Deal was fundamentally changed. The New Deal now had critics on the left — not just because more and more young scholars were radical, but also because time had carried many intellectuals beyond the liberal positions of the 1930s and beyond the reach of the Roosevelt charisma. When the critics had been on the right there was no close examination of the redistribution of money and power, since one of the conservatives' assumptions was that the New Deal was socialist in effect if not in name. But when scholars with strongly democratic sympathies began to scrutinize the New Deal there were hard questions about the actual degree of social change it had brought. The left of course has its own obsessive abstractions, but one of its intellectual virtues is a deep interest in the hard facts about the distribution of money and power in society. Had the New Deal redistributed income and wealth, political and economic power? In the struggle for federal favors, had business groups actually done as well or better than the unemployed, the old, the unemployable? Was the New Deal tax system progressive or regressive? What was the financial impact of unionism? Who were the beneficiaries of federal programs in agriculture? What was the size and nature of subsidies to extractive industry, the airlines, the merchant marine, the banks? Journalists and socialists asked such questions in the 1930s, but neither they nor interested scholars knew enough about the New Deal to give satisfactory answers. When these questions were asked again in the 1960s the shelves were filling with monographs that put the raw data in order. The combination of new perspectives and better historical evidence transformed the interpretation of the Roosevelt era.

The first sign that the New Deal was to be examined in the 1960s more critically by those who shared its social sympathies and purposes than by those who worried about capitalism came with the publication in 1963 of William E. Leuchtenburg's *Franklin D. Roosevelt and the New Deal: 1932–1940.* The book was a brilliant synthesis, compact and readable, but it was noticed at least as much for its critical stance as for its scholarly and stylistic virtues. Not since Broadus Mitchell's *Depression Decade* (1947) had a leading scholar found so many shortcomings in the New Deal record. At most points Leuchtenburg concluded that the situation had not permitted much more than the New Dealers had achieved, but his candid attention to the limited effects of New Deal recovery and reform measures sharply influenced interested scholars. It also signaled more critical essays to come, from men of less moderation and, in many cases, fewer hours of research.

Before the decade was over a diverse group of writers had attacked the New Deal from the left, making Leuchtenburg's 1963 book seem, by contrast, indulgent. Young radicals Brad Wiley and Jacob Cohen published sharp criticisms in the New Left press; Howard Zinn, author of a book on Fiorello LaGuardia, wrote a strongly critical essay on the New Deal that he published as an introduction to a book of primary materials on the 1930s; Barton Bernstein, a young Harvard-trained historian now at Stanford, published a well-researched essay in 1968, the most substantial New Left critique yet to appear; and in 1967 Paul Conkin, author of a prize-winning monograph on the New Deal community program, brought out a long interpretive essay that sadly logged the New Deal's failures. These authors pushed New Deal labor, relief, and social insurance policies to the background; they were much more interested in damage done to marginal farmers by AAA, the timidity of New Deal tax programs, the lavish aid given to creditors through the RFC and other agencies, the limited coverage and regressive financing of the Social Security program, the discrimination practiced against blacks in virtually all relief programs, the subsidies to businesses of all kinds, the failure to bring economic recovery.

Paralleling these efforts were numerous monographs whose findings added more dark tones to a portrait of the Roosevelt years that now stressed the defeat of liberal hopes. After thirty years the leftists of the 1930s — Norman Thomas, Mauritz Hallgren, John Dewey, the *New Republic* and *Common Sense* groups — had found their scholarly (and some not so

scholarly) inheritors. The liberal centrists by the end of the 1960s had a
new intellectual opposition; the argument was now between the center and
the left. Was the New Deal, as incremental reform within a capitalistic
framework, the only middle way between totalitarian extremes — and a
reasonably workable middle way at that? Or was it a device, witting or un-
witting, of conservatives, who used its showy campaigns and appealing
rhetoric to put down pressures for real reform and inadvertently perpetuate, perhaps even strengthen, an intolerable social system?

Thus we approach the fortieth anniversary of Roosevelt's inauguration, with historians at least as divided over the meaning of the New Deal
as were Roosevelt and Landon in 1936. Does this historiographical record
offer ground for encouragement or does it confirm the doubts of those who
say that the writing of recent history, like journalism and polemics, is
writing in sand? Both feelings in differing degrees are justified. First let us
accentuate the positive one. The accumulated literature on the New Deal
encourages the belief that historians can record the recent past with lasting
results. Much of the monographic writing is of excellent quality and durability, and, more important, there has been progress in the difficult task of
interpreting the whole. Disagreement among contending views has not exactly diminished, but over the last three decades it has moved from center-
right to center-left, and this is a clear gain. The right, in discussing the
New Deal, had a metaphysical bent and liked to argue that the expanded
governmental regulation of formerly private affairs was the End of Capitalism and Liberty as they had been enjoyed. The right riveted its eyes
on the laws and agencies of the liberal state and saw in the imposing legislative and bureaucratic structure of the New Deal a sort of European
tyranny. The liberals focused on the size and broadened agenda of the
government and interpreted the New Deal legislative record as a vast protection for the disadvantaged and the general public.

But in recent years, strong leftist interest in the location of money
and power and the conditions of life for working and marginal economic
classes has increasingly encouraged scholars to go behind the laws and agencies to measure who got what as a result of federal policy in the 1930s.
Such measurement almost invariably discloses less change in fundamentals
than the changed forms would imply. The scholars of the so-called New
Left specialize in this skepticism of formal gains, but they have not monop-
olized it. Liberal historians such as William Leuchtenburg, in *Franklin D.
Roosevelt and the New Deal* (1963); Frank Freidel, in *The New Deal in
Historical Perspective* (1959, 1965); David E. Conrad, in *The Forgotten
Farmers* (1965); James T. Patterson, in *The New Deal and the States* (1969),
probe hard to ascertain the actual size of New Deal accomplishments in

relief and redistribution and do not evade evidence of disappointing results.

As historians of both left and liberal-center show a sharpened interest in the realities of economic, political, and social power and advantages, scholarship is converging toward a certain consensus. The emerging
ground of agreement is not merely that the New Deal "saved capitalism" —
no liberal ever questioned this, though he may not have dwelt lovingly on
the point — but that the New Deal, while it *felt* revolutionary to contemporaries and while it made more changes in the functions of American government in five years than had been made in any comparable period since
the Founding, did not make changes that would justify that imprecise
word "revolutionary." In part this was because they fell short of some of
their goals, in part because their goals were not revolutionary. The New
Deal attempted and failed to ensure economic security for all, cradle to
grave; to sufficiently control the activities of enterprisers so as to eliminate
monopoly and the exploitation of men and environment; to shape political
institutions so that majorities could effectively focus their power; to foster
a cooperative ethic. It never intended to equalize wealth and income, to
achieve racial equality, to abolish or fundamentally alter capitalism. New
Deal–induced social changes fell far, far short of these ends, despite unprecedented governmental activity. And, since many of these ends were
those to which the New Dealers rolled up their sleeves in 1933, Paul Conkin
is surely right that a note of sadness and defeat is a part of the New Deal
story. This note was absent until the 1960s (except in the writing of Rexford Tugwell), and its appearance, not only in the writings of the New
Left but in the work of liberal authors like William Leuchtenburg, is the
surest sign that the argument over "revolution" has ended.

Although one need not expect a diplomatic protocol expressing a
consensus on the degree of social change effected by the New Deal and
signed by representatives from all historical factions, agreement is implicit
in the literature of the last ten years. Retrospect allowed historians to appreciate the durability of the class and attitude structures in America. In
the critical atmosphere of the 1960s, liberal scholars examined and reduced
their assessment of the New Deal's achievement in altering these structures
and raised a generation of young, radical scholars who wrote essays to ensure that this reduction was not understated. The outlines of the New Deal
achievement are now reasonably clear. There was no sweeping success in
income redistribution, elimination of poverty, organization of the unorganized, restraint of corporate power; there were barely measurable advances toward economic recovery and racial justice; there were modest steps
in organizing industrial labor in the northern cities, in underwriting the

economic security of landowning farmers and the unemployed, in liberal-izing the Democratic party, in restoring "faith" in ailing political and eco-nomic institutions. The primary issue now is, was this achievement a credit to the men who managed it or a permanent indictment of them and their ideas?

The writers of so-called radical history — Howard Zinn, Paul Con-kin, and Barton Bernstein — framed and pushed forward this new issue in the 1960s. Their stance is critical, and a critical tone can only rest on the argument that a better performance was possible. The liberal school has not capitulated. An article by Jerold Auerbach in 1969 reflects a widely shared conviction, that the New Deal achievement, however modest when measured against ideal standards, was admirable when measured against the circumstances of the 1930s. Personally, I vastly prefer this new contro-versy, and expect the 1970s to be an exciting time in New Deal scholarship. We are forced back to fundamental questions: are we to pass judgment, and, if so, by what standards is the past to be judged? Even so, we cannot fail to notice that the overtones of contemporary political and ethical com-mitments are still as strong as in the 1940s and 1950s, when the New Deal's political jeopardy charged historical discussion with such passion. The New Deal is still recent history, with all the distorting pressures that that in-volves. Liberalism is still a central issue in our political life.

I have compiled this anthology to present the best and most recent literature on the New Deal. But it is also intended to explore how men write the history of recent events. Like all history, recent history rests on factual evidence. Far more than is the case with events of other centuries, the interpretation of recent periods is influenced by contemporary pressures. Perhaps this anthology can clarify the effect of these pressures and their interaction with the "facts" of historical evidence. Ostensibly, I invite the student to think about the New Deal. Actually, he is invited to think about how to think clearly about the recent past.

In Part Two of this book, the reader will find seven interpretive essays on the New Deal. The essayists do not agree. In the usual anthology, the student is expected to choose the "correct" view. But I have found that students sometimes display a disconcerting coolness toward this assignment. They are shown that scholars come to different conclusions, but are not permitted to observe how they got there. This book is designed to lure the student into the discussion a bit farther than usual. Interpretive essays rest on evidence about the parts of the whole. Usually this evidence is invisible; only footnotes attest to its existence, and occasional quotations hint at its content. In Part One of this anthology the reader will find reprinted some of the evidence that undergirds the interpretive essays in Part Two. The evidence is drawn from primary and secondary sources, and illuminates the New Deal's effect in five areas: politics, labor, income distribution, race, and business.[2] In each area two views are offered, one emphasizing the sweep of New Deal social changes, the other underlining the limitations of its impact. After reading this evidence, the student may not know who is "correct," but he should begin to understand how intelligent men could have reached variant conclusions.

Special thanks are due to the General Editor of this series, Barton J. Bernstein, for his own valuable contribution to New Deal scholarship, and for his forebearance as I worked my way to conclusions at some variance from his own.

THE NEW DEAL
The Critical Issues

Part One
THE EVIDENCE

POLITICS: THE
REVOLUTIONARY NEW DEAL

The Revolt of the City

SAMUEL LUBELL

The argument that the New Deal brought revolutionary changes to American institutions and habits is most persuasive in the area of politics. Contemporaries knew that there had been no real economic recovery, and could conclude from the TNEC (Temporary National Economic Committee) hearings of 1938–41 that big business had not quite been brought to heel nor wealth significantly redistributed. But everyone agreed that the New Deal had fundamentally altered American politics, whether they thought of "politics" as the electoral process and formal institutions or more broadly as the functions and agenda of government.

The most dramatic political result of the New Deal was perhaps the transformation of the national Democratic party from a states-rights, fiscally conservative, minority party into a majority party with a strong urban base, lower-class sympathies, and a liberal, even a social-democratic program. The classic description of that change was written by journalist Samuel Lubell and is partially reprinted below. But this was only one political change among many. The size, power, and functions of the national government were greatly enlarged, and most of the new governmental duties were institutionalized in an invigorated executive branch. The Presidency gained authority at the expense of Congress and the Supreme Court and symbolized the new power of the American welfare state. New groups, ethnic and economic, gained access to the channels of political influence. In all, the New Deal seemed to have vastly accelerated the drift toward a centralized, powerful national government with democratic sym-

3

pathies and a clear mandate of intervention to ensure economic
security and social justice. It seemed to contemporaries, who
remembered the floundering Democratic party and irresolute
national government of the 1920s, the sharpest change in Amer-
ican political life since the days of Lincoln.

Much more than the third-term tradition was shattered when President Roosevelt took the oath of office again on Monday.

Who elected him? As in all elections, there were many crosscurrents, but the 1940 answer is simple and inescapable.

The little fellow elected him, because there are more of the little fellow and because he believed Mr. Roosevelt to be his friend and protector.

Roosevelt won by the vote of labor, unorganized as well as organized, plus that of the foreign born and their first and second generation descendants. And the Negro.

It was a class-conscious vote for the first time in American history, and the implications are portentous. The New Deal appears to have accomplished what the Socialists, the IWW and the Communists never could approach. It has drawn a class line across the face of American politics. That line seems to be there to stay. While thousands of wage earners, even voters on relief, voted for Willkie, we are talking here about groups as wholes.

Mr. Roosevelt is the first President to owe his election in such great measure to the teeming cities. On the farms and in the towns Mr. Willkie more than held his own. It was in the industrial centers that the Republican hopes were blacked out in factory smoke.

The Republican campaign had virtually no effect on this vote, the evidence argues. I doubt that anything Willkie might have done would have affected it. The election was not decided on the issues he debated, but on forces long at work — economic status, nationalities, birth rates. The rise of government as an employer on a scale rivaling the biggest business is a fourth. And the indications are that this vote might have gone to Roosevelt for a fourth or a fifth term as readily as for a third.

It is an American habit to forget an election quickly when the votes have been counted. We did so, as usual, and, so, few yet have grasped the

From pp. 43–44, 46–47, 57, 61–63 in *The Future of American Politics,*
Third Rev. Ed., by Samuel Lubell. Copyright © 1951, 1952, 1956, 1965
by Samuel Lubell. Reprinted by permission of Harper & Row, Publishers, Inc. This article originally appeared in *The Saturday Evening
Post* as "Post-Mortem: Who Elected Roosevelt?" Reprinted here by permission of *The Saturday Evening Post,* © 1941 The Curtis Publishing
Co.

fact that this was not just another election. The Republicans do not know what hit them; the Democrats, certainly as distinguished from the New Dealers, do not know what they hit the Republicans with. The New Deal has aimed at a bloodless revolution.

In 1940 it went a long way toward accomplishing it.

In numbers it was no great victory. Roosevelt won by the smallest plurality and the smallest percentage of the total vote since the neck-and-neck election of 1916. If his strength should diminish between now and 1944 at the same rate it did between 1936 and 1940, he would be beaten in 1944.

The opposition is taking comfort in these figures, but the 1940 vote upset the fundamentals of our old two-party system, and when the fundamentals are overturned, past-performance figures are worthless.

In considerable measure the vote was personal for Mr. Roosevelt. No one may say how far, if he does not run for a fourth term, he might be able to deliver this vote in 1944 to an heir. What is clear is that, once Roosevelt is out of the picture, this vote will not slip back automatically into its former slots. The political wars henceforth will be fought with new tactics and new weapons to unpredictable results.

I say this on the basis of a firsthand study of thirteen of the cities, from Boston to Seattle, which piled up the Roosevelt vote. . . .

DETROIT.

Roosevelt's greatest pluralities in Wayne County were registered in the Polish districts of Hamtramck, where precincts went twenty and thirty to one for him. More typical of the city as a whole, though, are two auto-workers precincts in the twenty-first ward which went for Roosevelt three to one.

Economically, these precincts fall into the great average sectors of Detroit. They are a food-stamp area; incomes run between $1,200 and $1,400 a year; neighborhood movies charge 20 cents admission; the well-kept private homes are worth between $2,500 and $5,000. "Sleeping room for rent" signs in many of the windows mirror the transient, half-boom, half-broke nature of auto-plant employment.

Workers in the two precincts are predominantly native white, better than half Protestant. In a random apartment house one finds such names as Baldwin, Walsh, Gibson, Calhoun, Costello, Powers, Snyder, Saltzgiver, and Solomon. Perhaps a fourth of the workers came up from the South during the 20's. Labor says that these "hillbillies," as they are known, were brought in because it was felt that they would be less inclined to join unions and would be easier to handle. Today the hillbillies are high in union councils.

Chrysler Local Seven, in the fore of the sit-down strike of 1937, has its headquarters in one precinct. The local has its own three-floor building, which at shift time becomes a buzz of activity. Four girls behind teller windows collect dues — the local claims 10,000 members. A stream of visitors pours in and out of the offices of the president and the shop committee.

Nearly fifty such United Auto Workers locals are scattered throughout the city. Their listings in the telephone book run to half a column. Only the state, federal, and municipal governments have longer listings. Like many another union, the UAW has become a big business, with its own white-collar opportunities. A stenographer working at Chrysler Seven is the daughter of an auto worker; the educational director is a young man in his thirties, fresh out of the plant. He still wears a work shirt and lumber jacket, but he sits at a desk with a telephone and a buzzer.

Even more so than with the Irish in Boston, Roosevelt, to these auto workers, is the "friend" who gave them recognition. The New Deal enabled them to build their union. It taught them the strength of their numbers and with the feeling of power has come a growing class-consciousness. The workers themselves use the phrase. "I'm franker than you," one local official replied when I asked him why he voted for Roosevelt. "I'll say it, even though it doesn't sound nice. We've grown class-conscious."

A Catholic priest in the precinct confessed, "If I ever attacked Roosevelt from the pulpit, it would be the end of me here."

Listening to these auto workers, one got the feeling that nothing Willkie could have said or done would have changed these votes. John L. Lewis had no effect. In their minds the cleavage between workingman and "economic royalist" is sharply drawn. One also got the feeling that, given the same choice, these workers would vote again and again for Roosevelt, regardless of whether it was the third, fourth or fifth term. . . .

BROOKLYN.

From city to city the dividing line fluctuates somewhat. If we think of the economic voting as falling into horizontal strata, then there also have been vertical vote movements cutting across economic lines and lifting the Roosevelt vote. These, naturally, would be most evident in the dividing zones. As major influences of this sort could be listed:

Organized labor reaching up into the better-paid skills.

The government, as an employer sprinkling jobs through all middle-class groups.

The whole body of New Deal benefits, from relief to FHA mortgages. Precisely in this economic range are New Deal votes thickest.

Nationalistic and religious sympathies stirred by Hitlerism, as with the Jews, the Poles, the Scandinavians, and the Czechs. Where these sympathies coincide with a low economic status as with the Poles, the Roosevelt pluralities are enormous. Where they cut across higher economic rungs, like among better-income Jews, wards normally Republican swing Democratic or have their majorities cut, while Democratic-inclined wards go Roosevelt by land-slide proportions.

In Brooklyn's Eighteenth Assembly District, Roosevelt won by about four to one, for a plurality of 70,000. The neighborhood is 65 per cent Jewish and 25 per cent Irish Catholic. Perhaps one in three is foreign born. There are a few slum shacks; there is a small Negro section; in one corner of the district are walk-up tenements occupied chiefly by needle-trades workers. One-time Socialists, they voted for Roosevelt on the American Labor Party ticket.

HARLEM.

How great has been the impact of this urban revolt upon the traditional Republican line-up can be seen in the Negro vote. Only in St. Louis, which continues to draw them from the South, do the Negroes still seem divided in their allegiances between the party of Lincoln and the party of Roosevelt. Harlem's Seventeenth Assembly District went better than seven to one for the New Deal.

Probably 50 per cent of Harlem's Negroes are getting relief of some kind. Older Negroes — they're most likely to be Republican — shake their graying heads ruefully and mutter, "Our people are selling their birthrights for a mess of pottage."

To the younger Negroes the WPA and relief mean not only material aid but a guaranty that no longer must they work at any salary given them, that they are entitled — they emphasize the word — to a living wage. Through the WPA, Harlem's Negroes have had opened to them white-collar opportunities which before had been shut, such as the music and art and writers' projects. Negroes, too, remember that Mrs. Roosevelt visited Harlem personally, that President Roosevelt has appointed more Negroes to administrative positions paying around $5,000 a year than any President before him. Each time Roosevelt makes such an appointment, the *Amsterdam News,* Harlem's leading newspaper, headlines it in 72-point type. Every young Negro gets a vicarious thrill thinking, "There may be a chance up there for me.". . .

In many a Harlem home hangs a rotogravure photograph of the new emancipator: some families have spent 50 cents to have it framed.

A young police reporter on the *News* summed it up when he remarked, "Negroes feel Roosevelt started something."

"Something" certainly has been started. In 1932 Roosevelt became President in a popular recoil against the depression. His third-term victory, however, is the result of an upsurging of the urban masses. In the New Deal they have found their leveling philosophy; under it they have been given recognition through patronage, benefits, and new opportunities; they have been awakened to the consciousness of the power of their numbers.

A LITTLE MATTER OF BIRTH RATES

In the winter of 1910 Congress received the longest report ever submitted by a government investigating body up to that time. From early 1907 a special commission had been studying almost every imaginable aspect of immigration, filling forty-two fat volumes with its findings. Buried in that statistical mountain was at least one table of figures which was to prove peculiarly prophetic for our own times.

This table showed that a majority of the children in the schools of thirty-seven of our leading cities had foreign-born fathers. In cities like Chelsea, Fall River, New Bedford, Duluth, New York and Chicago more than *two out of every three* school children were the sons and daughters of immigrants.

Viewed in today's perspective, it is clear that those figures forecast a major political upheaval some time between 1930 and 1940. By then all of these children, plus baby brothers and sisters not enrolled in school, would have grown to voting age. Massed as they were in the states commanding the largest electoral vote, their sheer numbers would topple any prevailing political balance.

No matter what else had happened, the growing up of these children of the 13,000,000 immigrants who poured into the country between 1900 and 1914 was bound to exert a leveling pull on American society. As it was, the depression — striking when most of them had barely entered the adult world — sharpened all their memories of childhood handicaps. When Roosevelt first took office, no segment of the population was more ready for "a new deal" than the submerged, inarticulate urban masses. They became the chief carriers of the Roosevelt Revolution.

The really revolutionary surge behind the New Deal lay in this coupling of the depression with the rise of a new generation, which had been malnourished on the congestion of our cities and the abuses of industrialism. Roosevelt did not start this revolt of the city. What he did do was to awaken the climbing urban masses to a consciousness of the power in their numbers. He extended to them the warming hand of recognition, through patronage and protective legislation. In the New Deal he supplied the leveling philosophy required by their sheer numbers and by the hungers stimulated by advertising. In turn, the big-city masses furnished the votes which re-elected Roosevelt again and again — and, in the process, ended the traditional Republican majority in this country. . . .

Not only does this generation hold the balance of political power in the nation. It also constitutes a radically new political force in American history. The old Republican dominance was rooted in the Civil War and the transcontinental expansion which followed. Most of the immigrants who peopled our larger cities came to these shores long after the Civil War, even after the exhaustion of free lands in the West. To their children and grandchildren the loyalties of Appomattox and the Homestead Act were details in history books rather than a family experience passed down from grandfather to grandson.

Never having known anything but city life, this new generation was bound to develop a different attitude toward the role of government from that of Americans born on farms or in small towns. To Herbert Hoover the phrase "rugged individualism" evoked nostalgic memories of a rural self-sufficiency in which a thrifty, toiling farmer had to look to the marketplace for only the last fifth of his needs. The Iowa homestead on which Hoover grew up produced all of its own vegetables, its own soap, its own bread. Fuel was cut and hauled from the woods ten miles away, where one could also gather walnuts free. "Sweetness" was obtained from sorghums. Every fall the cellar was filled with jars and barrels which, as Hoover observes in his memoirs, "was social security in itself."

To men and women who regulated their labors by the sun and rain, there was recognizable logic in talking of natural economic laws — although even among farmers the murmur for government intervention grew louder, as their operations became more commercialized and less self-sufficient.

In the city, though, the issue has always been man against man. What bowed the backs of the factory worker prematurely were not hardships inflicted by Mother Nature but by human nature. He was completely dependent on a money wage. Without a job, there were no vegetables for his family, no bread, no rent, no fuel, no soap, no "sweetness." Crop failures, plagues of grasshoppers or searing drought could be put down as acts of God. Getting fired or having one's wages cut were only too plainly acts of the Boss.

A philosophy that called for "leaving things alone" to work themselves out seemed either unreal or hypocritical in the cities, where nearly every condition of living groaned for reform. The wage earner had to look to the government to make sure that the milk bought for his baby was not watered or tubercular; he had to look to government to regulate the construction of tenements so all sunlight was not blocked out. If only God could make a tree, only the government could make a park.

Neither the Republicans nor the New Dealers seem to have appreciated how sharp a wrench from the continuity of the past was involved in the rise of this big-city generation. . . .

The depression vote of 1932 still mirrored the orbit of conflict of the old Republican order. The GOP cleavage had been mainly a struggle between the "progressives" of the Midwest and Far West against the industrial East. Roosevelt's first campaign was directed primarily toward splitting off this "progressive" vote. His best showing came in the Western and Mountain states. All six states he lost — Pennsylvania, Delaware, Connecticut, Vermont, New Hampshire and Maine — were in the East.

The shift in the basis of Roosevelt's appeal "from acreage to population," to use Raymond Moley's phrase, occurred in 1935. Moley credits the change to Huey Long's "Share Our Wealth" agitation and to Roosevelt's ire over the Supreme Court's declaring the NRA unconstitutional. To steal Long's thunder, Roosevelt proposed a "soak the rich" tax bill, which, Moley feels, marked the beginning of the conservative-liberal split inside the Democratic party. Whatever the exact turning point, 1935 saw more social legislation enacted than in any other year in the nation's history — the "wealth tax," the Wagner Labor Relations Act, the Social Security Law, the creation of WPA, the Public Utilities Holding law, the start of the Rural Electrification Administration.

Not only in Washington but throughout the country 1935 was the year of decision. To go back to the old order or to move forward to something different? That was the question posed for decision in 1935, in countless different ways, in every phase of life. . . .

In 1932 one fourth of the Democratic campaign funds was contributed by bankers. In 1936 bankers accounted for a mere 3 per cent of the Democratic party's war chest. (Their total contributions to the Democrats were only about a third of the $750,000 spent by organized labor.)

Particularly in rural areas, the 1936 vote showed that sizable numbers of voters were ready to return to the Republicanism of their ancestors. Winston County, which had seceded from Alabama during the Civil War to remain loyal to the union, swung back to the Republican party in 1936; so did thirty-two counties in Missouri, all but eight bone-dry by tradition. Less than a dozen wheat counties in the whole country had stayed Republican in 1932. Four years later, most of the wheat counties were on their way back to the Republican party.

In the industrial centers, however, the political allegiances that had grown out of the Civil War were uprooted for good. In New York, New Jersey and Pennsylvania, alone, the Democratic vote leaped by roughly 1,800,000. Despite the depression, in 1932, Roosevelt failed to carry a dozen cities with 100,000 or more population — Philadelphia, Scranton and Reading in Pennsylvania; Canton, Youngstown and Columbus in Ohio; Gary, Duluth, Des Moines, Grand Rapids and Springfield, Massachusetts. Every one swung for Roosevelt in 1936 and except for Grand Rapids have remained Democratic since.

A dramatic glimpse into the nature of this hidden political revolution will be found by comparing the 1928 and 1936 vote in our major cities. While Smith won six of every ten voters in some cities, in others he drew only three out of ten. This disparity had narrowed by 1932, but wide divergences in voting still prevailed in different parts of the country. With the 1936 election, as the table below shows, the voting of nearly all our major cities hit a common level.

Whether the cities are heavily foreign born or native American in make-up, Catholic or Protestant, with large numbers of Negroes or of whites up from the South, did not make too much difference in their 1936 vote. Nor whether the city had a strong labor tradition like San Francisco or an open shop tradition like Los Angeles, nor whether it was located on the East or West coast or in the Midwest.

Cities High Smith			*Cities Low Smith*		
City	*Dem. % 1928*	*Dem. % 1936*	*City*	*Dem. % 1928*	*Dem. % 1936*
Lawrence	71	73	Flint	19	72
Boston	67	63	Wichita, Kansas	24	64
Lowell	64	61	Los Angeles	28	67
Fall River	64	67	Akron	31	71
New York	60	75	Des Moines	31	55
New Haven	57	65	San Diego	32	65
Milwaukee	53	76	Seattle	32	64
New Bedford	52	65	Duluth	32	71
Cleveland	52	76	Canton	34	66
St. Louis	51	66	Spokane	35	71
San Francisco	49	72	Detroit	37	65
Chicago	48	65	Indianapolis	39	57
Pittsburgh	47	67	Philadelphia	39	60
Baltimore	47	67	Youngstown	39	74

A new nationalizing force had clearly been injected into American politics. In the past American political realignments have always followed sectional lines. The Revolt of the City, however, had drawn the same class-conscious line of economic interest across the entire country, overriding not only regional distinctions but equally strong cultural differences.

POLITICS: THE
CONSERVATIVE NEW DEAL

Federalism in the Style of the 1930's

JAMES T. PATTERSON

New Deal changes in the size and agenda of government and in the constituencies to which it answered seemed revolutionary to contemporaries, whether they approved of them or not. New Dealers cited these political alterations with pride; socialists like Norman Thomas sadly admitted that they had destroyed the Socialist party; and conservatives like Herbert Hoover thought that these changes spelled the end of liberty, individualism, and the Constitution. But in recent years, the political changes of the 1930s have begun to seem much more limited in extent and effect than contemporaries guessed.

Every year some new study is published that increases our awareness of the New Deal's limitations. The national government may have gained power during the New Deal, but, as James T. Patterson argues below, state and local governments remained in conservative hands and blunted federal power when it reached out into the localities. Walter D. Burnham has shown that the New Deal did not really awaken to political participation the masses that Huey Long tried to reach and Roosevelt seemed to reach. The New Deal only briefly interrupted a long-term trend toward political apathy and nonvoting in America, a development associated particularly with the lower classes. Grant McConnell and Theodore Lowi, among others, have described the capture of the New Deal regulatory apparatus by the very interest groups it was supposed to regulate. James M. Burns has argued that the President failed to make the structural changes in the Democratic party that would have kept it a strongly liberal party even after his death.

In summary, the changes in American politics that seemed so great in the 1930s did not go as far as was originally thought. They did not produce anything like the economic alterations one would have predicted from the goals of the welfare state and its new constituencies among the disadvantaged. To some extent this relatively conservative resultant was shaped by the war and the failure of FDR's successors to develop policies to consolidate and to extend his gains. But even by 1939–40 the New Deal "political revolution" must be seen, in retrospect at least, as having only limited potential for producing substantial socio-economic change. Entrenched economic elites may "lose" the Presidency, lose control of public policy in important areas, and find party platforms written with an eye toward their natural economic enemies. But while these elites are displaced politically, they do not thereby lose their energy, economic power, confidence, experience, determination, and control over the means of production and the media.

So, the establishment accommodated the new political forces and institutions. The price was a sharing of political power with the better organized of the "out" groups and of economic power with the state, along with higher lobbying fees to guarantee that the newcomers' share was small. Some call this "co-optation," and condemn it as a device for smothering genuine social change. Others, seeing new groups gain a stake in the American political — and through it the economic — system, judge the New Deal's political changes to have been timely and extensive enough to prevent violent revolution, and see in them the praiseworthy genius of the American political system.

Patterson, a professor of history at Indiana University, in the monograph reprinted here, focuses on New Deal relations with state governments. It is a splendid case study in the process whereby New Deal changes in the functions and size of the federal government were quietly absorbed into the vast network of institutions, habits, and attitudes that had managed the society's energies for generations.

No two people, it seemed, agreed on the New Deal's impact on the states during the 1930's. Friendly observers spoke of a "new federalism," a potentially cooperative relationship enriched by matching funds.[1]* Others,

From James T. Patterson, *The New Deal and the States: Federalism in Transition* (copyright © 1969 by Princeton University Press), pp. 194–198, 200–207. Reprinted by permission of Princeton University Press.
* [See pp. 180–181 for notes to this article. — Ed.]

conceding the blessings bestowed by the national administration, countered that the New Deal was discriminatory — that some states basked in the warmth of presidential friendship while others shivered outside in the cold. Conservatives perceived not a generous father but an autocratic Leviathan. "We are all beginning to look to Uncle Sam to be Santa Claus," one Democratic governor complained in 1935. "I think the toughest problem that we as governors have is to stay away from it if we can." [2] And liberals, reflecting a fourth view, disagreed sharply on all counts, maintaining that federal timidity was stranding the nation in the miasmatic conservatism of the 1920's. "Since 1930," one critic charged in 1949, "state government has dismally failed to meet responsibilities and obligations in every field. . . . The federal government has not encroached upon state government. State government has failed." [3]

Various improvements in state government during the decade seemed to support defenders of the thesis of cooperative federalism. One was administrative efficiency. Eleven states passed reorganization statutes during the decade, making a total of 26. Many others, acting in piecemeal fashion, removed administrative control and financial responsibility from the archaic local units which had formerly dominated the field.[4] It was no accident that the home rule movement languished in the 1930's: states seemed better answers than counties or towns to the economic problems of the era.[5]

A related development was the expansion of the merit system in the late 1930's. One authority remarked in 1939 that "the past two years have probably seen more progress in the field of public personnel administration than any previous period in our national history." Five states, the first since 1920, passed workable statutes in 1937, and 6 others applied the merit system to various departments, most often in the realm of public welfare.[6] The trend toward state merit systems, revived after a lapse of more than fifteen years, continued steadily if unspectacularly through the 1940's, 50's and 60's. . . .

The New Deal can take some credit for the improvements which were made. Its insistence during the lifetime of the FERA on a single state agency for welfare and its later requirement of 1939 of civil service procedures in social security stimulated administrative efficiency in the states.

The New Deal also hastened the spread of social legislation, some of which reached the statute books in the little New Deal states. And even in the majority of states where little immediate effect was visible, it transformed the nature of argument. Before the New Deal, states rights remained a vital if negative dogma which enabled people like Byrd of Virginia and Ritchie of Maryland to achieve national prominence. Even Brandeis and Roosevelt had stressed a more affirmative version. But in showing what positive government could do, the New Deal forced politicians to recognize that states rights without state activism must perish. As Governor Olin Johnston of South

Carolina warned his colleagues in 1935, "There has been a continuous de-
crease of state powers because . . . the states have not used them, and the
people wanted government. If a government does not measure up to its
responsibility by the exercise of its powers . . . the powers will not be there
. . . they will be exercised by the mobs, by the rabble, or something. . . . It
is God's and nature's law." [7] Even conservatives readily understood this
logic.

The Roosevelt years also altered — conservatives said warped — state
political patterns. Appealing to previously ignored groups, the New Deal
stimulated increases in political participation in many states.[8] Most of these
new voters were underprivileged — Negroes, unemployed, unskilled workers,
immigrants. They tended to vote Democratic in national elections and in so
doing to force both parties in competitive states to promise more liberal
services.

The New Deal cannot take all the credit for this development. Although voter participation did increase during the decade, the trend had already begun with the nomination of Smith in 1928. Moreover, uninspiring,
job-seeking Democrats all too often cashed in on Roosevelt's electoral magic
without in any way selling progressive ideas on the state level. But even
though few states enacted significant reforms in the 1930's, the trend started
in 1928 and accelerated by the New Deal spurred many politicians in both
parties to listen to long-silent urban voices. In this sense, the New Deal did
indeed promote, however slowly and accidentally, the spread of urban programs in the states.

Above all, the combination of national policy and depression forever
transformed federal-state relations. Take, for instance, the governor of 1925:
he could expect a few congressional dollars for highways, agricultural extension work, and vocational education. If he was a Republican — and most were
— he traveled to Washington once or twice a year to confer with the president
and be photographed for the home folks. Otherwise he expected little, and
worried still less about the bickering on Pennsylvania Avenue.

His successor in 1940 inhabited a different world. While purely in-
trastate matters continued to dominate the governor's time, national policy
intimately affected the economic health of his state and his own political
future. Like it or not, he usually played along with the New Deal, and if
he too often refused to press for progressive reforms, he was even less likely
to reject the matching money which his constituents found so appealing.
Partly because of federal activism, the American state of 1940 spent more,
taxed more, and provided much more than it had two decades before. And
three decades later its importance had grown even further, following many
of the same guidelines and policies on grants that had been established from
1933 to 1940. . . .

But liberals were also unhappy, justifiably so. Though labor legislation in some states was more progressive than in the 1920's, it was short lived, and after the sitdown strikes of 1937 a reaction set in, halting further gains. In a short time state right-to-work and criminal syndicalism laws appeared with alarming frequency. The record of the states in relief spending was equally disappointing. Despite some advances in administration, social workers were less optimistic in 1940 than they had been a few years earlier. Especially disheartening were the scanty state contributions for general relief. Because the WPA let states provide for unemployables, and because the federal formula for aid to aged, blind, and dependent children required no minimum state contribution, the needy in many areas fared almost as badly as they had in the early days of the depression. And although all states cooperated with the unemployment compensation program, few surpassed the niggardly minimum requirements.

State financial policy also veered to the right during the decade. While a few progressive income and corporate taxes reached the books, the most striking trend was the sales tax movement. Because states were already seeking new sources of revenue before 1930, such a development would probably have occurred anyway, but federal policy accelerated it. Increased income levies passed in the Hoover and Roosevelt administrations forced states to turn elsewhere, and the insistence by New Dealers that states contribute a share to welfare costs intensified the search. Far from "soaking the rich," states remained as regressive in raising revenue as they had been in the past.

The New Deal was not only unable to force progressive labor, welfare, and tax policies on the states, but one may question whether it inspired those gains which were made. Did the New Deal deserve credit for the advances in labor law — or was the organized political power of the CIO more important? Did federal policy awaken some states to their welfare responsibilities, or did the depression leave them no choice? And why did a few states tighten public utility regulation — because the New Deal set an example, or because the conduct of some utility executives was so flagrant? Were the state policies of the 1930's the result of federal guidelines or of economic necessity?

The New Deal was certainly important; try to imagine what states would have done without money and exhortation from Washington. Yet it is equally hard to understand the occasional advances in state legislation in the 1930's without recognizing that they occurred in a time of crisis. Localities alone simply could not provide for relief, education, and highways, and the states had begun to stumble into the breech even before Roosevelt inaugurated the New Deal. The centralization of American life was forcing the states to assume local functions. Nothing since that time has reversed this invincible trend.

The liberal critics have the strongest case. While state activity expanded in the 1930's, the change was far from dramatic; indeed, the growth in state services in the 1950's and 1960's has been much more impressive. The New Deal produced neither federal dictation, a completely cooperative federalism, nor a new state progressivism. Instead, it helped create a rather flat mixture of achievement, mediocrity, and confusion. For all the supposed power of the New Deal, it was unable to impose all its guidelines on the autonomous 48 states.

LABOR: THE
REVOLUTIONARY NEW DEAL

The End of the Turbulent Years

IRVING BERNSTEIN

One of the most striking changes in American society during the Roosevelt years was effected in the occupational life of the working man. Before the New Deal, those who had a job in manufacturing earned an average weekly wage of $17.05 and had almost no protection against wage reductions or layoffs. Just over 3 million men in a nonagricultural work force of 23 million were organized into unions, and their unions were precarious. By the end of the 1930s workers in industries affected by interstate commerce were assured a 40¢ hourly wage and time and a half over eight hours a day; many were assured benefits under the unemployment insurance provisions of the Social Security Act in the event of layoff; and the number of unionized workers had tripled to nearly 9 million, a development that promised those workers greater leverage in the industrial decisions that so affected their lives — wages, hours, working conditions, retirement, job security.

Minimum wages, maximum hours, and unemployment insurance were New Deal measures, and while unionization came through private efforts, it was stimulated both generally by the friendly climate of the New Deal toward labor ("President Roosevelt wants you to join a union," John L. Lewis said in 1933–34) and in particular by the federal guarantee of collective bargaining under the Wagner Act. The labor vote veered to Roosevelt in the 1930s and stayed there out of appreciation for the New Deal's active role in improving the lives of America's blue-collar workers. In the passage below, Irving Bernstein, a foremost authority on New Deal labor policies and the labor movement between

the wars and currently with the Institute of Industrial Relations,
UCLA, enumerates the dramatic improvements that came in the
1930s — unionization spreading to include the vital mass-produc-
tion industries and all of the attendant gains for industrial de-
mocracy, worker compensation, job security.

In the spring of 1940 George Korson, the folklorist, visited the coal camps of the southern Appalachian region. He knew that the unionization of this area in the thirties had spurred a new burst of bituminous minstrelsy and that local miners' unions opened and closed their meetings with song. In Trafford, Alabama, he found an aged, blind, crippled, and unlettered Negro miner, Uncle George Jones, who had joined the United Mine Workers in 1894. He lived in a ramshackle windowless cabin. Uncle George had composed a song that Korson recorded, entitled, "Dis What De Union Done." It went this way:

In nineteen hundred an' thirty-two
We wus sometimes sad an' blue,
Travelin' roun' from place to place
Tryin' to find some work to do.
If we's successful to find a job,
De wages wus so small,
We could scarcely live in de summertime —
Almost starved in de fall.

Befo' we got our union back,
It's very sad to say,
Ole blue shirts an' overalls
Wus de topic of de day.
Dey wus so full of patches
An' so badly to'n,
Our wives had to sew for 'bout a hour
Befo' dey could be wo'n.

Now when our union men walks out,
Got de good clothes on deir backs,
Crepe de chine and fine silk shirts,
Bran' new Miller block hats;

From *The Turbulent Years.* Copyright © 1969 by Irving Bernstein.
Reprinted by permission of the publisher, Houghton Mifflin Company.

> Fine silk socks an' Florsheim shoes,
> Dey're glitterin' against de sun,
> Got dollars in deir pockets, smokin' good cigars —
> Boys, dis what de union done.

In this song Uncle George voiced his perception of the labor history of the thirties: The rise of the union had transformed poverty and despair into plenty and hope.[1]*

What, in fact, had happened?

The most important development that took place was the dramatic increase in the size of the labor movement. If one uses the National Bureau of Economic Research series, constructed by Leo Wolman and Leo Troy on conservative criteria, the membership of American unions (excluding Canadian members) rose from 2,805,000 in 1933 to 8,410,000 in 1941. This constituted an almost exact tripling in size. Perhaps even more significant, for the first time in the history of the nation unions enrolled a substantial fraction of those at work, by 1941, 23 per cent of nonagricultural employment. Further, the prospect at the close of this period was that rapid growth both in absolute numbers and in the share of employment would continue for at least the duration of the war.

While expansion was evident in all industry groups, it was most marked in manufacturing, transportation, and mining. Wolman made the following estimates of the per cent of wage and salaried employees organized:

	1930	1940
Manufactures	8.8%	34.1%
Transportation, communication, and public utilities	23.4	48.2
Building	54.3	65.3
Mining, quarrying, and oil	21.3	72.3
Services	2.7	6.7
Public service	8.3	10.2

Thus, by 1940 those industry groups with heavy concentrations of blue-collar workers — mining, construction, transportation, and manufacturing — were highly unionized, and those with predominantly white-collar employment — the services and government — were overwhelmingly unorganized. In effect,

* [See p. 181 for notes to this article. — Ed.]

the notable advances of the thirties had penetrated deeply into the unorganized sectors of the manual labor force; the gains in the nonmanual areas were slight.

The largest and most significant increases in membership occurred in manufacturing industries. Here it is important to note that manufacturing at that time was by far the biggest of the industry groups, representing more than one third of all nonagricultural employment. Wolman's calculations of the per cent of production workers organized in manufactures are as follows:

	1935	1941
Metals	10.2%	43.3%
Clothing	47.6	64.4
Food, liquor, and tobacco	11.3	32.5
Paper, printing, and publishing	30.3	41.0
Leather and leather products	12.4	34.0
Chemicals, rubber, clay, glass, and stone	4.7	15.4
Textiles	7.5	14.3
Lumber and woodworking	6.5	11.8

.   .   .

In "Dis What De Union Done," Uncle George said that the UMW had raised the wages of Alabama coal miners. He was indubitably correct. Average weekly earnings in bituminous coal in the nation advanced from $14.47 in 1933 to $30.86 in 1941 and the increase in the mines about Trafford may have been more. But when one moves from the specific to the general, it becomes far more difficult to assess the impact of growing unionism upon the condition of workers. This is because of the great size and diversity of the American economy, the disparity among collective bargaining systems, the subtlety in assigning causes to results, and the inadequacy of the statistics. Despite these impediments, it seems worthwhile to draw a few generalizations, recognizing both that they are not universally applicable and that, in some cases, they are impossible to prove.

There can be no doubt that the rise of unionism in the thirties led to a significant increase in wages. Arthur M. Ross demonstrated this in an analysis of the movement of real hourly earnings between 1933 and 1945 in sixty-five industries grouped by the extent of employment covered by collective bargaining agreements. He found a direct relationship between the per cent of unionization and the per cent of increase in earnings. Thus, union members enjoyed a more rapid rise in wages than nonmembers. Moreover, Ross pointed out, unions also raised the wages of unorganized workers by setting standards of equity for them and their employers and by prodding the latter into granting higher wages in order to keep the union out.

Another wage impact of the new unions, almost certainly, was to narrow differentials in earnings. By comparison with other industrial nations, American differentials were exceptionally wide prior to the Great Depression. The CIO unions in manufacturing industries, in particular, compressed the spread between the skilled and the unskilled by negotiating wage increases across-the-board in cents per hour, rather than per cent. For example, a difference of 100 per cent between an unskilled rate of 50¢ and a skilled rate of $1.00 diminished to 83 per cent when each was pushed up 10¢. Probably this narrowing of skill differentials was relatively modest prior to 1941 because the recession that began in 1937 restrained wage increases for about three years. During the thirties, as well, southern manufacturing industries narrowed historic wage differentials with the North. While unionization was a factor, the NRA codes and the Fair Labor Standards Act of 1938 also contributed to this result.

An important achievement of the new unionism was the introduction of the seniority principle. As might be expected at a time of serious unemployment, seniority was mainly applied to layoffs, transfers, and rehires, and to a lesser extent to promotions. In some industries seniority in layoffs was linked to work-sharing. That is, if the work force must be reduced, the hours of all employees were cut first and thereafter individuals would be laid off in accordance with length of service. One effect of the use of seniority was to restrict management's discretion both in selecting the worker it considered best qualified for the job and in making arbitrary or discriminatory choices. Another was to provide job security for employees with longer service.

Perhaps the most significant accomplishment of the new unions was to establish grievance procedures — what they called industrial democracy and what Sumner H. Slichter named industrial jurisprudence. At the outset this took the form of creating a shop-steward system in the plant and of compelling the employer to deal with it in the disposition of grievances. This led shortly to the erection of hierarchically arranged steps with increased levels of authority on each side through which grievances passed in accordance with time limits. Towards the end of the period a growing but small number of collective bargaining agreements provided for arbitration as the terminal step in the procedure, utilizing an impartial person to render a final and binding award. At the same time the umpire system began to emerge in which a "permanent" arbitrator served on all cases during the life of the agreement. Aside from older arrangements of this sort in the needle trades, hosiery, and anthracite coal, two notable new umpireships were established — in the Pacific Coast longshore industry in 1938 and under the General Motors–AW agreement in 1940. Dean Wayne L. Morse of the University of Oregon Law School served as the West Coast arbitrator, and Professor Harry A. Millis of the University of Chicago was umpire under the General Motors agreement until 1941, when he became chairman of the NLRB. Professor George W. Taylor of the University of Pennsylvania, formerly the impartial chairman under agreements in the full-fashioned hosiery and the Philadelphia men's clothing industries, succeeded him as umpire.

While these procedures for the most part admitted grievances over the whole range of shop issues, their most significant immediate impact was in the area of discipline and discharge. The employer was now required to show cause for taking such action, and the worker who appealed to the grievance procedure was afforded representation and many other elements of due process. Here, again, management's power was narrowed. Workers won protection against arbitrary or discriminatory punishment.[2] . . .

It was more than happenstance that the great cases that tested the validity of the Wagner Act should lie at the center of the constitutional crisis of 1937. This was because the period witnessed a change in American law so profound as to constitute a revolution. Most of the principles that received statutory and judicial expression in the thirties, to be sure, had roots extending back to an earlier period, in some cases deep into the nineteenth century. But there were two characteristics of public policy in the New Deal era that distinguished it fundamentally from these antecedents.

The first was comprehensive and permanent regulation by government. The National Labor Relations Act and the Railway Labor Act did more than establish rules to control the initiation and conduct of collective bargaining; these statutes also set up administrative agencies to enforce these rules. Several of the states followed the federal example by passing "little" Wagner Acts and by creating "little" Labor Boards.

The second was a fundamental shift in the posture of public policy on collective bargaining from neutrality to affirmation. Earlier, government, by its statutory silence, assumed that the contest between labor and management was an essentially private matter. While it was lawful for workers to organize and bargain collectively, as William M. Leiserson wrote, "the law recognized the equal freedom of the employers to destroy labor organizations and to deny the right of employees to join trade unions." The courts took an impartial position, notably by applying the Sherman Act's proscription against contracts, combinations, and conspiracies in restraint of trade to unions as well as to corporations. A legal system under which government played a neutral role had the effect of tipping the balance of bargaining power in most American industries in favor of employers. The turn to affirmation found most dramatic expression in Section 1 of the Wagner Act. This premise of the statute asserted that "inequality of bargaining power between employees who do not possess full freedom of association or actual liberty of contract, and employers who are organized in the corporate or other forms of ownership association" burdened commerce, aggravated depressions, reduced wages, and depressed the purchasing power of wage earners. Thus, it now became "the policy of the United States" to remove obstructions to commerce "by encouraging the practice and procedure of collective bargaining." The courts joined in the movement to affirmation, especially by removing unions from the reach of the Sherman Act insofar as they engaged in bargaining functions, and by treating peaceful picketing as a protected form of freedom of speech under the First Amendment.

While responsive to the needs of a troubled industrial society, this basic change in public policy had qualities of a historical accident insofar as the Wagner Act was concerned. It is entirely possible, perhaps probable, that no Congress in modern American history except the 74th could have mustered majorities for such a bill in both the House and the Senate. The usual combination of Republicans and Southern Democrats would have prevented this. Yet the measure was brought in at the precise rare moment when it could be passed. Further, the National Labor Relations bill was in no sense an Administration proposal. President Roosevelt, in fact, showed little interest in and less support for Senator Wagner's bill until the penultimate stage when the Supreme Court, by nullifying NRA, left him no option. It seemed almost as though the nation had stumbled into a basic change in policy.

This governmental commitment to collective bargaining would lead to a number of significant consequences. The first was to spur the growth of union membership. There were, of course, other reasons to help explain the expansion of membership — an improved economic climate, the CIO campaigns in the mass-production industries, the AFL response to rival unionism. But the law laid the legal foundation. The National Labor Relations Act and the Railway Labor Act served both as a stimulus to organization and as a shield against interference by employers with its achievement.

Second, belligerent antiunion practices of employers substantially disappeared from American industrial relations. Within a few years of the passage of the Wagner Act such devices as industrial espionage, professional strikebreaking, antiunion private police, industrial munitioning, and company-dominated unions fell into disuse and the incidence of discrimination against and discharge for union membership was significantly reduced. This was a great victory for civil liberties in the shop. As against the employer, the law now guaranteed to the worker freedom of speech, freedom of assembly, and freedom of association. It also sharply reduced the level of violence in American industry, a notable gain in a society with a high propensity towards the use of force.

A third result was to diminish the need for and the incidence of the most difficult form of strike, that over union recognition. The representation machinery of the National Labor Relations Board and the National Mediation Board became a substitute for the work stoppage over organization; the peaceful election was the alternative to a test of economic power. While many employers in the early years declined to accept these representation procedures, after 1939 compliance improved and the relative number of strikes over recognition declined.

Another impact, fourth, was to undermine the appeal of Marxism, particularly of the Communist Party, to American workers. It was the realization of the prediction of such supporters of the Wagner bill in 1935 as Lloyd Garrison and Harry Millis, in the words of the former, "the safety measure" theory. This worked out in two ways. The more important was to strengthen a labor movement overwhelmingly committed to business unionism by increasing the volume of its business — collective bargaining. The second was to show that one of the fundamental tenets of Marxism, that the state under capitalism must serve as the instrument of the ruling class, was incorrect.

A fifth consequence was to strengthen industrial democracy, broadly defined. The representation election itself was a demonstration of the democratic process at work. Civil liberties were now legally underwritten in industry. More significant still, collective bargaining, particularly the grievance procedure, compelled the employer to share information and power in the decision-making process in the shop. In Milton Derber's terms, "unilateral control" gave way to "bilateralism."

Sixth, government regulation led inevitably to the "legalization" of collective bargaining; that is, the lawyers made a grand entrance. The quasi-judicial character of the Labor Board and the frequency of appeals to the courts made their services necessary. Insecure employers who could afford the luxury also brought them into negotiations and into arbitrations, and unions increasingly followed this example. The law schools introduced the systematic teaching of labor relations law; the law journals filled their pages with labor articles; commercial services published Board and court decisions; a specialized bar emerged, one part serving employers and the other unions; collective bargaining agreements, reflecting the lawyer's influence and style, became longer, more formal, more involved, more guarded in language; some arbitrators, notably Wayne Morse, "judicialized" the arbitration process.

A seventh result of federal intervention was to give the CIO a short-run advantage in its struggle with the AFL. This was because the CIO unions grasped more quickly than many of their more hide-bound AFL rivals the gains to be made by employing the Board's machinery, because the early NLRB showed some favoritism to the CIO, and because the Wagner Act helped to undermine the principle of exclusive jurisdiction. But this edge wore off after a few years when the AFL affiliates learned to use the Board, when Leiserson replaced Donald Wakefield Smith and Millis supplanted Warren Madden, and when exclusive jurisdiction lost much of its relevancy. By the time of Pearl Harbor, if not a year or two earlier, the CIO and the AFL stood equal before the government.

Eighth, the federal commitment to the regulation of collective bargaining was to prove permanent. The Wagner Act, viewed as an exercise in American politics, concluded the era of neutrality. That statute, reflecting the pro-labor sentiment of the 74th Congress, confined regulation to the conduct of employers. But, given the assurance of some future swing in the political pendulum, already evident in some of the states, the legislature would certainly amend the law to restrict unions, both in the bargaining process and in the conduct of their internal affairs.

This was because, finally, American employers, though by 1941 coming into substantial compliance, refused to accept the law as the final word. They were determined to turn the statute against unions and to overhaul the "G – – D – – – Labor Board." [3] . . .

President Roosevelt held an unusual press conference on April 15, 1937. Those who attended were the nation's leading newspaper publishers and editors, not the reporters. It was, of course, off-the-record and the discussion was frank. As a group, the publishers were hostile to Roosevelt. The great majority had opposed his re-election the preceding November, had fought his court plan, had rejected the Wagner Act. Only three days earlier the Supreme Court had upheld the constitutionality of the statute. This had been especially galling to the publishers because many of them faced the prospect of the unionization of their newspapermen and because the Associated Press, which they controlled, had failed to persuade the court that the Wagner Act abridged the freedom of the press protected by the First Amendment. They were angry and worked the President over on the labor question. With his usual deftness, he responded philosophically.

They wanted to know why he failed to condemn the illegality of the sit-down strikes publicly. Roosevelt point out that the lawyers for the American Liberty League had declared the Wagner Act unconstitutional and that the National Association of Manufacturers and the Chamber of Commerce had advised employers to disregard it. "It is not nearly as serious to trespass on somebody's property — that is a misdemeanor — as it is to violate a Federal statute." But the labor people were beginning to realize that sit-downs were "wrong" and were also "damned unpopular." After all, "labor cannot get very far if it makes itself unpopular with the bulk of the population of the country." The sit-down crisis would blow over. "It will take some time, perhaps two years, but that is a short time in the life of a nation."

A publisher was worried about the American Newspaper Guild. The

President replied, "I think you are going to have a bad time, quite frankly, for three or four years." The union people would change their leaders often and "gradually they will get people who have both feet on the ground all the time." This was the case with the new unions generally. They were going through "growing pains." They required several years of "education," time to develop leaders who would "see the whole picture instead of just the passionate picture of a new movement."

He concluded on a confident note. The nation must adjust to collective bargaining. It would be learned "only by experience and we have to go through that experience before we find a satisfactory solution." Ultimately, "we are going to get a workable system." The President, that is, foresaw the close of the turbulent years.[4]

LABOR: THE
CONSERVATIVE NEW DEAL

The Economic Effects of Unionism

GEORGE H. HILDEBRAND

Irving Bernstein's interpretation of unionism is an established view and widely held. As labor historian Walter Galenson wrote in 1960, unionism was an "almost revolutionary change in the power relationships of American society." But this view has met with some dissent. The labor developments of the 1930s now seem less than revolutionary. Both friends and enemies overestimated the effects of unionism. They both feared and hoped that unions would acquire the power to participate in management decisions on prices, standards, and industry policy generally. This did not happen. Another fundamental change, the power to extract from profits a greater share for labor, also did not materialize, as George Hildebrand, former Deputy Undersecretary of Labor for International Affairs in the Department of Labor, indicates in the selection below.

Two decades of careful study have persuaded most scholars that unionization has been of limited financial help to the worker and has hardly hurt the employer at all. The evidence cited by Hildebrand, along with a study by H. G. Lewis in 1963, suggests that at best unions have won for their members a slight wage advantage over nonunionized workers (perhaps 5 per cent), but that none of this came from a squeeze on profits. Employers pass on their higher labor costs to the consumer (i.e. the worker). In short, unionization has been one of the least important factors in the improved economic situation of the American worker, whatever he may think. Through no fault of the unions, their pressures for a greater share of the national wealth have stimulated

*both inflation and automation. The reasons for this, as Hildebrand
briefly indicates, seem to lie in a combination of union weakness
(unionism has yet to reach a majority of the nonagricultural
work force) and conservatism.*

*Even if unionism failed to redistribute income, its contribution
to job security and its diminution of the labor violence of the
pre-World War II period should not be minimized. Whatever
the effects of unionism, the New Deal may not take sole or even
chief credit for them. Roosevelt and most of his advisors were
cool to labor; its influential friends were among congressional
progressives, especially Senator Robert Wagner. The dynamic
surge of industrial unionism, symbolized by the CIO, forced
political concessions from the New Deal and accounted for the
huge increase in union membership after 1935 (in 1937 alone
there were 3 million new members). And even granted the friendship of men like Wagner and LaFollette, the spontaneous surge
of unionization after 1935, and the slightly reluctant but nonetheless unprecedented friendliness of the Roosevelt government,
the 1930s might not have been a successful decade for American
unionism. As David Brody pointed out in an essay published in
1964, the acceptance by employers of the Wagner Act's guarantee of collective bargaining was very much in doubt until the
war forced a more cooperative climate. In this case as in so many
others, significant social changes beyond the power of the New
Deal were achieved during the war.*

The upsurge of American unionism is now nearly a quarter-century
old. Looking at its impacts upon the economy, there are those who see unionism as a promise, those who view it as a menace, and those who think its
power largely illusory. Partly this divergence in views springs from differences
in speculative thought. Partly, too, it stems from the inherent technical difficulty of isolating and testing unionism relative to other major forces affecting
the performance of our economy.

Nonetheless the past decade has witnessed a great amount of research
and considerable progress in this field. In this chapter I propose to review and
to evaluate this work. . . . Does unionism have the power to alter overall
income distribution? . . .

From George H. Hildebrand, "The Economic Effects of Unionism," in
Neil W. Chamberlain et al., *A Decade of Industrial Relations Research
1946-1956* (New York: Harper and Brothers, 1958), pp. 98-101, 103-06,
137. Reprinted with permission.

If unionism has this redistributive power, it should show up in an increase in the employees' share of the national income, in a leveling of personal incomes, or both together. True, it has been argued that unionism has had the concealed effect of preventing labor's share from falling. However, as Levinson has pointed out,[1]* this assumes that long-run capital investment has been largely substitutive for labor, rather than complementary to it — a theme with overtones of Marx's impoverishment of the proletariat. No evidence has yet been advanced to show clear dominance of the substitution effect, and so this claim must fail.

To prove the redistributive power of unionism, it must also be shown that diversion of property income to wages, or leveling of personal incomes, can be attributed directly to collective bargaining or to the political influence of unionism, and not to other forces. . . .

Findings of leading studies. Though unionism attempts to control market forces to raise money wage rates, the most significant fact yielded by recent studies of income share behavior here and in England is that thus far collective bargaining has had little observable influence upon share distribution.[2] Burkhead, Johnson, and Denison all have found some long-run gain in labor's share, but none of them even mentions bargaining as a factor. Levinson also has observed a secular increase and credits collective bargaining with some influence, but only because it was supported by a peculiarly favorable economic environment. Phelps Brown and Hart have noted a small long-run increase in the United Kingdom and reach conclusions similar to Levinson's regarding the role of bargaining.

Despite differences of method and definition, all of these studies indicate that the upward shift in the employees' share has been relatively small, while showing the familiar inverse movement to the business cycle. The authors explain its secular rise mainly by influences extraneous to bargaining itself: the great growth in the government sector of the economy (Johnson, Denison, Levinson); decline of the proprietorship industries and rise of labor-intensive production (Johnson, Denison, Levinson); and government policies affecting rents, the interest rate, and full employment (Levinson, Phelps Brown, and Hart). . . . Finally, it is apparent from comparison of these studies that wage gains over the long run have not directly cut into the profits of enterprise. . . .

There is little evidence in these studies to support the inference that collective bargaining has significantly increased labor's relative share of the national income or has diverted profits to wages.[3] Nor is there convincing support for the thesis that collective bargaining has checked an otherwise inevitable decline in labor's relative share — inevitable because the rapid rise

* [See pp. 181–182 for notes to this article. — Ed.]

in capital investment per worker is supposedly labor-displacing in character.

However, unionism also has political influence. Undoubtedly it has helped to shape government policies that in turn have affected income shares. By pressing strongly for the postwar full employment program even at the risk of some inflation, the unions have helped invoke policies that may perhaps have increased labor's absolute income share by preventing serious slumps, though the inflationary phases may have aided profits at the expense of wages. Price control probably checked a decline in labor's relative share during World War II, when marked economic expansion occurred.[4] However, the most important redistributive influences have been taxes — on corporate profits, employers' payrolls, and personal incomes; and transfers — social security and private welfare benefits.[5] Clearly, unionism has politically supported these redistributive policies. However, they have enjoyed a broad base of middle-class support as well, which makes it difficult to assess the decisiveness of the unions' political role. . . . Without middle-class support, its political program could hardly have been decisive. Besides, collective bargaining could not have greatly compressed the wage structure if basic trends had not operated in the same direction. Bargaining has not been able to divert much property income directly to wages, nor is there strong basis for a belief that it has done much to improve the relative positions of very low wage workers.

Why has collective bargaining had so little effect upon relative shares? The available evidence suggests strongly that over the past quarter-century collective bargaining itself has not significantly changed relative shares, while profits before taxes have been successfully maintained. . . .

Part of the answer has been suggested by Clark Kerr: so far American unionism has had neither the incentive nor the power to penetrate deeply enough into economic decision-making to force a redistribution of shares.[6] For this penetration to work, the unions would either have to cripple the employers' freedom to innovate and to adjust employment and prices, or they would have to invoke political action to introduce a draconian system of price control or "fair shares" taxation. So far they have chosen neither course, no doubt because the rich yield of the American economy has given these alternatives so little attraction. Accordingly, so long as the economic environment continues to yield favorable returns to labor it seems unlikely that the unions would shift their goals to radical policies of redistribution. Both membership motivation and the requisite economic and political power are lacking. More likely the unions will continue to follow their customary practice of demanding a share of the fruits of progress through higher wages, shorter hours, and other benefits, allowing management adequate scope and incentive for the innovations required. . . . Of course the results of this research do not prove that unionism is a failure; only that it has not yet destroyed the resiliency and initiative of the entrepreneur, if indeed this were ever its intention.

Consider the evidence. Collective bargaining has not captured wages at the expense of profits. It has not greatly disturbed relative wages and the distribution of labor. Nor has unionism altered the rate of economic progress in any large way. True, unionism has helped foster creeping inflation, but even here only with the indispensable support of other more powerful economic groups. So far its main contributions lie elsewhere: shorter hours, a new system of wage compensation, a private social security system, more orderly plant wage structures, and a system of jurisprudence that regulates the employment relationship to reflect the interests of employees as well as those of management and consumers.

Granted that the evidence is not all in, the facts at hand suggest that it is a mistake to interpret modern unionism as an anti-capitalist institution.

INCOME DISTRIBUTION: THE REVOLUTIONARY NEW DEAL

The Fundamental Political Issue Today Is Taxation

HAROLD L. ICKES

Through all the convolutions of policy the New Deal's class over-tones showed clearly. In one way or another, Franklin Roosevelt meant to help the little man. To little men and big, this implied income redistribution. Roosevelt himself, in an occasional radical mood, declared for redistribution. Some of the first New Dealers thought that an economic formula could be found to help the underdog without actually squeezing the benefits from the invest-ing classes. But resentment of the rich was very strong in the 1930s, and Roosevelt probably would have made income and wealth redistribution an important part of the New Deal even had Huey Long never been so successful with his Share Our Wealth movement. Liberal economic theory pointed to inequali-ties of wealth as a prime cause of the depression, and the eco-nomic and political wisdom of Keynes' advice to borrow from the rich rather than tax them had yet to be widely appreciated.

As any contemporary could have told you, Roosevelt did tax the rich. The complaints that Secretary of the Interior Harold Ickes records below came from men who thought themselves hard hit by the tax laws of 1935 and 1936 and by the higher labor costs that NRA, the Wagner Act, and the Fair Labor Standards Act appeared to force upon employers. This legislating and com-plaining produced a very tenacious myth: the New Deal had brought revolutionary changes in the distribution of wealth and income in the United States. "The transformation in the dis-

*tribution of our national income," wrote economist Arthur F.
Burns in 1951, ". . . may already be counted as one of the great
social revolutions of history." Why should one doubt it? The
wealthy should have known, and they told of confiscatory taxation and the end of those financial incentives that are the heart
of the free enterprise system.*

Cissy Patterson has been spending the summer in her home on Long
Island and she asked me to spend the week end with her. I accepted, but with
this new development with regard to my speech and considering the way I
was feeling, I decided that I did not want to go. I called her on the telephone
Friday night to tell her that I had found I could not come, but she was so
insistent that I said I would go. She told me that she had been counting on
me and had made her plans accordingly and it didn't seem fair to let her
down. Moreover, I decided that it would do me good if I went.

I took the nine o'clock train Saturday morning to New York. My
night's sleep had done me good. I dictated to Mr. Cubberley all the way to
North Philadelphia and the dictation went pretty well, so that I was through
with what I wanted to do when we reached that point. Cissy's car met me at
the Pennsylvania Station in New York and I was driven out to her place,
which is near Port Washington, Long Island.

The place was originally owned by the late Burke Cochran, a very
eloquent Congressman for many years who had quite a checkered career.
Then it was owned for a period by Cosden, the man who made such a big and
sudden fortune in oil. He contrived to have the Prince of Wales (now King
Edward VIII) as his guest. That was before Cosden went broke. I think there
was an intervening ownership before it was bought by Mr. and Mrs. Elmer
Schlesinger, Mrs. Patterson then being Mrs. Schlesinger.

The house is a big frame, rambling structure on the top of a hill.
Not the kind of a house one would build now, but comfortable and roomy.
It is surrounded by some very beautiful trees and there is a vista down to
the harbor. J. Pierpont Morgan's yacht, *Corsair*, was anchored a short distance off the shore all the time I was at Cissy's. There are sixty-five acres of
land, and some little distance away Cissy has a bungalow where she goes to be
alone and work. There is a very lovely salt-water swimming pool on the place,
a big lawn, and nice gardens.

From Harold L. Ickes, *The Secret Diary of Harold L. Ickes: The First
Thousand Days, 1933–1936* (New York: Simon and Schuster, 1953), pp.
649–53. Copyright © 1953, by Simon & Schuster, Inc. Reprinted by permission of the publisher.

Saturday night we went to the Herbert B. Swopes' for dinner. There were fourteen at the table, among them Henry Luce and his wife. Luce is editor of *Time*. There was also a young Vanderbilt. I can only say for him that I hope he is not as dumb as he looks and acts. He didn't open his face, except for food, during the entire evening. Another interesting couple were Mr. and Mrs. William Randolph Hearst, Jr.

After dinner the men went into the library and the discussion turned on politics at once, although I did not bring up the subject. Later two other men came, one of them a Warburg and the other a man by the name of Lewis, who writes songs. With the exception of Swope and myself, both of whom were for Roosevelt, and of Lewis, who seemed to be open-minded, all the others were strong Landon men. . . .

Luce, who seems to be a very able man, was especially strong in his opposition to the President. He thinks that Roosevelt has offended and hampered business. Young Hearst opined that the unemployment problem would be taken care of by private industry if the President would only let business alone. I took issue with that by pointing out to him that there were a couple of million men out of work even during our most prosperous year in 1929, and I ventured the prediction that with business going full tilt there would be many more people than this out of work in the future. I said that business would not put a single extra man on that it could get along without, and I pointed to the fact that during the depression many industries, notably steel, had been improving their technological techniques so that it could turn out the same amount of product with fewer hands. . . .

Sunday morning Harry F. Guggenheim, former Minister to Cuba and son of Simon Guggenheim, came over to see Cissy. He had been out to the notification ceremonies at Topeka and was quite enthusiastic not only about Landon but about his acceptance speech. He is the only man I have yet met of either party who has had even faint praise for the acceptance speech. I asked him, as I had asked others the night before, what were the specifications to support the charge that Roosevelt was antagonistic to business. My discussion with Guggenheim clarified the whole thing in my mind. It became clear that, exactly as I had said in my speech at the University of Virginia, the fundamental political issue today is taxation. Roosevelt, according to these very rich people, is penalizing business and tearing it down because he has increased the income tax rates in the higher brackets and because he is taxing surpluses in corporation treasuries. This was the only reaction that I could get to my insistent questions asking what Roosevelt had done or proposed to do that was inimical to business.

As Guggenheim put it, under the Roosevelt policies, there will be no incentive, as of old, in the heart of any young man to make a great success in life. His initiative will be destroyed. He brought in the name of Henry Ford as an ideal for the youth of the future to emulate. I asked him what harm had been done to Henry Ford, as he is still a very rich man, to which he replied that when he dies his property will be broken up. I remarked that even so, Edsel Ford stood to inherit a least a couple of hundred millions and I thought that the ability to acquire and possess such a fortune as that might be enough incentive for any young man. It was this that gave me the answer and made it abundantly clear that it isn't anything that Roosevelt has done or proposes to do to hurt business directly but simply the fear of increased taxes that has made such a bitter enemy out of practically everyone in the class with which I was associated over the week end.

Swope, during the discussion at his house, gave it as his opinion that if Landon should be elected, there might be the very hell to pay in a few years. I followed up with the argument that I have made on other occasions that people won't indefinitely endure hunger and that if we do not give them an opportunity to earn enough to live on, sooner or later we will run the risk of revolution. I said that it might be a question of giving up a portion of our fortunes and saving the rest or having all of them taken away from us.

After I knew who young Hearst was, I took two or three occasions, without mentioning any names, to show how I felt about men being called communists who were simply trying to improve the social order and give the underdog a chance. I insisted that Roosevelt really had saved capitalism. However, there is no use trying to talk to men of that type. They do not know what has happened in the world, they haven't sense enough to appraise the social forces of this generation, and they cannot see ahead into the future any farther than the ends of their noses.

INCOME DISTRIBUTION: THE
CONSERVATIVE NEW DEAL

Was the New Deal a Social Revolution?

Douglass C. North

The idea that the New Deal redistributed wealth and income was not effectively challenged for years. Some empirical work just after the war, in particular Simon Kuznets' Shares of Upper Income Groups in Income and Savings *(1953), seemed to confirm once and for all that there had been a revolutionary redistribution of income as a result of the New Deal. But this confirmation was belied in the 1960s. The rediscovery of poverty in the early 1960s intensified interest in exactly where the money was in America, and recent books by Robert Lampmann, Herman Miller, and Gabriel Kolko, despite their disagreements, have shown that wealth is distributed today no more democratically than it was in 1910. Such changes as have occurred have hurt the top 5 per cent of income earners (Kuznets' study-group), but their losses accrued only to the top second and third of the income tenths. The vast middle ranges of American society are in about the same relative position they were before the First World War, and the bottom two income tenths have actually* lost *ground during the past fifty years, the 1930s not excepted.*

The study of income distribution is a difficult science, and trends in the 1930s are not entirely clear. But it is fair to summarize as follows: the New Deal failed to significantly redistribute income (although it may have prevented regressive redistribution); really heavy taxation of the rich came only with the war and was offset by a broadened tax base, which by 1944 had pulled into the federal income tax net an additional 35 million people who had formerly made too little money to be so honored.

*There was no revolution in income distribution under Franklin
Roosevelt.*

*Scholars are still trying to explain this surprising outcome,
and Douglass North, who teaches economics at the University
of Washington, provides a useful review of the problem below.
We know that Roosevelt was irresolute on the matter of taxation,
despite occasional strong statements such as the tax message of
June 19, 1935. We know that he allowed Congress to trim the laws
of 1935 and 1936 into quite modest revenue-producers. Roosevelt
was not much interested in taxation, and it must be said that
liberals generally failed to appreciate both the regressive impact
of pre-1935 taxes, especially state and local, and the potency of
taxation as an instrument of social reform. In addition to the
failure to write revenue laws that merited the hatred of the
rich, the administration based AAA funding on a regressive
processing tax, failed to hold the line on prices under NRA so
that the labor provisions would tax employers, and in 1935
financed the Social Security Act (old age insurance) by a regressive
payroll tax on employees. The fiscal aspects of the Social Security
system were especially disastrous to those who hoped for income
redistribution. Social Security taxes, write Joseph Pechman,
Henry Aaron, and Michael Taussig, "are particularly burdensome
on the poor. In the long run, both the employer and the employee payroll taxes are probably paid by the workers."*

*Few New Dealers, and no men of wealth, understood how parts
of the federal revenue apparatus largely canceled each other out,
or how the slight progressivity that Senator Pat Harrison and his
Senate Finance Committee had allowed in the federal revenue
system was nullified by regressive state and local taxes. Roosevelt
absorbed the hatred of the propertied classes and the gratitude
of the bottom two-thirds. But income redistribution, which so
stirred the political passions of the 1930s and helped sweep Roosevelt into office every four years for as long as he lived, had never
taken place at all.*

How successful was the New Deal in its efforts? Its success with respect to recovery was certainly far from complete. By 1940 a substantial share
of the labor force was still unemployed . . . ; this totaled 8 million people
in 1940, comprising almost 15 per cent of the labor force, and 10 per cent

From Douglass C. North, *Growth and Welfare in the American Past:
A New Economic History,* © 1966. Reprinted by permission of Prentice-
Hall, Inc., Englewood Cliffs, N.J.

were still unemployed in 1941 when the economy had begun to gird for war. The recovery that had shown promise in 1935 and 1936 was set back severely in 1937. Again, the policies of the Board of Governors of the Federal Reserve have frequently been blamed, in that they raised reserve requirements in the beginning of that year, so that the economy again fell back into the depths, re-emerging only by 1939. Certainly, the New Deal did not cause complete recovery, but an evaluation of its degree of success would have to be made against some hypothetical, alternative set of policies. One thing is clear, however: what the New Deal failed to do, World War II did with vigor. Between 1941 and 1942, when we suddenly became involved in global war, we again became a full-employment economy, remarkably illustrating how we could expand output and productive capacity and reorient ourselves to prosecute a war in a fashion and to a degree that amazed our allies and dismayed our enemies.

WAS THE NEW DEAL A SOCIAL REVOLUTION?

The New Deal provided hope and encouragement to millions in a desperate era. It equally produced violent epithets from businessmen and conservatives generally. Yet, viewed from a more detached perspective of more than a generation, what were the long-run consequences of the New Deal in terms of its effect on the welfare of American society? Was the New Deal really a new deal? Presumably, if it was, it (1) brought about a more fully employed economy, (2) accelerated the rate of growth of the economy, or (3) redistributed income in favor of that one-third of the nation who were ill-clothed, ill-housed, and ill-fed, to use Franklin D. Roosevelt's famous phrase. In order to do a careful appraisal, it would be necessary to spell out what hypothetical alternative we had in mind in each case. However, the necessary research has not yet been done, and at this point all we can do is to provide a more limited appraisal of the influence of New Deal policies.

With respect to full employment, we have already observed that the New Deal failed during the 1930's to accomplish its objective. Failure is not surprising in the light of governmental fiscal policy. A careful examination yields the conclusion.[1]* (1) In only two years during the 1930's was governmental fiscal policy (at all levels) significantly more expansionary (in terms of its effect on aggregate demand) than it had been in 1929. The two exceptions were 1931 and 1936, when large payments to veterans were made over the objection of both the Hoover and the Roosevelt administrations. (2) Federal government fiscal policies were somewhat more expansionary (in part as a result of the veterans' payments, opposed by the executive branch) than state and local government policies; and when all three are taken together, they

* [See p. 182 for notes to this article. — Ed.]

about cancel each other out in terms of any significant net effect. (3) The primary reason for this ineffectiveness was that taxes at every level of government expanded. All governments combined had run a deficit (spent more than they took in in taxes) in 1929, but from 1933 to 1939 (except 1936) all governments either ran a surplus (took in more than they spent) or had an approximately balanced budget.

Yet, the New Deal left one heritage that appears to have played an influential part in maintaining high levels of employment and income in periods of subsequent recession. These are the social security measures of old-age and survivors' insurance, unemployment insurance, and workmen's compensation. In periods of recession, they have maintained the income of unemployed workers and tended to limit the fall in income and to prevent vicious spiral results. . . . Social security measures appear to have developed some important, built-in stabilizers for mitigating subsequent recessions.

Did the New Deal affect the over-all growth rate of the economy? There is certainly no clear evidence on this subject. One would expect that New Deal measures that might have had some effect were (1) setting up regulatory bodies designed to improve the performance of business, with the result, presumably, of improving resource allocation, and (2) undertaking projects in areas where public investment might be assumed to have a higher social rate of return than private rate of return. Certainly, however, the results in both cases are equivocal at best. The regulatory bodies at times may have accomplished some improvements in resource allocation and industry performance; at other times, they proved to be handmaidens to the industries themselves, making unwise resource allocation and hampering rather than benefiting the performance of the industry. A continuing dilemma of regulatory agencies is that they can become vehicles whereby the regulated regulate the regulators, in the interest of the regulated — rather than that of the public.

I know of no over-all appraisal of government investment in water resources during the New Deal period. Perhaps the most important contribution was the impetus it gave to developing benefit-cost analysis, so that we could measure the rate of return on such projects and eventually extend our analysis to other types of government activity.

In many respects, the third issue was the one around which New Deal policy at the time became most controversial: the redistribution of income in the United States. For if the New Deal did not achieve full employment and if its implication for growth are at best equivocal, then the only way in which it could have benefited that one-third of the nation was by redistributing income in their favor, and it was clearly evident that the New Deal intended such results in a number of its policies. Specifically, policies that were aimed at encouraging the growth of trade unions — such as the

National Labor Relations Act and the Norris-LaGuardia Act — had the objective of expanding unionism in America, and it was commonly assumed
unions would thereby increase incomes going to labor. These acts, together
with the rivalry which developed between the American Federation of Labor
and the newly created Congress of Industrial Organizations, did expand trade
union membership from about 3 million in 1932 to 9 million in 1940. Similarly, the Fair Labor Standards Act, establishing minimum wages for workers, aimed at benefiting the lowest-income groups. The price-support program in agriculture, the subsidized low-cost housing for low-income groups,
and the social security program were all aimed in this direction. What were
their results?

Chart 1 shows disposable income of the top 1 per cent and top 5 per
cent of income groups between 1919 and 1946, and Chart 2 shows the share
of the top 1 per cent of wealth-holders in the United States. Both charts show
that wealth and income were becoming more unequally distributed in the
1920's, and both show that after 1929 the percentage of wealth and income

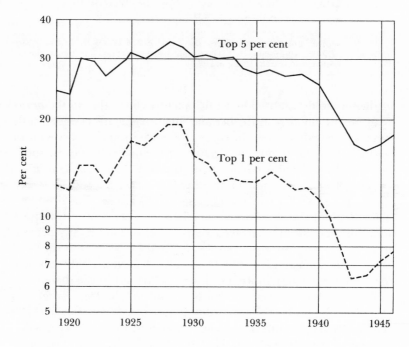

CHART 1. Per Cent Shares of Disposable Income Received by Top 1 Per
Cent and 5 Per Cent of Total Population, 1919–1946

Source: *Hist. Statistics* (Washington: GPO, 1960), Ser. G 131–46, p. 167.

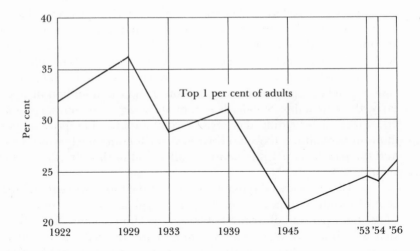

CHART 2. SHARE OF PERSONAL SECTOR WEALTH HELD BY TOP WEALTH-
HOLDERS, SELECTED YEARS, 1922–1956

Source: Robert J. Lampman, *The Share of Top Wealth-Holders in National Wealth,
1922–56*, (Princeton, N.J.: Princeton University Press for the National Bureau of
Economic Research, 1962), p. 25.

of the top holders falls. The wealth picture shows that in the period 1933 to
1939, wealth-holding again became somewhat more unequal, although the
income charts shows that the share of the top income-holder continues to fall
throughout. The significant decline in inequality comes in the war years,
however. It is equally evident that after war, wealth and income again became somewhat more unequally distributed. During the Thirties, there was
a decline in the share of the highest-income groups, but it appears to have
gone to middle-income groups. The lowest 20 per cent of consumer units, in
terms of their income, received 4.1 per cent of total family personal income
in 1935; they received 5 per cent in 1947 and 4.6 per cent in 1962.

In summary, it is not at all clear that New Deal measures provided
any significant redistribution of income. The fall in the share of top wealth-
and income-holders came about as a result of the Depression in 1929, and
there had already been a significant decline by the time the New Deal started.
The really significant fall is clearly related to the high progressive tax rates
imposed during World War II. Moreover, the redistribution from the very
rich appears to favor middle-income rather than lowest-income groups.

A careful examination of the measures designed to effect this income
redistribution suggests that this over-all result is not surprising. If incomes
were being redistributed in the 1930's, it was because the laws that were

passed either facilitated a relative rise in the low-income group or transferred income from higher-income groups to low-income groups. Minimum wage laws and promotion of trade unions were aimed at facilitating a relative rise in the low-income group, but their effectiveness in redistributing income in favor of low-income groups is debatable. It is not at all self-evident that minimum wage laws really raised wages of low-income groups. To the extent that they are effective, and that the minimum wage exceeds the value of output of workers, the long-run result will be more unemployment and therefore more inequality in income. Similarly, even though trade unions may raise wages of their members, it is a much debated point whether they raised wages over all. Labor's share of national income appears to have been increasing, but this is certainly not attributable to trade unions.[2] Therefore, if trade unions do manage to raise their wages but do not influence labor's share of national income, then they do so at the expense of three-quarters of the labor force, which is unorganized.[3] Since this includes most of the lowest-wage earners, the result appears likely to have made incomes more unequal, rather than more equal.

More effective results surely stem from the direct transfers of income from high- to low-income groups, as in the case of public housing and welfare payments. Their magnitude in the Thirties does not appear to have been significant, although the slight increase in the position of the lowest quintan of income earners in the 1940's suggests that the highly progressive tax rates combined with welfare measures in that decade temporarily improved the status of the lowest-income group. But that modest result came after the New Deal.

BLACKS: THE
REVOLUTIONARY NEW DEAL

The Negro and the New Deal Era

LESLIE H. FISHEL, JR.

Black Americans went into the 1930s voting Republican, as they had since Lincoln; by 1940 they were voting virtually en bloc for Franklin Roosevelt and the Democratic party. The total black vote was small, since most blacks still lived in the South where they were disfranchised, but the shift in black political allegiance to the Democratic party was nonetheless one of the most fundamental and far-reaching in American politics. The electoral college system strengthened the influence of heavily urbanized states, at least in presidential elections. As the black vote grew in northern and western cities, it became a crucial element in the liberal coalition that made the Democratic party the majority party for thirty years after the New Deal.

The reasons why blacks turned the picture of Lincoln to the wall and went over to the Democrats are summarized below by Leslie Fishel, Jr., President of Heidelberg College, in Ohio. The relief funds and employment opportunities that the New Deal brought to blacks were no more important than the general feeling, conveyed by Eleanor Roosevelt, Ickes, and Hopkins in their social affairs and appointment policies and by the great personal warmth of the President himself, that a breakthrough had come, that the Negro now had powerful friends in high places. Since Lincoln's day no administration had shown such sympathies. Blacks responded by transferring their deep political and personal loyalties to the party of the New Deal and Franklin Roosevelt.

44

The rhythm and the tone of the New Deal was set by the man in the White House, since Franklin D. Roosevelt was the spokesman and the master of his administration. His first public statement, the inaugural address of March 4, 1933, pierced the depression-fostered gloom and stabbed deftly and surely at the nation's physical and psychological ills. In stark contrast to his predecessor, Roosevelt recognized the prevailing despair, "the dark realities of the moment," and committed himself and his administration to a brighter future. He lashed out in Biblical terms against the profiteers and the selfish among the monied classes and laid down an emphasis which would characterize his administration more than he then realized: "The measure of the restoration lies in the extent to which we apply social values more noble than mere monetary profit." Identifying himself with the unemployed and underprivileged — "our greatest primary task is to put people to work" — he compared the depression to a war emergency and he warned that he was prepared to mobilize the resources of the federal government to fight it.

Like so many of FDR's speeches, including his informal radio fireside chats, the written version of this one paled on paper. His voice exuded warmth and a personal inflection which brought him close to his listeners. His own physical affliction and the way he bore it earned him deserved admiration and gave encouragement to those who had afflictions of their own, even a darker skin. John Gunther testified to Roosevelt's attraction for people as "concrete and intimate. . . . He set up goals in human terms that the average man could grasp for." The general public responded to his magnetism; one of his secretaries selected a list of salutations which were used on letters addressed to him, and they ran the gamut from "Dear humanitarian friend of the people" to "My Pal!" and "Dear Buddy." Almost all of his callers remarked on his personal charm and persuasiveness.

These characteristics of FDR the man, taken with his consummate ability to personalize his understanding of human exploitation and underprivilege, made him the most attractive President, for Negro citizens, since the Civil War. Robert Vann, publisher of the Negro weekly Pittsburgh *Courier,* who was brought into the 1932 campaign by some of Roosevelt's lieutenants, advised his race to "go home and turn Lincoln's picture to the wall. The debt has been paid in full." Yet, like Lincoln, Roosevelt's actual commitments to the American Negro were slim. He was more a symbol than an activist in his own right. His compassion, though real, was tempered by his own background, by the enormity of the decisions which came up to him, and by political considerations. An enthusiastic politician, he used political weights and measures on a political scale to judge the evidence, and the

"The Negro and the New Deal Era" from *The Negro American: A Documentary History* by Leslie H. Fishel, Jr., and Benjamin Quarles. Copyright © 1967 by Scott, Foresman and Company.

Negro was often found wanting. When Walter White, the executive secretary of the NAACP, obtained an audience through the good graces of Mrs. Eleanor Roosevelt to plead for the President's public support of the antilynching bill, FDR demurred because he needed Southern votes in Congress on other matters.

Nevertheless, the FDR image eventually became a favorable one; his picture hung in living rooms and infant sons carried his name. At first, though, Negroes waited to be shown. Their publications granted him the benefit of doubt when he spoke about justice and equality, in the hope that he was talking, too, to Negroes. He called lynching murder, remarked W. E. B. DuBois, and "these things give us hope." His acknowledgment, through his Secretary of Labor, of the National Urban League's survey of economic conditions among Negroes was, in the words of an *Opportunity* editorial, "an evidence of his deep interest in the Negroes' welfare." By midway through his first term, FDR had captured the admiration and affection of the Negro people and, with that, their votes. During the campaign of 1936, Negroes were outspoken in their support of the Democratic national ticket. Sixteen thousand Harlem residents traveled to Madison Square Garden in September of that year to attend a political rally, and sixty other cities held similar and simultaneous rallies. The New Yorkers mixed a rich fare of music and entertainment with leading New Dealers talking politics, but it was an African Methodist Episcopal Bishop, the Reverend C. Ransome, who symbolized the affair and its meaning by reading a "New Emancipation Proclamation." The vote in November was anticlimactic; the second Roosevelt had weaned the Negro away from the Republican party.

Roosevelt did not publicly associate himself with Negro projects or Negro leaders before 1935, but his programs and some of his associates were more aggressive. Early in 1933, he approved of a suggestion that someone in his administration assume the responsibility for fair treatment of the Negroes, and he asked Harold Ickes to make the appointment. A young white Georgian, Clark Foreman, came to Washington at Ickes' request to handle the task, and brought in as his assistant an even younger Negro of great promise, Robert C. Weaver. Foreman successfully made his way through the burgeoning maze of new agencies which were springing up and did a respectable job of calling to the attention of agency heads and their assistants an awareness of the special problems of Negroes. Along with Ickes, Daniel Roper, the Secretary of Commerce; Harry Hopkins, FDR's relief administrator; and Aubrey Williams, a Hopkins deputy, were sympathetic to committing the New Deal to work more generously with and for Negroes.

From the first, the various New Deal agencies carried the major burden of this emphasis, since they translated words into bread and butter, shelter and schooling. For the Negro, the most significant were the Federal

Employment Relief Administration (FERA), the National Recovery Administration (NRA), the Works Progress Administration, later called the Work Projects Administration (WPA), the Agricultural Adjustment Administration (AAA), the Tennessee Valley Authority (TVA), the National Youth Administration (NYA), the Civilian Conservation Corps (CCC), and the public housing efforts of several agencies. There were others in the alphabetical jungle which assisted Negroes, as whites, in more specialized ways, such as the Federal Writers' Project and the Office of Education studies. The very number of agencies added credence to the emergent fact that, for the first time, the federal government had engaged and was grappling with some of the fundamental barriers to race progress.

It was one thing to engage and grapple with a problem at the federal level, and another thing to implement it at lower levels. Most of the New Deal agency programs ran afoul of local laws and customs and most of them capitulated on very practical grounds. As a consequence, Negroes vigorously attacked the inequities, even while they appreciated the limited benefits. FERA, the first New Deal agency to work directly to alleviate the plight of the destitute, tried by locally administered dole and work-projects to pump more money into circulation. Until the end of 1935, when it was abolished, it administered most of the direct relief and work relief programs which the New Dealers initiated, distributing about four billion dollars. Its progress was dogged by racial discrimination, since the design of projects and allocation of funds remained in local hands. Jacksonville, Florida, Negro families on relief outnumbered white families three to one, but the money was divided according to proportions of the total city population. Thus 15,000 Negro families received 45 per cent of the funds and 5,000 white families got 55 per cent. Along the Mississippi River, from Natchez to New Orleans, Negroes were passed over for skilled jobs and frequently received less than the stipulated minimum wage. When the state of Georgia squeezed out of the FERA administrator the right to fix hourly wages for Negroes below thirty cents an hour, *Opportunity* mournfully questioned, "Does this presage the end of that heralded concern for the Forgotten Man?"

If the relief program raised questions of discrimination, the NRA brought howls of indignation. In the words of a Negro labor specialist, the NRA administrator, General Hugh A. Johnson, was "a complete failure" for not properly recognizing the Negro. The industrial codes established under NRA deferred to geographic wage and employment consideration so that the Negro worker generally earned less money for equal time and was frozen out of skilled jobs. A young Negro lawyer, John P. Davis, organized the Joint Committee on National Recovery in the fall of 1933 to persuade federal authorities to rectify these policies. "It has filed briefs, made appearances at public hearings," he wrote, and "buttonholed administrative officers relative to the elimination of unfair clauses in the codes," but to little avail. In self-defense, NRA officials explained the difficulty in bucking local customs, pointing out also that the NRA was responsible only for industrial workers. Agricultural laborers, domestic servants, and the service trades were not included, and most of the unskilled workers were exempted by statute from wage and hour minimums. "It is not fair," wrote an NRA administrator in a Negro journal, "to blame the NRA for not curing all these ills, if such they be, within a year." Until the Supreme Court decreed its demise in the spring of 1935, the NRA was a favored whipping boy for Negroes, as well as for others. "The Blue Eagle," a Virginia newspaper observed, "may be [for Negroes] a predatory bird instead of a feathered messenger of happiness."

The TVA and the AAA came under fire in the early years of the New Deal for similar reasons. Negro critics raged at the all-white model towns, such as Norris, Tennessee, which were established in conjunction with TVA. Homes for white workers on the project were substantial, while Negro workers lived in substandard temporary barracks. Skilled jobs went first to whites and most labor crews were segregated. TVA, it appeared to two observers in 1934, "aims to maintain the *status quo*." A year later, the situation seemed little better. In one sample two-week period, Negroes were 11 per cent of the working force, receiving only 9.5 per cent of the payroll. Under AAA, Negro tenant farmers and sharecroppers, as the most dispensable laborers, suffered first from the crop-reduction policy and found themselves without employment. Concerned about the evolving discriminatory pattern, the NAACP in 1934 devoted a major share of its energy to trying to prevent white landlords from illegally depriving their Negro tenants of crop-reduction bonuses.

Two New Deal programs for young people operated with a minimum of discrimination: the CCC and the NYA. The CCC established segregated camps in the South and in some parts of the North; the great bulk of the integrated camps were in New England. By 1935, its peak year, CCC had over a half million boys in camp. In general, Negroes stayed in CCC camps longer than whites, were not moved up to administrative posts in camps as readily as whites, and were restricted to less than 10 per cent of the total enrollment. Since the proportion of young Negro men in need was substantively higher than this, the quota system was actually inequitable. The NYA, which Mary McLeod Bethune served as administrator of Negro affairs, was shaped to help young men and women in school and with schooling. It grew out of the university and college student relief program established under FERA, and by the end of its first six months, in late 1935, had distributed more than forty million dollars. Conforming to existing state and regional patterns, the NYA still managed to help a critical age group among Negroes.

The debit side of the New Deal's efforts to assist Negroes fell far short of its material and psychological credits. Never before had Negro leaders participated in government affairs as freely and as frequently. The Department of Commerce had E. K. Jones, on leave from the National Urban League; the NYA had Mrs. Bethune; Interior had William H. Hastie and Weaver; the Social Security Board had Ira DeA. Reid; Labor had Lawrence W. Oxley; the Office of Education had Ambrose Caliver, to mention a few. Never before had there been so great a stress on improving the education of Negroes. Many relief programs included elementary education and training classes as part of the regimen. Negro colleges and universities received funds for buildings. The Office of Education, along with other agencies, began an important study of the status of Negro education.

Professional opportunities opened up in government, although not at the rate at which Negroes were graduating from college. For the first time, Negroes were employed as architects, lawyers, engineers, economists, statisticians, interviewers, office managers, case aids, and librarians. Nonprofessional white-collar jobs, which had rarely been within reach of the race, now became available to trained stenographers, clerks, and secretaries. While many of these jobs centered around programs for Negroes within the government, such as Negro slum clearance projects, Negro NYA offices, and the like, they broke the dam which had hitherto kept Negroes out of these kinds of positions.

Harold Ickes, a former president of the Chicago chapter of the NAACP, was the first New Dealer to be recognized as a tried friend. He quickly ended discrimination in his department and set the example by placing professionally-trained Negroes in responsible positions. He first drew FDR's attention to Hastie as a candidate for the federal judge vacancy in the Virgin Islands, and Roosevelt made the appointment in 1937. Ickes appeared at predominantly Negro functions and in 1936, on the occasion of an address at Howard University, even went so far as to wear a University of Alabama hood with his cap and gown because "it seemed to have the best color effect. . . ." While Ickes could not breach established segregation patterns in housing, one-eighth of the federal housing projects planned before the end of 1935 were in mixed neighborhoods. Approximately one-half of them were in Negro slum areas and, thanks to the negotiating skill of Ickes' assistant, Robert C. Weaver, the contracts for a substantial portion of these called for the employment of both skilled and unskilled Negro workers.

Eleanor Roosevelt, the New Deal's conscience, made it her business to reaffirm by word and deed her faith in the equality of opportunity for all. She included Negro and mixed organizations on her itineraries, welcomed mixed groups of adults and children to the White House, and spoke up for the race at critical times. In 1936, as part of a long memo on political strategy in the presidential campaign, she urged party leaders to ask respected Negroes like Mrs. Bethune to participate among Negro groups. The penalty for her unflagging advocacy of the Negro's cause was abuse or occasionally embarrassing questions. As the European war spread after 1939, she confronted questions about the Negro's loyalty. "Rarely," she told a group of New Jersey college women in 1940, "do you come across a case where a Negro has failed to measure up to the standard of loyalty and devotion to his country."

Eleanor Roosevelt was more than a symbol of the New Deal's conscience; she was a vehicle for approaching and influencing the President. She performed this service for Walter White when the antilynching bill was before Congress. When the DAR refused to allow Marian Anderson to sing in Constitution Hall, Mrs. Roosevelt was the intermediary who secured permission to use the Lincoln Memorial for the concert. It was useful for the President to have his wife serve in these varying capacities, absorbing some of the criticism, supplying him with information he could get from no other source, and sparking his conscience, when that was needed. This relieved the President from having to punctuate his speeches and press conferences with references to the Negro. Before 1935, these were almost nonexistent; after 1935, they increased in frequence and directness, but Roosevelt did not directly commit himself, as his wife did, until his famous Executive Order 8802 of June, 1941, established a Fair Employment Practice Committee to supervise all defense-contract industries.

In many ways, 1935 seemed to be a pivotal year for the President's public statements to and about the Negro. His annual message to Congress in January asserted that "in spite of our efforts and in spite of our talk, we have not weeded out the overprivileged and we have not effectively lifted up the underprivileged." Uplift and underprivilege were two words which Negroes understood, two words which footnoted their history; yet Roosevelt did not mention the Negro specifically. Shortly after that, he told WPA state administrators that "we cannot discriminate in any of the work we are conducting either because of race or religion or politics," and although he went on to speak of political pressures, the word "race" was there for Negroes to see. In two other public statements later in the year, FDR paid lip service to the accomplishments of the race and by 1936, an election year, he proclaimed his policy that "among American citizens there should be no forgotten men and no forgotten races." The transformation was more one of degree than of conviction; Roosevelt was beginning to speak to the Negro, however rarely, rather than to lump him without identification into massive generalizations. But his eye was ever on the balance of political forces and he never voluntarily came out foursquare for the Negro.

In perspective, Roosevelt's circumspection on some domestic issues was less significant than his New Deal legislative program. Labor unions received substantial encouragement from Section 7a of NRA and from the Wagner Act, although the White House maintained an equivocal position toward both labor and management. The jump in union memberships and the rise of the Committee on Industrial Organization, first within the AF of L and later as the independent Congress of Industrial Organizations (CIO), gained impetus from the newly established right to strike and the newly created federal board to mediate labor disputes. A strengthened labor movement confronted, as one of its problems, the question of Negro members. Older unions such as the United Mine Workers and the International Ladies Garment Workers Union welcomed Negroes without distinction. When the CIO broke from the AF of L, its nucleus of unions including the new and somewhat fragile organizations in the automobile, rubber, and steel industries accepted Negroes on an equal basis, except in those localities where race friction was high. The United Textile Workers attempted to do the same, but the existence of textile plants in southern states made this task more onerous. It was not enough for a union to resolve, as the CIO did, to accept members without regard to race, creed, or color, or even, as the UAW and the organizing committees of the steelworkers did, to offer Negro workers a chance to join up. Negroes still hung back, alternately tempted and frightened by management's offers and threats. The wave of the future was with the industrial unions, and *Opportunity*'s declaration to Negro steelworkers that it would be "the apotheosis of stupidity" for them to stay out of the union battling for recognizance in 1937, was prophetic. The success of the Brotherhood of Sleeping Car Porters, under the leadership of A. Philip Randolph, in gaining recognition as the bargaining agent with the Pullman Company after a twelve-year struggle, marked the beginning of the race's influence in national labor circles and on national labor policy. . . .

Toward the end of the 1930's the federal government turned more and more of its attention to the European conflict, the economy flourished as the industrial bastion of the embattled Allies, and the Negro had committed himself to the New Deal and to President Roosevelt. Polls in 1940 showed that Negro voters overwhelmingly supported Roosevelt for a third term, and the polls were right. The reason for this support was not difficult to surmise. Outside of what the Democratic Administration had tried to do directly and indirectly, the decade itself was marked with identifiable milestones of progress. In athletics, Jesse Owen was an Olympic champion, and Negro football players starred on many of the major college teams. Professional baseball still resisted, but its time was not far off. In interracial activities, conferences on a variety of subjects began to meet with overbearing regularity and, though self-consciously interracial, the pattern developed almost irrevocably. College students and adults met to talk about education, religion, economic matters, and of course, civil rights. Even in the South,

the indomitable Mrs. Bethune organized an interracial conference at the college she founded, and the white University of Florida tentatively sent delegates. In the deep South, interracial conferences were held on a segregated
basis; Eleanor Roosevelt told of attending one in Birmingham and inadvertently sitting in the colored section. "At once the police appeared to re-
mind us of the rules and regulations on segregation. . . . Rather than give in
I asked that chairs be placed for us with the speakers facing the whole group."
White Southerners began to speak up for the Negro. They were still a small
minority, but the mere fact that a white supervisor of schools in Georgia
would admit to the inequalities of segregated schools, or a white North Carolina legislator would question a decreased appropriation for a Negro college,
was a sign of change. The rise of Huey Long in Louisiana brought a different
attitude, one of ignoring race differences without changing race relationships.
The all-white Mississippi Education Association established a committee in
1938 to recommend ways in which students might study Negro life, and
several Northern newspapers in 1940 editorially acknowledged the importance of Negro History Week. The tide had turned, and Negroes credited
the turning to the New Deal.

BLACKS: THE
CONSERVATIVE NEW DEAL

A Black Inventory of the New Deal

JOHN DAVIS

*The federal government's dealings with black Americans in the
1930s contrasted so favorably with past administrations' that
blacks transferred their political allegiance to Roosevelt and his
party. But this signified only relative progress, not the attainment
of equal treatment. Research has confirmed what a few black
leaders knew at the time, that the New Deal discriminated against
blacks in its programs and that it deliberately rejected entreaties
by white liberals and blacks to correct its racial inequities and to
outlaw lynching and the poll tax.*

*The essay below by a young black attorney, John Davis, an
organizer of the National Negro Congress in the 1930s, detailed
the racial shortcomings of the New Deal as early as 1935. Recent
studies of New Deal programs, such as that by John Salmond
on the Civilian Conservation Corps (CCC) and by Raymond
Wolters on NRA and AAA, show that while Fishel may be right
about the subjective impact of the New Deal on blacks, the
objective impact was closer to that described by Davis. Federal
relief and recovery programs either hurt blacks, as did the crop
restriction measures of the agricultural program, or helped them
far less than their numbers and need warranted. In most cases,
these failures were even pointed out to officials all the way up to
the White House without effect.*

*To the President, whose racial attitudes were more liberal
and sympathetic than those of most whites of his time and of
any President since Lincoln, the political facts of life seemed to
limit what he could do for blacks. He included blacks on as many*

*relief rolls and work relief programs as he was permitted by
public opinion and by the prejudices of his own bureaucrats;
he allowed Eleanor to have her picture taken with blacks and in
other ways to agitate the national conscience; he spoke out finally
against lynching (1934) and the poll tax (1938) but without
endorsing any federal legislative solution. As he told the
NAACP's Walter White in 1934: "I did not choose the instruments with which I would work." Congressional power was
largely in southern hands, and Roosevelt felt he could not en-
danger his entire legislative program just to curb racial injustices
that were as old as the nation.*

*Much remains to be learned about New Deal–black interaction
in the 1930s. We know that Roosevelt avoided any clear challenge
to the biracial system and we have his explanation for this. But
we do not know whether he and others accurately assessed the
political risks and advantages in a more vigorous pursuit of racial
justice. The overwhelming majority of blacks apparently thought
he had done all he could, and more than they had expected.
But even of this we are not sure. What satisfied blacks in the
1930s, at any rate, would not do so ten years later. The war
accomplished much more change than the New Deal in black-
white relations. While FDR brought hope, the war brought jobs,
geographical mobility, the liberation of new perspectives. In four
short years, the war changed more situations and attitudes than
all the New Dealers with all their good intentions, and proved
again to be the Master Reformer.*

It is highly important for the Negro citizen of America to take inventory of the gains and losses which have come to him under the "New
Deal." The Roosevelt administration has now had two years in which to
unfold itself. Its portents are reasonably clear to anyone who seriously studies
the varied activities of its recovery program. We can now state with reasonable certainty what the "New Deal" means for the Negro.

At once the most striking and irrefutable indication of the effect of
the New Deal on the Negro can be gleaned from relief figures furnished by
the government itself. In October, 1933, six months after the present administration took office, 2,117,000 Negroes were in families receiving relief in the

John Davis, "A Black Inventory of the New Deal," *Crisis*, XLII (1935),
pp. 141–45. Reprinted from *The Crisis* with the permission of Crisis
Publishing Company, Inc.

United States. These represented 17.8 per cent of the total Negro population
as of the 1930 census. In January, 1935, after nearly two years of *recovery
measures,* 3,500,000 Negroes were in families receiving relief, or 29 per cent
of our 1930 population. Certainly only a slight portion of the large increase in
the number of impoverished Negro families can be explained away by the
charitable, on the grounds that relief administration has become more humane. As a matter of fact federal relief officials themselves admit that grave
abuses exist in the administration of rural relief to Negroes. And this is re-
liably borne out by the disproportionate increase in the number of urban
Negro families on relief to the number of rural Negro families on relief. Thus
the increase in the number of Negroes in relief families is an accurate indication of the deepening of the economic crisis for black America.

The promise of NRA to bring higher wages and increased employment to industrial workers has glimmered away. In the code-making process
occupational and geographical differentials at first were used as devices to
exclude from the operation of minimum wages and maximum hours the bulk
of the Negro workers. Later, clauses basing code wage rates on the previously
existing wage differential between Negro and white workers tended to continue the inferior status of the Negro. For the particular firms, for whom
none of these devices served as an effective means of keeping down Negro
wages, there is an easy way out through the securing of an exemption specifically relating to the *Negro* worker in the plant. Such exemptions are becoming more numerous as time goes on. Thus from the beginning relatively few
Negro workers were even theoretically covered by NRA labor provisions.

But employers did not have to rely on the code-making process. The
Negro worker not already discriminated against through code provisions had
many other gauntlets to run. The question of importance to him as to all workers was, "as a result of all of NRA's maneuvers will I be able to buy more?"
The answer has been "No." A worker cannot eat a wage rate. To determine
what this wage rate means to him we must determine a number of other factors. Thus rates for longshoremen seem relatively high. But when we realize
that the average amount of work a longshoreman receives during the year is
from ten to fifteen weeks, the wage rate loses much of its significance. When
we add to that fact the increase in the cost of living — as high as 40 per cent
in many cases — the wage rate becomes even more chimerical. For other
groups of industrial workers increases in cost of living, coupled with the part
time and irregular nature of the work, make the results of NRA negligible.
In highly mechanized industries speed-up and stretch-out nullify the promised result of NRA to bring increased employment through shorter hours.
For the workers are now producing more in their shorter work periods than
in the longer periods before NRA. There is less employment. The first suf-

ferer from fewer jobs is the Negro worker. Finally the complete break-down of compliance machinery in the South has cancelled the last minute advantage to Negro workers which NRA's enthusiasts may have claimed.

The Agricultural Adjustment Administration has used cruder methods in enforcing poverty on the Negro farm population. It has made violations of the rights of tenants under crop reduction contracts easy; it has rendered enforcement of these rights impossible. The reduction of the acreage under cultivation through the government rental agreement rendered unnecessary large numbers of tenants and farm laborers. Although the contract with the government provided that the land owner should not reduce the number of his tenants, he did so. The federal courts have now refused to allow tenants to enjoin such evictions. Faced with this Dred Scott decision against farm tenants, the AAA has remained discreetly silent. Farm laborers are now jobless by the hundreds of thousands, the conservative government estimate of the decline in agricultural employment for the year 1934 alone being a quarter of a million. The larger portion of these are unskilled Negro agricultural workers — now without income and unable to secure work or relief.

But the unemployment and tenant evictions occasioned by the crop reduction policies of the AAA is not all. For the tenants and sharecroppers who were retained on the plantations the government's agricultural program meant reduced income. Wholesale fraud on tenants in the payment of parity checks occurred. Tenants complaining to the Department of Agriculture in Washington have their letters referred back to the locality in which they live and trouble of serious nature often results. Even when this does not happen, the tenant fails to get his check. The remainder of the land he tills on shares with his landlord brings him only the most meagre necessities during the crop season varying from three to five months. The rest of the period for him and his family is one of "root hog or die."

The past year has seen an extension of poverty even to the small percentage (a little more than 20 per cent) of Negro farmers who own their own land. For them compulsory reduction of acreage for cotton and tobacco crops, with the quantum of such reduction controlled and regulated by local boards on which they have no representation, has meant drastic reduction of their already low income. Wholesale confiscation of the income of the Negro cotton and tobacco farmer is being made by prejudiced local boards in the South under the very nose of the federal government. In the wake of such confiscation has come a tremendous increase in land tenantry as a result of foreclosures on Negro-owned farm properties.

Nor has the vast public works program, designed to give increased employment to workers in the building trades, been free from prejudice. State officials in the South are in many cases in open rebellion against the ruling of PWA that the same wage scales must be paid to Negro and white labor. Compliance with this paper ruling is enforced in only rare cases. The majority of the instances of violation of this rule are unremedied. Only unskilled work is given Negroes on public works projects in most instances. And even here discrimination in employment is notorious. Such is bound to be the case when we realize that there are only a handful of investigators available to seek enforcement.

Recently a move has been made by Negro officials in the administration to effect larger employment of Negro skilled and unskilled workers on public works projects by specifying that failure of a contractor to pay a certain percentage of his payroll to Negro artisans will be evidence of racial discrimination. Without doubting the good intentions of the sponsors of this ingenious scheme, it must nevertheless be pointed out that it fails to meet the problem in a number of vital particulars. It has yet to face a test in the courts, even if one is willing to suppose that PWA high officials will bring it to a test. Percentages thus far experimented with are far too low and the number of such experiments far too few to make an effective dent in the unemployment conditions of Negro construction industry workers. Moreover the scheme gives aid and comfort to employer-advocates of strike-breaking and the open shop; and, while offering, perhaps, some temporary relief to a few hundred Negro workers, it establishes a dangerous precedent which throws back the labor movement and the organization of Negro workers to a considerable degree. The scheme, whatever its Negro sponsors may hope to the contrary, becomes therefore only another excuse for their white superiors maintaining a "do-nothing" policy with regard to discrimination against Negroes in the Public Works Administration.

The Negro has no pleasanter outlook in the long term social planning ventures of the new administration. Planning for subsistence homesteads for industrially stranded workers has been muddled enough even without consideration of the problem of integrating Negroes into such plans. Subsistence Homesteads projects are overburdened with profiteering prices for the homesteads and foredoomed to failure by the lack of planning for adequate and permanent incomes for prospective homesteaders.

In callous disregard of the interdiction in the Constitution of the United States against use of federal funds for projects which discriminate against applicants solely on the ground of color, subsistence homesteads have been planned on a strictly "lily-white" basis. The more than 200 Negro applicants for the first project at Arthurdale, West Virginia were not even considered, Mr. Bushrod Grimes (then in charge of the project) announcing that the project was to be open only to "native white stock." As far north as Dayton, Ohio, where state laws prohibit any type of segregation against Negroes, the federal government has extended its "lily-white" policy. Recently it has established two Jim-Crow projects for Negroes. Thus the new administration seeks in its program of social planning to perpetuate ghettoes of Negroes for fifty years to come.

An even more blatant example of this policy of "lily-white" reconstruction is apparent in the planning of the model town of Norris, Tennessee, by the Tennessee Valley Authority. This town of 450 model homes is intended for the permanent workers on Norris Dam. The homes are rented by the federal government, which at all times maintains title to the land and dwellings and has complete control of the town management. Yet officials at TVA openly admit that no Negroes are allowed at Norris.

TVA has other objectionable features. While Negro employment now approaches an equitable proportion of total employment; the payroll of Negro workers remains disproportionately lower than that of whites. While the government has maintained a trade school to train workers on the project, no Negro trainees have been admitted. Nor have any meaningful plans matured for the future of the several thousand Negro workers who in another year or so will be left without employment, following completion of work on the dams being built by TVA.

None of the officials of TVA seems to have the remotest idea of how Negroes in the Tennessee Valley will be able to buy the cheap electricity which TVA is designed to produce. They admit that standards of living of the Negro population are low, that the introduction of industry into the Valley is at present only a nebulous dream, that even if this eventuates there is no assurance that Negro employment will result. The fairest summary that can be made of TVA is that for a year or so it has furnished bread to a few thousand Negro workers. Beyond that everything is conjecture which is most unpleasant because of the utter planlessness of those in charge of the project.

Recovery legislation of the present session of Congress reveals the same fatal flaws which have been noted in the operation of previous recovery ventures. Thus, for example, instead of genuine unemployment insurance we have the leaders of the administration proposing to exclude from their plans domestic and agricultural workers, in which classes are to be found 15 out of every 23 Negro workers. On every hand the New Deal has used slogans for the same raw deal.

The sharpening of the crisis for Negroes has not found them unresponsive. Two years of increasing hardship has seen strange movement among the masses. In Chicago, New York, Washington and Baltimore the struggle for jobs has given rise to action on the part of a number of groups seeking to boycott white employers who refuse to employ Negroes. "Don't Buy Where You Can't Work" campaigns are springing up everywhere. The crisis has furnished renewed vigor to the Garvey Movement. And proposals for a 49th State are being seriously considered by various groups.

In sharp contrast with these strictly racial approaches to the problem, have been a number of interracial approaches. Increasing numbers of unemployed groups have been organized under radical leadership and have picketed relief stations for bread. Sharecroppers unions, under Socialist leadership in Arkansas, have shaken America into a consciousness of the growing resentment of southern farm tenants and the joint determination of the Negro and white tenants to do something about their intolerable condition.

In every major strike in this country Negro union members have fought with their white fellow workers in a struggle for economic survival. The bodies of ten Negro strikers killed in such strike struggles offer mute testimony to this fact. Even the vicious policies of the leaders of the A. F. of L. in discrimination against Negro workers is breaking down under the pressure for solidarity from the ranks of whites.

This heightening of spirit among all elements of black America and the seriousness of the crisis for them make doubly necessary the consideration of the social and economic condition of the Negro at this time. It was a realization of these conditions which gave rise to the proposals to hold a national conference on the economic status of Negroes under the New Deal at Howard University in Washington, D.C., on May 18, 19 and 20. At this conference, sponsored by the Social Science Division of Howard University and the Joint Committee on National Recovery, a candid and intelligent survey of the social and economic condition of the Negro will be made. Unlike most conferences it will not be a talk-fest. For months nationally known economists and other technicians have been working on papers to be presented. Unlike other conferences it will not be a one-sided affair. Ample opportunity will be afforded for high government officials to present their views of the "New Deal." Others not connected with the government, including representatives of radical political parties, will also appear to present their conclusions. Not the least important phase will be the appearance on the platform of Negro workers and farmers themselves to offer their own experience under the New Deal. Out of such a conference can and will come a clear-cut analysis of the problems faced by Negroes and the nation.

But a word of caution ought to be expressed with regard to this significant conference. In the final analysis it cannot and does not claim to be representative of the mass opinion of Negro citizens in America. All it can claim for itself is that it will bring together on a non-representative basis well informed Negro and white technicians to discuss the momentous problem it has chosen as its topic. It can furnish a base for action for any organization which chooses to avail itself of the information developed by it. It cannot act itself.

Thus looking beyond such a conference one cannot fail to hope that it will furnish impetus to a national expression of black America demanding a tolerable solution to the economic evils which it suffers. Perhaps it is not too much to hope that public opinion may be moulded by this conference to such an extent that already existing church, civic, fraternal, professional and trade union organizations will see the necessity for concerted effort in forging a mighty arm of protest against injustice suffered by the Negro. It is not necessary that such organizations agree on every issue. On the problem of relief of Negroes from poverty there is little room for disagreement. The important thing is that throughout America as never before Negroes awake to the need for a unity of action on vital economic problems which perplex us.

Such a hope is not lacking in foundation upon solid ground. Such an instance as the All India Congress of British India furnishes an example of what repressed groups can do to better their social and economic status. Perhaps a *"National Negro Congress"* of delegates from thousands of Negro organizations (and white organizations willing to recognize their unity of interest) will furnish a vehicle for channeling public opinion of black America. One thing is certain: the Negro may stand still but the depression will not. And unless there is concerted action of Negroes throughout the nation the next two years will bring even greater misery to the millions of underprivileged Negro toilers in the nation.

BUSINESS: THE
REVOLUTIONARY NEW DEAL

They Hate Roosevelt

MARQUIS CHILDS

*What was the New Deal? There may not be much firm ground in
this matter anymore, but surely one descriptive statement is as
valid now as it ever was: the New Deal was antibusiness. Like
the liberal tradition before and after it, as Arthur M. Schlesinger,
Jr., has said, the New Deal was an effort by nonbusiness elements
in American society to discipline and reform the business community. To be sure, the New Deal's approach to business was not
always hostile. From 1933 to mid-1935, it tried to coax business
into economic expansion by stressing cooperation and by avoid-
ing tax and antitrust policies that might offend capital. When
business responded neither with increased investment nor even
with any measurable political gratitude, the New Deal after 1935
became more openly antibusiness and pursued labor, antitrust,
and fiscal policies that businessmen almost unanimously protested
and fought. But even in the first period, the overall opposition of
businessmen to the New Deal was sizable.*

*Certainly few things seemed as clear in the 1930s as the anti-
business orientation of the New Deal and the anti–New Deal
orientation of American business. In proof, one might cite the
volumes of criticism leveled at Roosevelt in business journals, annual conventions, and country clubs where businessmen gathered.
Marquis Childs, the chief Washington correspondent of the St.
Louis* Post-Dispatch, *vividly describes such criticism in the selection below. One might further list — and the list would eventually be quite long — the New Deal legislation that restricted the
power of capitalists, enlarged the countervailing power of their*

*work force, raised their costs, taxed their profits, and put gov-
ernment directly into competition with them. The core of that
list would be the core of the New Deal: the Wagner Act, the
Fair Labor Standards Act, the Wealth Tax Act of 1935, the
Public Utilities Holding Company Act, the Securities and Exchange Act. Judging by the comments of businessmen in the
1930s (the textbooks agree), this was the New Deal. And these
same businessmen would agree with liberal historians that the
resulting economic system was not capitalism at all, but a significantly different hybrid, a uniquely American, compensated economy in which much of the power and freedom of businessmen
was subjected to political controls. There was even consensus that
businessmen did not like the new arrangements. The only matter
in question for years seemed to be: was this nearly revolutionary
shift of power a good thing or not? On the question of who had
done what to whom, there seemed complete agreement.*

A resident of Park Avenue in New York City was sentenced not long
ago to a term of imprisonment for threatening violence to the person of
President Roosevelt. This episode, with the conclusions as to the man's probable sanity, was recorded at length on the front pages of the newspapers of
the land. In itself it was unimportant. Cranks with wild ideas are always to
be found here and there in any large community. Yet it was significant as a
dramatically extreme manifestation of one of the most extraordinary phenomena of our day, a phenomenon which social historians in the future will
very likely record with perplexity if not with astonishment: the fanatical
hatred of the President which to-day obsesses thousands of men and women
among the American upper class.

No other word than hatred will do. It is a passion, a fury, that is
wholly unreasoning. Here is no mere political opposition, no mere violent
disagreement over financial policies, no mere distrust of a national leader
who to these men and women appears to be a demagogue. Opposition, disagreement, distrust, however strong, are quite legitimate and defensible,
whether or not one agrees that they are warranted. But the phenomenon to
which I refer goes far beyond objection to policies or programs. It is a consuming personal hatred of President Roosevelt and, to an almost equal degree, of Mrs. Roosevelt.

Marquis Childs, "They Hate Roosevelt," *Harpers Monthly*, 172 (May,
1936), pp. 634–36, 638, 640–41; Marquis Childs, *They Hate Roosevelt!*
(New York: Harper and Brothers, 1936), p. 26. Reprinted with permission of the author and Harper & Row, Publishers, Inc.

It permeates, in greater or less degree, the whole upper stratum of American society. It has become with many persons an *idée fixe*. One encounters it over and over again in clubs, even in purely social clubs, in locker and card rooms. At luncheon parties, over dinner tables, it is an incessant theme. And frequently in conversation it takes a violent and unlawful form, the expression of desires and wishes that can be explained only, it would seem, in terms of abnormal psychology.

In history this hatred may well go down as the major irony of our time. For the extraordinary fact is that whereas the fanatic who went to prison had lost his fortune and, therefore, had a direct grievance, the majority of those who rail against the President have to a large extent had their incomes restored and their bank balances replenished since the low point of March, 1933.

That is what make the phenomenon so incredible. It is difficult to find a rational cause for this hatred. I do not mean, of course, that it is difficult to find a rational cause for criticism, even passionately strong criticism, of the New Deal. One may quite reasonably be convinced that its policies are unsound, that its leaders are hypocritical, that its total influence is pernicious. But the venom to which I refer is of a sort seldom found among men and women who have not been personally hurt, and badly hurt, by those whom they excoriate.

Some members of this class have undoubted grounds for feeling personally hurt. Some, for example, have found themselves with income still depleted, and have warrant for attributing the still sorry state of their investments to various measures sponsored by the Administration. Yet others have prospered exceedingly since March, 1933; and certainly on the average they find their present circumstances much improved.

As the New Dealers themselves have been at pains to point out, taxes on the rich have not been materially increased. Secretary Ickes, speaking before the Union League Club in Chicago recently, developed this at length, showing that a man with a net income annually of $50,000 would pay no more to the Federal government in taxes this year than he paid last year; with $60,000 annually he would pay $90 additional; with $80,000 he would pay $775 more, and on an income of $1,000,000, an added $1,875. And although a new tax program is being drafted as this is written, probably no small proportion of the burden will be placed upon the mass of consumers through processing or excise taxes.

Surely the explanation does not lie in the trifling changes made thus far. Nor would the fear of inflation seem to account for it. In the first place, the rise in prices from 1933 to date has, by and large, helped these people more than it has hurt them. Witness the long advance in the stock market, which has doubled, tripled, or quadrupled the prices of stocks — and indeed has multiplied some of them by ten. In the second place, there is no denying that, conversely, the deflation of 1929–1933 did great damage to the fortunes of the rich. In the third place, fears of the future possibilities of the credit-inflation policy of the Administration, whether justified or not, are at any rate not fears of immediate or definitely predictable trouble. Finally — and still more important — the rich are seldom the victims of inflation. It is well known that most of the very wealthy profited from the German inflation. Long before the storm breaks large investments have been safeguarded by diversification in real property or in stocks adapted by their nature to adjust to swiftly changing price levels. Many wealthy persons have already begun to shift their holdings to such things as farm land.

That there is a widespread conviction among the wealthy that they are being butchered to make a Roman holiday for the less fortunate is undeniable. But it is certain that as a class the wealthy have suffered relatively less than any other from the economic events of the past three years; and in that single word *relatively* there is a world of meaning. As for their feeling that butchery has at least been intended by the Roosevelt Administration, let us glance for a moment at some opinions from the other side of the fence.

A great many liberals, and certainly all radicals, complain that President Roosevelt's chief mission has been to save the fortunes of the very rich. Economists for the American Federation of Labor estimated in the annual report for 1935 that in the course of that year corporate profits — dividends and so forth — had increased forty per cent, while real wages had increased slightly less than two per cent. What is more, the wage increase had been in part offset by a corresponding increase in the work-week of an hour and a half.

Surveying the present state of the nation — stock-market boom, crowded Florida resorts, thronged night clubs, the revival of luxury spending — one might almost imagine the fury of the rich to be part of a subtle plot to return Mr. Roosevelt to office. For surely such uncritical vituperation, such blind hostility, must contribute to that end. Is that it then? To throw the workers and the farmers off their guard, the American rich are simulating this rage against the man who — if one listens to the other side — has been their savior?

But such choler could not be simulated. Anyone who has seen it now and then at close range must be aware that it is too authentic for that.

While this phenomenon has gone virtually unrecorded, it is familiar to most middle-class people to-day. Indeed, it has had its influence upon the middle class. There are those who have been only too eager to pick up crumbs of emotion dropped from the rich man's table. In general, however, the violence of the hatred varies directly with the affluence of the social group. The larger the house, the more numerous the servants, the more resplendent the linen and silver, the more scathing is likely to be the indictment of the President.

It may be useful to record certain recent examples of the present temper of the two per cent, if only because the rapid shifting of events may leave slight evidence of it for the notebook of the social historian. In the following scenes I have altered names and circumstances just enough to prevent identification; but the episodes are not only in essence true, they are being duplicated daily wherever the very fortunate congregate. . . .

Let me turn to a characteristic scene. This one is in Florida. James Hamilton is the head of a firm of commodity brokers in Chicago. During the Roosevelt Administration the Hamilton firm has made a handsome profit handling various products for the Commodities Credit Corporation. And in other indirect ways Hamilton has profited from the great increase in governmental activity. He owns a considerable block of stock, inherited from his grandfather, in a flour milling company, and into the treasury of this closely owned firm the Supreme Court dumped a sum in impounded processing taxes greater than the net profits for 1928 and 1929.

But even the warm sun of Florida cannot moderate one degree James Hamilton's grim antipathy to the President and his every word and deed. At Miami Beach he sits on the porch of the cabana he has leased at one of the best beach clubs and vituperates. The President has deliberately tried to destroy the foreign market for our cotton, to the profit of Brazil. One may talk in vain about the decline in soil fertility in the cotton States, about the world movement toward national self-sufficiency, about trends and tendencies existing long before Mr. Roosevelt came into office. It is breath wasted. The President, says James Hamilton, is ruining the farmers of the middlewest by permitting the importation of corn. He will not hear you if you point out the exact number of bushels of corn that have been imported, a negligible number, or the fact that it is in considerable part corn unsuited for feeding to cattle, not to mention the graph that shows clearly how the farmers' purchasing power has mounted.

With James Hamilton is his son, James Hamilton III, also a partner in the firm. The younger Hamilton specializes in Roosevelt horror stories. He repeats with a knowing air, as having come from the inner councils, all the preposterous canards that have passed through the country by word of mouth during the past year. Many of these are built round the report that the President is insane. A number of versions of this story have become familiar. The commonest one has to do with the strange laughter with which the President greets his visitors, a laughter that — if one were to believe the story — continues foolishly and irrelevantly during most of the interview. . . .

Attempting to trace the rise of the current hate one falls into useless conjecture. If one might have a graph such as only an omniscient statistician could produce, showing the development of this animosity year by year, it would be interesting to superimpose upon it a graph representing the rise that has occurred since 1933 in every index of price and production. My guess is that there would be a fairly close correspondence. To be sure the animosity was a little slow in developing. In the spring and summer of 1933, when prices were rising fast from the panic levels of the banking crisis, there was among the rich a great deal of resentment at the tendency in Washington to blame the bankers for all that had happened, there was uneasiness over the wholesale legislation introduced by the Administration, and over the President's inflationary tendencies, but there was little real denunciation of Roosevelt. That came later. Since the latter part of 1933, however, it has increased in volume and in unanimity — and never faster, apparently, than during the sustained advance of the stock market and the less uniform but, nevertheless, hopeful advance of business during 1935.

This phenomenon might be perplexing to the future historian. The usual evidence of history is that men and women whose fortunes are rising do not turn against the government in power. Yet apparently every ten-point rise in common stocks within the past year or two has but added to the confidence with which its major beneficiaries have conducted their attack, has but added to their anger at having to pay high taxes on their winnings. Here are some pertinent questions for the psychologist. Is the memory of fear, once we have recovered from that fear, an intolerable thing? No one can deny that there was panic in February and March of 1933 among those who stood to lose most by a sharp break with the past. And does gratitude toward the hero of the hour turn upon itself in proportion as the crisis is left behind? . . .

The lines to-day are more sharply drawn and there is no sign of any truce. A major war would serve of course, as it did for Wilson, to dissolve the fury. But nothing less than that would reconcile Mr. Roosevelt's enemies to his presence in the White House.

There is a much earlier historical figure with whom Mr. Roosevelt would appear to have something in common. That, as has been pointed out, is the wise Turgot who tried briefly to restore some order and reason to the France of Louis XVI. As comptroller general, he favored restricting the monopoly privileges enjoyed by certain powerful corporations. He wanted to reform the royal household and restrain the more fantastic and flagrant extravagances of the court. He succeeded in abolishing many of the artificial impediments that had been put in the way of free trade. At the same time he proposed to ameliorate the lot of the petit bourgeois and the long-suffering peasants by removing the tax on salt and other burdensome levies.

For all his wisdom, M. Turgot lasted only a little more than two years. The rich and the powerful were outraged at what this radical proposed to do. Why, he struck at the very foundation of orderly government. The arguments of the time could almost be taken from current newspaper headlines. At any rate M. Turgot was removed as comptroller general, his reforms swept into the wastebasket.

And here, perhaps, is a happy exemplar for Mr. Roosevelt. Turgot retired to his country estate where he devoted himself to peaceful study and the pleasant pursuits of leisure. He died in 1781, quietly in his bed; which was not the lot, if one recalls correctly, of those who sent him into exile.

BUSINESS: THE
CONSERVATIVE NEW DEAL

Partial Planning for Business
Under the New Deal

ELLIS W. HAWLEY

*The traditional interpretation of the relation between business
and government in the 1930s has seemed satisfactory for years. It
holds that the public, through its national government, expanded
its invasion of the private sector, over the strenuous objections
of all businessmen. Until the 1960s no noted scholar doubted this
interpretation or suggested that it might have been the other way
around, that private enterprise might have captured public power
for its ends. But in 1964 the business community (the sophisticated
part of it) accepted a deliberate deficit in order to stimulate the
economy. Later in the year, the country's leading businessmen
appeared to support the Democrat Lyndon B. Johnson against a
Republican who proposed to dismantle the New Deal. It seemed
time to question exactly for how long and precisely in what
respects American business had found the welfare state so con-
genial.*

*Events of the 1960s told nothing about the 1930s, but they
did revive some curiosity about aspects of the 1930s that had not
been exhaustively studied. No one expected a reexamination of
business political views and activities in the 1930s to reveal
that businessmen had in some heretofore concealed way really
liked Harry Hopkins, Eleanor Roosevelt, the WPA, the Undis-
tributed Profits Tax, and repeated deficits. But evidence already
in hand suggested that certain businessmen at certain times
strongly supported federal economic intervention. Interest in the*

68

*careful delineation of such political activity had been stifled by
the old stereotype (a joint creation of New Dealers and businessmen) of business-government relations in the 1930s. By the mid-
1960s this stereotype had weakened, and a reexamination was
possible.*

*Historians have always known that Roosevelt and the New
Deal had supporters in the business community — men like
Gerard Swope, Bernard Baruch, Henry and W. Averill Harriman,
and Joseph P. Kennedy. But the relation of these men to New
Deal policy and the political involvement of the industries and
banking houses they represented have not been rigorously studied.
Squeezed away in histories of the 1930s, there exist pedestrian
agencies manned by un–New Dealish Democrats, complex regulatory measures, subsidies, and tax laws that were incompatible
with dramatic narrative. Historians had not concealed lending
agencies such as the RFC, the Farm Credit Administration, the
Home Owner's Loan Corporation, or the subsidies to the avia-
tion and merchant marine industries, or the Robinson-Patman
and Miller-Tydings fair trade laws. They were just not interested
in them. This may have been due to an assumption, nowhere
directly argued, that these laws were not as important as relief
and reform measures, but it is certainly true that they were complex and difficult to describe with verve or drama. The monographic work available on economic regulation was done by
political scientists and economists. Businesses did make gains in
the 1930s through federal legislation, but businessmen talked and
voted as if these gains were unimportant. Historians have generally accepted their perspectives on the matter.*

*Ellis Hawley, who teaches history at the University of Iowa,
devotes a part of his brilliant study,* The New Deal and The
Problem of Monopoly *(1966), to an analysis of the search by
natural resource and transportation industries in the 1930s for the
haven of public utility status against the profit-killing pressures
of overproduction and fierce competition. The book is thoroughly
researched and readable, and it is by a historian who keenly senses
historical continuities. Hopefully, it may initiate further scholarly
interest in the relation of government to business in the 1930s.
Then we may go beyond the rhetoric of businessmen and measure
exactly who got what, and how, from the activist, liberal state
under FDR. And as we learn about what businessmen gained
and lost through politics, we may be reminded of Joe Kennedy's
statement that he would gladly give up half of what he had if the
government would protect his enjoyment of the other half, and
we may conclude that Roosevelt did not drive nearly so hard a
bargain.*

As the economist Paul Homan surveyed New Deal policy in 1936, he concluded that the dominant theme was a type of partial planning or government-supported cartelization. Many industries were no longer interested in such programs; others were unwilling to pay the price of public supervision; still others could not win the necessary political support. But for those that wanted government aid and that possessed the right combination of public sympathy, acute problems, political strength, internal cohesion, and effective symbols for justifying a departure from competitive standards, the aid was available. Two such industries were bituminous coal and crude oil production. Both were competitive industries in which private arrangements had failed to achieve market stability. Both possessed an effective lobby, one through the influence of a politically powerful labor union, the other through tightly-knit trade associations and the support of oil-state politicians. Both were natural resource industries, in which the potent symbol of conservation could be used to overcome the objections of antitrusters and mask a program of market controls.[1]* . . .

There were . . . proposals for "Guffeyizing" such sick industries as lumber, the apparel trades, and anthracite coal. Yet none of these possessed the basic prerequisites necessary to secure a program of publicly supported market controls, at least in any form that its leaders would be willing to accept. Generally speaking, the proposed programs could not be adequately disguised. They lacked the support of a powerful, cohesive lobby with the right political connections. And their supporters were unable to come up with strong alternative ideals that could be used to justify a departure from competitive standards.[2]

There were other areas of the economy, however, where these basic prerequisites did exist. In the transportation industries, and to some extent in the distributive and service trades, it was possible to develop programs and rationales similar to those for bituminous coal and crude oil production. Consequently, it seems advisable to consider these areas next and note the trends toward partial planning and counterorganization that were underway there. . . .

In the United States the term "public utility" generally conjures up a vision of an inherently monopolistic industry providing essential public

From Ellis W. Hawley, *The New Deal and the Problem of Monopoly: A Study in Economic Ambivalence* (copyright © 1966 by Princeton University Press; Princeton Paperback, 1969): pp. 205, 224, 226–29, 231–34, 244–45, 276–78, 483–85. Reprinted by permission of Princeton University Press.
* [See pp. 182–183 for notes to this article. — Ed.]

services, one in which the nature of the service, the large amounts of capital required, and the presence of high fixed costs of all combine to produce large economies of scale and make any competitive duplication of facilities wasteful and inefficient. It is usually conceded, too, that in dealing with such "natural monopolies," society may resort to public regulation. Since the purpose of this presumably is to protect consumers, the industries concerned are expected to resist its establishment as long as possible. But under depression conditions like those of the nineteen thirties, these commonly held assumptions were of doubtful validity. On the contrary, for a number of declining, overly competitive, or particularly depressed industries, the status of a public utility became a means of economic salvation, a way to enter the haven of publicly regulated monopoly and use the power of the state to stabilize prices, reduce competition, and insure profitable returns on overcapitalized structures.

One field in which this perversion of the public utility concept was especially noticeable was that of transportation. Under depression conditions and in view of the threat posed by newer forms of transport, the leaders of the older transportation industries had begun advocating a broad extension of the public utility approach, an extension they justified by appealing to past precedents, arguing that transportation was a "natural monopoly," or stressing things like public safety or national defense. And the result was a mixture of controls, protection, subsidies, and publicly sponsored cartels, a system in which the government became not only a regulator, but a protector, supporter, and provider as well.[3]

For a long period in America, inland transportation had meant railroad transportation. During the nineteen thirties, the railroad industry remained a highly important one. It still hauled approximately two-thirds of the nation's freight, employed about a million men, and used about one-fifth of the nation's coal, fuel oil, steel, and lumber. In terms of total investment, it was outranked only by agriculture; and since a large proportion of railroad securities were held by financial and fiduciary institutions, distress for the railroads could spell financial disaster for the whole community, a fact that made politicians extremely reluctant to tamper with railroad financing.

For a number of years, however, railroading had been a declining industry. The advent of automobiles had produced a steady drop in passenger traffic, a decline of about sixty-six per cent from 1920 to 1933. A good deal of freight, too, was being diverted to motor trucks, barges, and pipelines. And such developments as the shift from coal to natural gas or the tendency to locate plants closer to raw materials and markets had also reduced the demand for railroad services. Finally, on top of these problems, came the depression. Demand fell sharply; the newer forms of transportation captured an even larger share of the market; and the result was a drastic decline in railroad revenue, a drop of about fifty per cent from 1929 to 1933. Under the circumstances, a sanely financed and conservatively managed industry would have been in trouble. The railroads, with their fixed costs, heavy bonded indebtedness, overexpanded and obsolescent plant, and legacy of financial manipulation, never had a real chance. By 1933 one-sixth of the nation's railroad mileage was in the hands of receivers, and many of the remaining companies were nearly bankrupt.[4]

In the face of declining demand, railroad managers tended to blame their difficulties upon excessive competition or unfair subsidization of their rivals. The solution, they seemed to think, was a program of cartelization, under which the power of the state could be used to control facilities, raise rates, protect invested capital, and restrict their competitors. By 1933, such a program was already well advanced. Even before World War I the railroads had developed an elaborate system of rate-making conferences, which in practice initiated most rate changes and inhibited rate cutting. Following the war, the Transportation Act of 1920 gave legal sanction to the cartel principle, to the idea of equalizing returns between weaker and stronger systems and adjusting rates so that the carriers as a whole (or in separate rate groups) would earn a fair return of 5.5 per cent on the value of their property. With the onset of the depression, the demands for financial assistance, further consolidation, and higher rates had brought some aid from the Hoover Administration. The Reconstruction Finance Corporation, for example, had made government loans available; a new bankruptcy law had facilitated financial reorganization; and the ICC had allowed some rate increases.[5]

With the advent of the New Deal, railroad leaders and investors renewed their demands for economic aid, and because of past precedents and the special position of the industry, the new Administration listened sympathetically. After consulting with industrial spokesmen, a special transportation committee, headed by Joseph Eastman of the ICC, worked out a plan for a federal coordinator of transportation. After further adjustments to meet the objections of the railroad unions and other interested parties, the plan resulted in the Emergency Railroad Transportation Act of 1933, a measure that seemed thoroughly compatible with the prevailing philosophy of industrial self-government. Under its provisions, the nation's railroads were divided into three regional groups, each under a coordinating committee chosen by the member carriers. Such committees, together with the Federal Coordinator, were to devise measures for reducing waste, pooling facilities, and eliminating any unnecessary duplication of services. . . .

The Emergency Railroad Transportation Act was not the only attempt to legislate prosperity for the railroads. After all, most of the "destructive competition" seemed to come from the newer forms of transportation; consequently, it was not surprising that the railroads should attempt to do something about this threat from their new rivals. The trucking industry, in particular, had become a major worry, had inspired a long series of railroad-sponsored motor carrier bills, and had produced a growing conviction on the part of railroad leaders, their dependents, and their allies on the state and federal railroad commissions that the public would benefit greatly if trucking could be converted into a public utility.

During the nineteen twenties the truckers themselves were far from enthusiastic about the alleged benefits of public regulation. But with the coming of the depression, the drastic drop in demand, and the resulting struggle for available markets, the attitude of some of the larger trucking firms began to change. Their position, they felt, was seriously threatened by the appearance of cut-rate, "fly-by-night" operators, who, with the aid of truck dealers and manufacturers, managed to get a truck on credit, to eke out a living on cut rates until they lost it, and in the process to force down wages and disrupt the whole rate structure. Under the circumstances, there was growing support in trucking, bus, and teamster circles for some type of regulation, some system that would establish minimum rates and wages and eliminate irresponsible operators.

In 1933, then, many truckers welcomed the establishment of an NRA code. Most of them, particularly the smaller truckers and contract carriers, continued to prefer the code to any type of special legislation. The suggestions for a separate motor carrier act continued to come primarily from the railroads, the railroad commissions, or the Federal Coordinator of Transportation; and, as trucking spokesmen pointed out, they almost invariably proposed that the new controls be entrusted to the "railroad-minded" Interstate Commerce Commission. This was true of the Wheeler bill that was passed by the Senate in April 1935. For a time, this measure encountered strong opposition, not only from shippers and automobile manufacturers, but also from the American Trucking Associations and most other trucking leaders.[6]

The turning point came with the Schechter decision, which in effect converted the American Trucking Associations from an opponent into an active sponsor of special legislation. As a result, the Wheeler bill now moved through Congress with relative ease and by August 1935 had become the Motor Carrier Act, a measure that gave the ICC broad regulatory powers over most interstate motor carriers. Common carriers now had to secure certificates of public convenience and necessity, contract carriers to secure permits, and brokers to secure licenses, all of which would be issued as a matter of right to those operating in June 1935, but whose issuance in the future would depend upon the discretion of the ICC. The Commission could also fix maximum and minimum rates for common carriers and minimum rates for contract carriers; it could supervise the issuance of trucking securities; and it could establish maximum hours and safety rules, not only for common and contract carriers, but for private carriers as well. Thus, through control over entry, required adherence to filed rates, and the establishment of higher standards of financial responsibility, safety, and labor practices, the ICC could reduce competitive disturbances, both within the industry and between the truckers and the railroads.

In practice, there was a good deal of complaint about the time-consuming, cumbersome, and cautious manner in which the act was implemented. Enforcement, too, was difficult, and the friction between the railroads and truckers persisted, resulting in frequent charges of favoritism on both sides. Yet there was little disposition to do away with the act. It did bring greater stability, a minimum-rate floor, fewer and larger trucking firms, more rate bureaus, and a reduction in the cost advantage of low-cost carriers. In both trucking and railroad circles, there was a general feeling that the new system provided some protection against the cut-rater and the chiseler and that consequently, even though the trucking industry possessed few of the traits of a "natural monopoly," the policy of treating it as a public utility should be continued.[7] . . .

By 1938, the main trends in transportation policy seemed firmly established. When declining demand led to excess capacity and intense competition, the transportation leaders reacted by advocating some type of cartelization. In case after case, the use of the appropriate symbols had produced the desired results. Public sympathy had been won, the defenders of competitive values had been silenced, and the government had moved in to establish rate floors, control entry, promote coordination and consolidation, provide special favors, and keep out the chiselers. Most transportation leaders and regulatory officials, moreover, remained convinced that a return to competition would be "unnatural" and "economically dangerous." . . .

It was extremely difficult to discern any over-all pattern or integrating theme in the politically-inspired partial planning of the post-NRA period. Yet insofar as there was any common thread at all, it could probably be found in the concept of counterorganization, in the idea of using the government to promote the organization of economically weak groups so that they might hold their own against stronger rivals. Theoretically, such an approach might have been used to promote economic expansion, which after all was the crying need of the time. If the government could have selected and built up the right groups, those whose natural interests lay in a larger output, fuller employment, and low-cost, high-volume operations, if it could have distinguished between original and countervailing power and concentrated on developing the latter, and if it could have persuaded or forced the organized groups involved to follow their long-range interests, then it might have been possible to increase consumer purchasing power, build a mass market, and thus achieve the economic balance necessary for sustained growth.

In reality, though, the post-Schechter version of counterorganization and partial planning rarely stimulated much expansion, nor was its ability to do so a prime consideration in selecting the areas in which it should be applied. On the contrary, government intervention depended upon the desire, political strength, and ideological appeals of the pressure groups involved; and since these groups were producer-oriented and imbued with a depression psychology, the end product was almost always restrictive in nature. In the farm program, for example, the emphasis was upon higher farm prices and restricted output, not upon lower costs, greater consumption, and stiffer bargaining by farm consumers. In labor union circles, the major goals were higher wages and job security, not fuller employment, cheaper goods, and maximum efficiency. In the "sick" industries and the transportation field the typical program was designed to arrest technological innovation and protect inefficiency, not to encourage economic progress or ease the transition to newer, cheaper, and more productive methods of providing the necessary goods and services. And in the distributive trades the whole legislative effort was directed against the mass distributors and aimed at protecting inefficient merchants, penalizing consumers, and preventing the development or use of countervailing power, not at reducing the costs of distribution, offsetting the market power of manufacturers, and passing the economies along to consumers.

The type of planning that was possible, then, might help to check deflationary forces and provide temporary relief to individual groups, but in the process it seemed to make over-all expansion more difficult than ever. As some of the national planners pointed out, it was creating a situation where organized economic groups were fighting furiously against each other for larger shares of an ever-shrinking pie. Unless they changed their attitudes and goals, they would condemn the nation to permanent depression.[8] The great need was for a larger product, for some arrangement or program that would stimulate growth and counteract the restrictive tendencies inherent in pressure-group planning. Since over-all planning for this purpose was politically impossible, a number of planners were now turning to the underconsumptionist and spending ideology associated with the British economist, John Maynard Keynes. Under the circumstances, this offered an attractive alternative, one that would avoid the complications and difficulties of structural reform and yet provide a politically feasible way to stimulate expansion. . . .

The general effect of this whole line of New Deal policy might be

summed up in the word counterorganization, that is, the creation of monopoly power in areas previously unorganized. One can only conclude, however, that this did not happen according to any preconceived plan. Nor did
it necessarily promote economic expansion or raise consumer purchasing
power. Public support of monopolistic arrangements occurred in a piecemeal,
haphazard fashion, in response to pressure from specific economic groups and
as opportunities presented themselves. Since consumer organizations were
weak and efforts to aid consumers made little progress, the benefits went primarily to producer groups interested in restricting production and raising
prices. In the distributive trades, the efforts to help small merchants tended,
insofar as they were successful, to impede technological changes, hamper
mass distributors, and reduce consumer purchasing power. In the natural
resource and transportation industries, most of the new legislation was designed to restrict production, reduce competition, and protect invested capital. And in the labor and agricultural fields, the strengthening of market
controls was often at the expense of consumers and in conjunction with business groups. The whole tendency of interest-group planning, in fact, was toward the promotion of economic scarcity. Each group, it seemed, was trying
to secure a larger piece from a pie that was steadily dwindling in size.

From an economic standpoint, then, the partial planning of the post-
NRA type made little sense, and most economists, be they antitrusters, planners, or devotees of laissez-faire, felt that such an approach was doing more
harm than good. It was understandable only in a political context, and as
a political solution, it did possess obvious elements of strength. It retained
the antitrust laws and avoided any direct attack upon the competitive ideal
or competitive mythology. Yet by appealing to other goals and alternative
ideals and by using these to justify special and presumably exceptional departures from competitive standards, it could make the necessary concessions
to pressure groups interested in reducing competition and erecting govern-
ment-sponsored cartels.[9] Such a program might be logically inconsistent and
economically harmful. Perhaps, as one critic suggested at the time, it combined the worst features of both worlds, "an impairment of the efficiency of
the competitive system without the compensating benefits of rationalized collective action." [10] But politically it was a going concern, and efforts to achieve
theoretical consistency met with little success.

Perhaps the greatest defect in these limited planning measures was
their tendency toward restriction, their failure to provide any incentive for
expansion when an expanding economy was the crying need of the time. The
easiest way to counteract this tendency, it seemed, was through government
expenditures and deficit financing; in practice, this was essentially the path
that the New Deal took. By 1938 Roosevelt seemed willing to accept the
Keynesian arguments for a permanent spending program, and eventually,

when war demands necessitated pump-priming on a gigantic scale, the spending solution worked. It overcame the restrictive tendencies in the economy, restored full employment, and brought rapid economic expansion. Drastic institutional reform, it seemed, was unnecessary. Limited, piecemeal, pressure-group planning could continue, and the spending weapon could be relied upon to stimulate expansion and maintain economic balance.

Part Two
THE INTERPRETATIONS

THE REVOLUTIONARY
NEW DEAL

An Attempt to Revolutionize
the American System of Life

HERBERT C. HOOVER

Early appraisals of the New Deal almost uniformly stressed the extensive changes it brought to American life. A few leftists in the 1930s insisted that the New Deal had only minimally repaired capitalism, but liberals and conservatives, agreeing for once, drowned them out. To them the New Deal was a turning point in American history; and they were the majority. The following essay expresses the conservative (or anti–New Deal) view of that turning point, written by the man who was not only the best-known but one of the most dedicated and well-informed critics of the New Deal — Herbert Hoover.

Today, this essay and all anti–New Deal writing from the right in the 1930s (with the possible exception of Walter Lippmann's The Good Society) *sounds not only hysterical but silly. The New Deal was not socialism. It did more to prevent socialism than A. Mitchell Palmer's raids, the American Legion, or the Sears-Roebuck catalogue. The federal government under FDR was not all-powerful. It was, if anything, too weak to do what was plainly necessary. The New Deal involved no "hideous dangers." There was only the possibility of some carelessly spent money, squandered energy, and a slightly larger federal bureaucracy — all of these paltry beside the comparable excesses of 1917–18. And above all, "freedom" was not synonymous with the absence of federal intervention. All this is so obvious today that some explanation must be given for including this essay in an anthology.*

The first and best justification is that many people felt this way in the 1930s and 1940s, and their strong convictions are not only a part of the historical reputation of the New Deal but were an important political force helping shape events during Roosevelt's lifetime. Hoover's views are paralleled in memoir form by Raymond Moley's After Seven Years *(1939) and in scholarly form by Edgar E. Robinson's* The Roosevelt Leadership *(1955). A second good reason for including an interpretation that time has dealt roughly with is the fact that in this passage Hoover, in that hyperbolic way of his, raised at least one fundamental question about the New Deal. The New Deal, as he argues so earnestly, did* not *bring recovery, and the ex-President's explanation of this may not be so wide of the mark. Capitalism cannot be made to work, he argues, where political power is in the hands of liberals who continually interfere with the market mechanism in order to provide social services the market does not produce or who interrupt and redirect the natural activities of the profit motive in accordance with their own notions of what society needs. Who can say, based on the experience of the last forty years, that Hoover is wrong? The New Dealers could not make capitalism work at anything like reasonable efficiency, even with their unprecedented spending on humanitarian projects. Liberals after FDR have kept the economy functioning only with massive defense purchases. Time and again, since 1940, war and cold war have provided the effective rationale (no liberal politician has ever discovered another one) for the degree of federal spending required to stave off serious economic decline. Perhaps Hoover was right that there was and is no middle way between capitalism and socialism, and that war was and is necessary to rescue the liberal experiment.*

In my last address a few weeks after the election of 1932 I said:

You will expect me to discuss the late election. Well, as nearly as I can learn we did not have enough votes on our side. . . . My country has given me the highest honor that comes to man. . . . That is a debt I can never repay.

Only a few rare souls in a century, to whose class I make no pretension

Herbert C. Hoover, *The Memoirs of Herbert Hoover: The Great Depression 1929–1941* (New York: The Macmillan Company, 1952), pp. 350–51, 354–56, 386–89, 471–72, 475–76, 484–85. Reprinted with permission of The Herbert Hoover Foundation.

count much in the great flow of this Republic. The life stream of this nation is the generations of millions of human particles acting under impulses of advancing ideas and national ideals gathered from a thousand springs. These springs and rills have gathered into great streams which have nurtured and fertilized this great land over the centuries. Its dikes against dangerous floods are cemented with the blood of our fathers. Our children will strengthen the dikes, will create new channels, and the land will grow greater and richer with their lives.

We are but transitory officials in government whose duty is to keep the channels clear and to strengthen and extend their dikes. What counts toward the honor of public officials is that they sustain the national ideals upon which are patterned the design of these channels of progress and the construction of these dikes of safety. What is said in this or in that political campaign counts no more than the sound of the cheerful ripples or the angry whirls of the stream. *What matters is — that God help the man or the group who breaks down these dikes, who diverts these channels to selfish ends. These waters will drown him or them in a tragedy that will spread over a thousand years.*

My memoirs would be incomplete without an appraisal of the attempts to break down the dikes of American freedom — and its consequences.

The period from 1933 to 1941 may be viewed from two angles: first, as an attempt to revolutionize the American system of life, and second, as a mere continuation of the Great Depression into its sixth phase by inept economic action. It was, in fact, both — the first being largely the cause of the second. My interest in my country could not be ended by an election, especially as I knew the character and purposes of the men coming into power were not those of traditional America.

Demonstration of the rightness of the American manner of life, and the disaster to my countrymen following departure from it, requires an objective account of the social, economic, and governmental forces in action.

What had been, up to the election, an ideological debate was now transformed into a reality of national experience. In adopting the New Deal, most of the American people did not realize that they had departed from the road of free men. Our people had never been conscious of ideological systems. They had simply lived and breathed our own American manner of life. Moreover, they were little acquainted with the meaning of the abstract terms used in such philosophies. They did not believe that hideous dangers to their freedom lurked in generous-looking but distorted use of such phrases as "Liberalism," "New Deal," "Economic Planning," "Planned Economy," "Production for Use" and "Redistribution of Wealth." A people traditionally willing to "try anything once" welcomed such ideas — at first.

I shall prove that the penalty was nine years more of the Great Depression which ended in name only with the absorption of our man power and energies in war.

There should be lessons to free men in this experience. . . .

During Roosevelt's first eight years the guiding phrases of the New Deal were not "Communism," "Socialism," and "Fascism," but "Planned Economy." This expression was an emanation from the caldrons of all three European collectivist forms. The phrase first popularized by Mussolini, and often mouthed by the Communists and the Socialists, was itself a typical collectivist torture of meaning. It was not a blueprint, but a disguise. It meant governmental execution and dictation. Ever since George Washington we have planned, with changing times, the necessary development of government within the limits of freedom. Our public schools, public works, safeguards to health, conservation, reclamation of the desert, creation of parks, highways, the beautification of cities, regulatory laws, and standards of conduct were proofs.

By a series of invasions of the judicial and legislative arms and the independence of the states, accompanied by such measures as managed currency, government operation of some industries and dictation to others, "Planned Economy" quickly developed as a centralization of power in the hands of the President, administered and perpetuated by an enormous Federal bureaucracy. It was an attempt to cross-breed Socialism, Fascism, and Free Enterprise.

The illusion of the advocates of this mixture was that they could have parts of economic collectivism and yet maintain representative government, the personal liberties, and the productivity of the nation. They were totalitarian "liberals." They believed that free initiative and creative individualism could survive without economic freedom. Their further illusion was that any economic system would work in a mixture of others. No greater illusions ever mesmerized the American people. The ultimate end would be to transform the people into a government of men and not of laws.

I believe that any objective student of social forces will agree that these men did their best to create a traditional "mass movement" to accomplish their aims. Such mass movements had been successful in the case of Russian Communism, German National Socialism, and Italian Fascism. All these movements sprang from the soil of postwar misery, the strivings for power, greed for the possessions of others, boredom with the routines of life, yearnings for adventure, or just frustration. These mass movements had many common characteristics. They exaggerated the miseries of the times. They condemned the existing economic and social systems as bankrupt. They cried, "Emergency! Emergency!" They promised Utopia. They envisaged a national devil. They stifled criticism with smearing and misrepresentation through the powerful agencies of government propaganda. They subjugated the legislative and judicial arms and purged their own party oppositions.

They spent public moneys in subsidies to pressure groups. They distributed patronage to their adherents. They sought ceaselessly for more power.

The New Deal imitated all these methods, but it was successful in producing only a transitory rash of a "mass movement." It failed to produce the dynamism which had made such revolutions effective. The traditional American love of freedom and devotion to constitutional processes ultimately proved too deep for its schemes to work.[1]*

It may be said at once that during the eight years under discussion here the New Deal, despite its "Planned Economy" and its gadgets, the doubling of national expenditures, debt, and bureaucracy, totally failed to restore employment. During those eight years the numbers of persons unemployed and on relief proved each autumn to be about the same as they had been on the day Roosevelt was elected.

I will show that at the same time twelve great nations with free economy had, within two or three years, recovered from the worldwide depression and risen to levels of prosperity higher than even in the boom year of 1929.

During these eight years America continued to wallow in the Great Depression. In the end Roosevelt turned from the "New Deal" to international affairs and with the wrappings of war covered the utter debacle of "Planned Economy."

All of this will unfold as this narrative proceeds. . . .

ROOSEVELT'S OWN IDEAS OF PERSONAL POWER

In my account of the election of 1932, it is shown that Roosevelt was not backward in his forecasts of what was coming for the American people by way of revolution from American principles and traditions of free men. Some of them may well be recalled.

Stripped of oratorical trimmings, on May 22, 1932, he said:

> That which seems more important to me in the long run is the problem of *controlling by adequate planning the creation and distribution of those products which our vast economic machine is capable of yielding.* . . .
>
> It seems to me probable that our physical economic plant will not expand in the future at the same rate at which it has expanded in the past. We may build more factories, but the fact remains that we have enough now to supply all of our domestic needs, and more, if they are used.

He said in Detroit on October 2nd:

> We know that some measures of regularization and planning for balance among industries and for envisioning production as a national activity must be devised.

* [See pp. 183–184 for notes to this article. — Ed.]

> We must set up some new objectives; we must have new kinds of management.

And at Albany on October 6th Mr. Roosevelt implied such controls of trade as would prevent international competition and would regulate domestic production, saying:

> More realistic mutual arrangements for trade, substituted for the present system, . . . will make possible the approach to a national economic policy at home which will have as its central feature the fitting of production programs to the actual probabilities of consumption.

In addition to his illuminating speeches during the campaign of 1932, statements from him during the first eight years are ample confirmation.

I omit his habitual defamation of the "Haves," "Plutocrats," "Economic Royalists," and his straw men set up to represent a non-existent economic system.

On June 24, 1933, he said:

> Long before Inauguration Day I became convinced that individual effort and local effort and even disjointed Federal effort had failed and of necessity would fail and, therefore, that a rounded leadership by the Federal Government had become a necessity both of theory and of fact.

Again on January 4, 1935, he said:

> The outlines of the new economic order, rising from the disintegration of the old, are apparent.

On January 3, 1936, he said:

> In thirty-four months we have built up new instruments of public power. In the hands of a people's Government this power is wholesome and proper. . . . [In wicked hands] such power would provide shackles for the liberties of the people.

He returned to this idea of instruments of power in a statement of January 20, 1937:

> We are beginning to wipe out the line that divides the practical from the ideal; and in so doing we are fashioning an instrument of unimagined power for the establishment of a morally better world.

It may be remarked that the essence of representative government in this Republic is government by law. There is at least a tradition that no man shall possess the power to shackle the liberties of the people. It might be remarked further that the word "liberalism" comes from the word "liberty" and not from the word "shackles."

Through all these solemnly intoned pronouncements there ran the constant divergence between appearance and reality.[2]

There can be no dispute that Roosevelt was surrounded by many purposeful men who knew where they were going, who wrote his statements and, more important still, his legislative proposals and his executive "directives."

The economic views of the President's associates were no better stated than by Rexford Tugwell, who was indeed the ideologic philosopher of the Planners. He said:

> It is . . . a logical impossibility to have a planned economy and to have business operating its industries, just as it is also impossible to have one within our present constitutional and statutory structure. Modifications in both, so serious as to mean destruction and rebeginning, are required.

In another place he said:

> The challenge of Russia to America does not lie in the merits of the Soviet system, although they may prove to be considerable. The challenge lies rather in the idea of planning, of purposeful, intelligent control over economic affairs. This, it seems, we must accept as a guide to our economic life to replace *the decadent notions of laissez-faire philosophy*.[3]

On still another occasion he said:

> Planning will become the function of the Federal Government — either that, or the Planning agency will supersede the Government, which is why, of course, such a scheme will be assimilated to the State.[4]

Roosevelt frequently denied any dictatorial tastes, but a small side evidence is indicative. That was the daily issuance of Executive Orders in peacetime. In his first term alone, he issued 1,486 such orders, as against an average of 166 for each previous four years of Presidents since George Washington. And that 143 years included four wars which necessitated more than the usual executive action. Such a quantity of orders constantly emphasized Congressional surrender of its responsibilities. Aside from legislation and administrative jobs, the mere formulation of these orders, which had the effect of law, gave vast opportunities to the "inner core."

Students who wish to arrive at the subcurrents around Roosevelt would do well to examine the platform of the Socialist party of 1932 and observe the uncanny fulfillment of its recommendations by Roosevelt's first administration. A student should also examine the many parallels of argument in Roosevelt's speeches of January 3, 1936, and June 27, 1936, with the program of the Communist International (Moscow), September 1, 1928. And all the New Deal acts should be contrasted with the Democratic platform of 1932, which Roosevelt endorsed "100 per cent." . . .

I shall try, by the cold application of statistics, to sum up the final proof:

1. That the Great Depression extended from 1929 to 1941;

2. That recovery from the Great Depression came quickly to other nations of free economy; but, as a consequence of the New Deal devices, it never came to the United States under Roosevelt during peacetime;

3. That the primary cause of this failure was the New Deal attempt to collectivize the American system of life;

4. That the Great Depression was ultimately in name ended only by war.

The indexes of the number of unemployed, the number on relief, and the subnormal productivity are the infallible proof that the Great Depression extended until the man power and energies of the American people were absorbed in military action.

The currently published American Federation of Labor figures on unemployment show:

July, 1932	Depression low point	12,300,000
October, 1932	Roosevelt's election	11,586,000
January, 1933		13,100,000
1934		13,282,000
1935		12,058,000
1936		12,646,000
1937		10,002,000
1938		10,926,000
1939		11,369,000
1940		10,656,000

After January, 1940, war production and large mobilization for the armed forces began to have some effect; but even at Pearl Harbor (December, 1941) more than 8,000,000 were still unemployed.

Different authorities vary greatly on the number of unemployed at any one time. I have chosen the American Federation of Labor's currently reported January figures because the only real census of unemployment during this period, taken in November, 1939, corroborated their estimates. Roosevelt stated this census as follows:

This check-up indicated that there were, as of November, 1937, about 11,000,000 totally unemployed or emergency workers. . . .

The number of partly unemployed determined after the check-up census
was placed at 5,500,000. . . .[5]

Thus at this time the actual number unemployed was greater than
11,000,000 totally unemployed, and compares with the A. F. of L. estimate
of two months later of 10,926,000 unemployed.

The contention is made that New Deal measures were a success because there was an annual increase in the number of workers for whom jobs
were provided. That explanation hardly holds water because the increase of
workers came from the increase of population; therefore more services, and
jobs, were required to support the increase.

It might be observed that the 1940 figure was only about 1,000,000
less than the number unemployed the day Mr. Roosevelt was elected, eight
years before. . . .

CAUSES OF THE UNITED STATES' FAILURE TO RECOVER

The reasons for this failure of the United States to recover were obvious. The first was the setback caused by the wholly unnecessary bank panic.
More important than this temporary blow was the whole New Deal collectivism. There is no middle road between any breed of collectivist economy and
our American system. Aside from any question as to whether such high productivity as that of the United States could be maintained under either pure
communism, fascism, or socialism, even parts of these systems certainly cannot be mixed with free enterprise. The reasons why there can be no mixture
are clear. In the American kind of free economy, production and distribution
are generators from which flow long transmission lines of initiative, employment, and opportunity. Once these lines are interfered with at any point the
whole current is weakened.

The American system is based upon the confidence, hopes and the
judgment of each man in conducting his business affairs upon his judgment.
He determines his prices in relation to demand, supply and competition. His
policies are based upon endless chains of contracts and agreements. If only
one link be touched, the whole chain weakens and the expected results are
frustrated. Also, under "planned economy" the actions of government and
bureaucrats are unpredictable. At once men become hesitant and fearful.
Every time the planners inject their dictation into some region of private
enterprise, somehow, somewhere, men's minds and judgments become confused. Initiative and enterprise slacken; production and consumption slow
down. At once unemployment is increased, and every fear is accelerated.
Then more drastic powers and more government agencies are demanded by
the planners. And thus the cancer of power over men grows by creating its
own emergencies.

An examination of our economy during the depression indicates the precise spot of stagnation. And in locating this spot we give proof of the destructive forces which were induced by New Deal collectivism. . . .

At the end of eight years of the New Deal, any examination of the causes of its failure to secure economic recovery must needs consider its own seeds of destruction.

The recognition of Russia on November 16, 1933, started forces which were to have considerable influence in the attempt to collectivize the United States, particularly through the labor unions. We saw government conducted by "emergencies," purges, propaganda, bureaucracy, hate, the turmoil of class conflict — all of collectivist pattern. We saw an era of the deepest intellectual dishonesty in public life. We saw the growth of executive power by the reduction of the legislative arm, with few exceptions, to a rubber stamp. We saw the Congressional powers over the purse practically abandoned. We saw the subjection of the Supreme Court to the collectivist ideas of the executive. We saw the independence and responsibility of the states undermined by huge Federal subsidies directly to the citizens.

Thus the four great pillars of free men were weakened. As a result of eight years of the New Deal, there was not more but less liberty in America. And, unique among the nations of the world free of collectivism, we had not ended the Great Depression. Its vast unemployment and its huge numbers on relief were only ended by war. But out of these years of New Dealism and the necessary expansion of control measures by the war came a partial redemption of America from collectivism.

From this and the necessary expansion of collectivist measures during the war, there came a revulsion in the public mind. A first real turning away from collectivism came with the Congressional election after the war (1946). In the new Congress, Republicans with the aid of conservative Democrats repealed — according to an estimate by a responsible member — some 70,000 New Deal and war rules, regulations and orders, which went far to restore the American system. It has since had some setbacks, but that the American system has survived at all is proof of its vitality.

The Third American Revolution

Carl N. Degler

In the essay below, originally published in 1959, Carl Degler strongly propounds the view that the cumulative impact of the New Deal changes was revolutionary. Unlike Hoover, Degler, who teaches history at Stanford University, sees its changes as enhancing freedom and democracy, as well as laying the foundation for the economic prosperity that eluded the New Dealers in the prewar years. Degler lucidly expresses here a view shared by many leading historians of modern America. This interpretation has recently come under attack by younger historians who do not see much change in the 1930s. Degler, they would say, sees change because he concentrates on areas such as the role of government, voting, and labor relations, where there was a great deal of eye-catching institutional alteration. But, the critics insist, these alterations left the basics undisturbed — the profit system, the prevailing distribution of wealth, private ownership of the means of production.

Degler published a revised version of Out of Our Past *in 1970 (the passage below is from the revised edition), but he had not changed his argument noticeably since 1959. Although his footnotes and bibliography show his awareness of the new critical interpretations of the New Deal, Degler continues to stress the fundamental changes produced under Franklin Roosevelt. He does not argue that the New Deal brought a new economic and political system (only Hoover, in this book, argues that), for of course it did not. Rather, he finds it revolutionary by comparison with any previous period in American history. New Left historians' reference is their vision of a really different (and better) society; Degler's is the American past. So, too, was it most contemporaries' standard. They remembered the 1920s, felt deeply the dramatic alteration in the tone of public life, and saw all around them substantial changes — federal relief, rising agricultural prices through crop limitation, unionization, regulation of the securities market. They felt a great discontinuity between Hoover and Roosevelt, and Degler's essay reflects with considerable fidelity the sensibility of the time.*

If it is argued that contemporaries were bad judges of what was really happening around them, this must be acknowledged as much for the 1930s as for today. A dynamic President replaces a dour one, the state doubles and triples its functions and begins

*to answer to constituencies other than business — such changes
seemed far-reaching to men who vividly remembered yesterday.
But time has shown us that capitalism remained unimpaired,
that the rich found ways to remain rich while the poor continued
their numberless sufferings. Flawless history would record both
what people felt and what was actually happening at the fundamentals of social organization. Degler's essay is perhaps stronger
at the first task than at the second.*

THE END OF LAISSEZ FAIRE

Perhaps the most striking alteration in American thought which the
depression fostered concerned the role of the government in the economy.
Buffeted and bewildered by the economic debacle, the American people in
the course of the 1930's abandoned, once and for all, the doctrine of laissez
faire. This beau ideal of the nineteenth-century economists had become, ever
since the days of Jackson, an increasingly cherished shibboleth of Americans.
But now it was almost casually discarded. It is true, of course, that the rejection of laissez faire had a long history; certainly the Populists worked to
undermine it. But with the depression the nation at large accepted the government as a permanent influence in the economy.[1]*

Almost every one of the best-known measures of the federal government during the depression era made inroads into the hitherto private pre-
serves of business and the individual. Furthermore, most of these new measures survived the period, taking their places as fundamental elements in the
structure of American life. For modern Americans living under a federal
government of transcendent influence and control in the economy, this is
the historic meaning of the great depression.

Much of what is taken for granted today as the legitimate function of
government and the social responsibility of business began only with the
legislation of these turbulent years. Out of the investigation of banking and
bankers in 1933, for example, issued legislation which separated commercial
banking from the stock and bond markets, and insured the bank deposits of
ordinary citizens. The stock market, like the banks, was placed under new
controls and a higher sense of responsibility to the public imposed upon it by
the new Securities and Exchange Commission. The lesson of Black Tuesday

From pp. 384–394, 396–400, 403–404, 406–413 in *Out of Our Past*, Re-
vised Edition, by Carl N. Degler. Copyright © 1959, 1970 by Carl N.
Degler.
* [See pp. 184–186 for notes to this article. — Ed.]

in 1929 had not been forgotten: the classic free market itself — the Exchange — was hereafter to be under continuous governmental scrutiny.

The three Agricultural Adjustment Acts of 1933, 1936, and 1938, while somewhat diverse in detail, laid down the basic lines of what is still today the American approach to the agricultural problem. Ever since the collapse of the boom after the First World War, American agriculture had suffered from the low prices born of the tremendous surpluses. Unable to devise a method for expanding markets to absorb the excess, the government turned to restriction of output as the only feasible alternative. But because restriction of output meant curtailment of income for the farmer, it became necessary, if farm income was to be sustained, that farmers be compensated for their cut in production. Thus was inaugurated the singular phenomenon, which is still a part of the American answer to the agricultural surplus, of paying farmers for *not* growing crops. The other device introduced for raising farm prices, and still the mainstay of our farm policy, came with the 1938 act, which provided that the government would purchase and store excess farm goods, thus supporting the price level by withdrawing the surplus from the competitive market. Both methods constitute a subsidy for the farmer from society at large.[2] . . .

Perhaps the most imaginative and fruitful innovation arising out of the depression was the Tennessee Valley Authority, which transformed the heart of the South. "It was and is literally a down to earth experiment," native Tennesseean Broadus Mitchell has written, "with all that we know from test tube and logarithm tables called on to help. It was a union of heart and mind to restore what had been wasted. It was a social resurrection." For the TVA was much more than flood and erosion control or even hydroelectric power — though its gleaming white dams are perhaps its most striking and best-known monuments. It was social planning of the most humane sort, where even the dead were carefully removed from cemeteries before the waters backed up behind the dams. It brought new ideas, new wealth, new skills, new hope into a wasted, tired, and discouraged region.

At the time of the inception of the TVA, it was scarcely believable that the "backward" South would ever utilize all the power the great dams would create. But in its report of 1956, the Authority declared that the Valley's consumption of electricity far exceeded that produced from water sites: almost three quarters of TVA's power is now generated from steam power, not from waterfall. In large part it was the TVA which taught the Valley how to use more power to expand its industries and to lighten the people's burdens. Back in 1935, Drew and Leon Pearson saw this creation of consumer demand in action. "Uncle Sam is a drummer with a commercial line to sell," they wrote in *Harper's Magazine*. "He sold liberty bonds before, but never refrigerators."

Measured against textbook definitions, the TVA is unquestionably socialism. The government owns the means of production and, moreover, it competes with private producers of electricity.[3] But pragmatic Americans — and particularly those living in the Valley — have had few sleepless nights as a consequence of this fact. The TVA does its appointed job, and apparently it is here to stay. For when the Eisenhower administration sought to establish an alternative to the expansion of the TVA power facilities by awarding a contract for a steam plant to a private firm — Dixon-Yates — friends of the TVA in and out of Congress forced the cancellation of the contract. And despite Eisenhower's unfortunate reference to it as "creeping socialism," the TVA has been absorbed into that new American Way fashioned by the experimentalism of the American people out of the wreckage of the Great Depression.

Undoubtedly social security deserves the appellation "revolutionary" quite as much as the TVA; it brought government into the lives of people as nothing had since the draft and the income tax. Social security legislation actually comprises two systems: insurance against old age and insurance in the event of loss of work. The first system was completely organized and operated by the federal government; the second was shared with the states — but the national government set the standards; both were clear acknowledgment of the changes which had taken place in the family and in the business of making a living in America. No longer in urban America could the old folks, whose proportion in the society was steadily increasing, count on being taken in by their offspring as had been customary in a more agrarian world. Besides, such a makeshift arrangement was scarcely satisfying to the self-respect of the oldsters. With the transformation of the economy by industrialization, most Americans had become helpless before the vagaries of the business cycle. As a consequence of the social forces which were steadily augmenting social insecurity, only collective action by the government could arrest the drift.

To have the government concerned about the security of the individual was a new thing. Keenly aware of the novelty of this aim in individualistic America,[4] Roosevelt was careful to deny any serious departure from traditional paths. "These three great objectives — the security of the home, the security of livelihood, and the security of social insurance," he said in 1934, constitute "a minimum of the promise that we can offer to the American people." But this, he quickly added, "does not indicate a change in values."

Whether the American people thought their values had changed is not nearly as important as the fact that they accepted social security. And the proof that they did is shown in the steady increase in the proportion of the population covered by the old-age benefit program since 1935; today farm workers as well as the great preponderance of nonfarm workers are included in the system. Apart from being a minimum protection for the individual and society against the dry rot of industrial idleness, unemployment insurance is now recognized as one of the major devices for warding off another depression.

It is true, as proponents of the agrarian life have been quick to point out, that an industrialized people, stripped as they are of their economic self-reliance, have felt the need for social insurance more than people in other types of society. But it is perhaps just as important to recognize that it is only in such a highly productive society that people can even dare to dream of social security. Men in other ages have felt the biting pains of economic crisis, but few preindustrial people have ever enjoyed that surfeit of goods which permits the fat years to fill out the lean ones. But like so much else concerning industrialism, it is not always easy to calculate whether the boons it offers exceed in value the burdens which it imposes.

For the average man, the scourge of unemployment was the essence of the depression. Widespread unemployment, permeating all ranks and stations in society, drove the American people and their government into some of their most determined and deliberate departures from the hallowed policy of "hands off." But despite the determination, as late as 1938 the workless still numbered almost ten million — two thirds as great as in 1932 under President Hoover. The governmental policies of the 1930's never appreciably diminished the horde of unemployed — only the war prosperity of 1940 and after did that — but the providing of jobs by the federal government was a reflection of the people's new conviction that the government had a responsibility to alleviate economic disaster. Such bold action on the part of government, after the ineffective, if earnest approach of the Hoover administration, was a tonic for the dragging spirits of the people.[5]

A whole range of agencies, from the Civil Works Administration (CWA) to the Works Progress Administration (WPA), were created to carry the attack against unemployment. It is true that the vast program of relief which was organized was not "permanent" in the sense that it is still in being, but for two reasons it deserves to be discussed here. First, since these agencies constituted America's principal weapon against unemployment, some form of them will surely be utilized if a depression should occur again. Second, the various relief agencies of the period afford the best examples of the new welfare outlook, which was then in the process of formation.

Though in the beginning relief programs were premised on little more than Harry Hopkins' celebrated dictum, "Hunger is not debatable," much more complex solutions to unemployment were soon worked out. The relief program of the WPA, which after 1935 was the major relief agency, was a case in point. In 1937, *Fortune* magazine commented on "the evolution of unemployment relief from tool to institution" — a recognition of the importance and duration of relief in America. "In 1936, the federal government was so deeply involved in the relief of the unemployed," *Fortune* contended, "that it was not only keeping them alive, but it was also giving them an opportunity to work; and not only giving them an opportunity to work but giving them an opportunity to work at jobs for which they were peculiarly fitted; and not only giving them an opportunity to work at jobs for which they were peculiarly fitted, but creating for them jobs of an interest and usefulness which they could not have expected to find in private employment." The statement somewhat distorts the work of the WPA, but it sums up the main outlines of the evolution of the relief program.

The various artistic and cultural employment programs of the WPA are excellent examples of how relief provided more than employment, though any of the youth agencies like the Civilian Conservation Corps or the National Youth Administration (it subsidized student work) would serve equally well. At its peak, the Federal Writers' Project employed some 6,000 journalists, poets, novelists, and Ph.D.'s of one sort or another; unknowns worked on the same payroll, if not side by side, with John Steinbeck, Vardis Fisher, and Conrad Aiken. The $46 million expended on art — that is, painting and sculpture — by the WPA in 1936–37 exceeded the artistic budget of any country outside the totalitarian orbit — and there art was frankly propagandistic. *Fortune,* in May, 1937, found the American government's sponsorship of art singularly free of censorship or propaganda. The magazine concluded that "by and large the Arts Projects have been given a freedom no one would have thought possible in a government run undertaking. And by and large that freedom has not been abused." During the first fifteen months of the Federal Music Project, some fifty million people heard live concerts; in the first year of the WPA Theater, sixty million people in thirty states saw performances, with weekly attendance running to half a million. T. S. Eliot's *Murder in the Cathedral,* too risky for a commercial producer, was presented in New York by the Federal Theater to 40,000 people at a top price of 55 cents.

"What the government's experiments in music, painting, and the theater actually did," concluded *Fortune* in May, 1937, "even in their first year, was to work a sort of cultural revolution in America." For the first time the American audience and the American artist were brought face to face for their mutual benefit. "Art in America is being given its chance," said the British writer Ford Madox Ford, "and there has been nothing like it since before the Reformation. . . ."

Instead of being ignored on the superficially plausible grounds of the exigencies of the depression, the precious skills of thousands of painters, writers, and musicians were utilized. By this timely rescue of skills, tastes, and talents from the deadening hand of unemployment, the American people, through their government, showed their humanity and social imagination. Important for the future was the foresight displayed in the conserving of artistic talents and creations for the enrichment of generations to come.

The entrance of the federal government into a vast program of relief work was an abrupt departure from all previous practice, but it proved enduring. "When President Roosevelt laid it down that government had a social responsibility to care for the victims of the business cycle," *Fortune* remarked prophetically in 1937, "he set in motion an irreversible process." The burden of unemployment relief was too heavy to be carried by local government or private charities in an industrialized society; from now on, the national government would be expected to shoulder the responsibility. "Those who are on relief and in close contact otherwise with public matters realize that what has happened to the country is a bloodless revolution," wrote an anonymous relief recipient in *Harper's* in 1936. The government, he said, has assumed a new role in depressions, and only the rich might still be oblivious to it. But they too "will know it by 1940. And in time," they will "come to approve the idea of everyone having enough to eat." [6] Few people escaped the wide net of the depression: "Anybody sinks after a while," the anonymous reliefer pointed out. "Even you would have if God hadn't preserved, without apparent rhyme or reason, your job and your income." That the depression was a threat to all was perhaps the first lesson gained from the 1930's.

The second was that only through collective defense could such a threat be met. By virtue of the vigorous attack made upon the economic problems of the thirties by the government, the age-old conviction that dips in the business cycle were either the will of God or the consequence of unalterable economic laws was effectively demolished. As recently as 1931, President Hoover had told an audience that some people "have indomitable confidence that by some legerdemain we can legislate ourselves out of a world-wide depression. Such views are as accurate as the belief that we can exorcise a Caribbean hurricane." From the experience of the depression era, the American people learned that something could and ought to be done when economic disaster strikes. No party and no politician with a future will ever again dare to take the fatalistic course of Herbert Hoover in 1929–33.

As the enactment of the Employment Act of 1946 showed, the prevention of depression now occupies top listing among the social anxieties of the American people. The act created a permanent Council of Economic Advisers to the President, to keep him continuously informed on the state of the economy and to advise him on the measures necessary to avoid an economic decline. And the Joint Committee on the Economic Report does the same for Congress.

Today political figures who indignantly repudiate any "left-wing" philosophy of any sort readily accept this inheritance from the depression. "Never again shall we allow a depression in the United States," vowed Republican candidate Eisenhower in 1952. As soon as we "foresee the signs of any recession and depression," he promised, ". . . the full power of private industry, of municipal government, of state government, of the Federal Government will be mobilized to see that that does not happen." . . .

The evident acceptance of the new obligations of government in the economy on the part of the first Republican administration since the New Deal is strikingly suggestive of the shock which the depression dealt conventional economic thought in America.

REVOLUTION IN POLITICS

In passing through the dark valley of the depression, Americans discarded more than conventional economics; they also revised their political preferences. Like downswings in other times, the depression of the thirties spawned a number of ephemeral political aberrations like the Share the Wealth of Huey Long, the oldsters' rebellion led by Dr. Francis E. Townsend, and the soured Populism of Father Coughlin's crusade for Social Justice. But the most portentous shift in popular political thought was the Roosevelt Revolution — the raising of the Democratic party to the predominant position in American political life. As the War for the Union became the stock in trade of the Republicans after 1865, so the Great Depression became the Democrats' primary justification; they have made as steady use of the tattered shirt as the Republicans did of the bloody shirt. And the tactic has worked; during the fifties and sixties, as the national elections show, there have been many more Democrats than Republicans in the country. Although Republican Eisenhower was elected by large majorities in 1952 and 1956, only in his first election was he able to carry a Republican Congress into office with him. Not since 1848 has a winning President failed to bring a House of Representatives of his own party into power. Eisenhower's failure to do so in 1956, despite his immense personal popularity, and Nixon's inability to do so in 1968 suggest that most American voters are still loyal to the Democratic party, despite their willingness to support an occasional Republican Presidential candidate. The grip of the depression on the American psyche has barely loosened a full generation after 1940. . . .

Perhaps the most unexpected result of the revolution was the transfer of the Negro vote from the Republicans, where it had lain for three generations, to the Democrats. . . .

In the depths of the depression, even though there was some dissatisfaction with Hoover among Negro leaders, it is clear that the rank-and-file black voter clung to his Republican faith. The name Franklin Roosevelt carried no magic for Negroes in 1932. In the black wards of Chicago that

year, Roosevelt picked up only 23 per cent of the vote — a ratio smaller than
Al Smith's in the prosperous year of 1928. It was the same among the Negroes
in Cleveland; Detroit Negroes awarded F.D.R. only a little more than a
third of their votes.

By 1936, however, the somersault had been executed. At that election Chicago's Black Belt gave Roosevelt 49 per cent of its votes; the Negroes
of Cleveland went all out for the President — 62 per cent — even though in
1932 they had awarded Hoover 72 per cent of their ballots. Roosevelt gar-
nered almost two thirds of the Negro vote in Detroit, and the four Negro
wards in Philadelphia each gave him a majority of 5,000. The swing to the
Democrats had been forecast in 1934, when the first Democratic Negro congressman in American history was elected from Chicago. Between 1936 and
1940, exactly half of the eighteen Negroes elected to state legislatures were
Democrats. Though a tendency has been developing among some Negro
leaders since the Second World War to be more critical of their new Democratic allies, Samuel Lubell reported that in the election of 1950 there was
"less of a break among Negroes than among any other major group in the
Roosevelt Coalition." Despite the fact that civil rights had become a super-
charged issue in the country at the time of the 1956 elections, Negroes, particularly in the North, continued to adhere to their recent Democratic
conversion.[7]

What brought about this dramatic reversal? Part of the answer, of
course, lies in the demographic facts of migration, but, as the Negro voting
in 1932 demonstrates, the really operative force was the Roosevelt administration's recognition of the Negro. It is noteworthy that very little of the
Democratic appeal to the Negro before 1940 can be illustrated in pronouncements or even in particular pieces of legislation. Only rarely does one find
in the literature of Franklin Roosevelt and his New Deal such self-conscious
appeals to the Negro as, say, in Harry Truman's Fair Deal or in Lyndon
Johnson's famous address at Howard University in 1964.

There are several reasons for this. Primary, of course, is the fact
that Truman's Fair Deal developed after the Roosevelt regime had already
given the Negro a bigger and higher platform from which to articulate his
demands. Moreover, because F.D.R., as a working politician, was always
conscious of his party's southern wing, he would rarely antagonize the
Southerners on the race issue alone. Furthermore, Roosevelt as a leader was
only tangentially aware of the Negro as a special case, as a minority to be
singled out for exceptional treatment or concern. It was Eleanor Roosevelt,
not Franklin, who went out of her way to be racially democratic and to concern herself with minority problems.

Nonetheless, the Roosevelt administration in its relatively undra-
matic fashion did much for the Negro, and this too stemmed from both the

character of Franklin Roosevelt and the underlying philosophy of his administration. Just as the federal government found a place for the artist, so its humane outlook could not exclude the Negro. Thus if white men were to be given relief work, so must Negroes; and if so, then why not on an equal basis? "We are going to make a country in which no one is left out," the President said in another connection. And there was nothing to suggest that he had any mental reservations about race when he said it. Besides, although F.D.R. would do little publicly to antagonize his southern allies on the race question, his political perspicacity told him that in the North his power was heavily dependent upon city machines, many of which could or did benefit from Negro votes.

From the very outset the Democratic regime in Washington accepted the black man. Negroes were sprinkled through almost all its agencies either as advisers or as employees in a lesser capacity. The administration consulted and bestowed office upon nonpolitical Negroes (the Republicans had generally used Negroes as political appointees) like William H. Hastie, later to be the first Negro federal judge; Robert C. Weaver, the economist who later, under Lyndon Johnson, became the first Negro to sit in the Cabinet; and Mrs. Mary Bethune, the educator. When low-cost housing went up, Negroes got their share; Negro youths were welcome in the CCC and the NYA just as the whites were, though in the former the races were segregated. Recreational centers, hospitals, and schools were built for Negroes with federal money. Evenhandedly distributed federal relief funds were a gift from heaven to the black man, who was traditionally "hired last and fired first." As one Negro newspaperman told Samuel Lubell, "The really important thing about WPA is that it is a guarantee of a living wage. It means Negroes don't have to work for anything people want to give them." In the votings conducted by the AAA among farmers and those supervised by the National Labor Relations Board among workers, Negroes were treated the same as white men, even though in the South these same black men were excluded from political elections. In short, the Roosevelt administration took a number of concrete steps toward accepting the Negro as a full citizen — a simple innovation of portentous consequences. It would be difficult hereafter for any party in power to do less.

All the credit for converting the Negro from his Republicanism, however, should not go to positive acts of the Democratic administration; the objective economic and social environment also deserves some. Negroes, for example, began to secure jobs in a greater variety of occupations than ever before; under the impact of the depression, some employers were willing to hire Negroes for the first time, if only because the black worker accepted lower wages. Moreover, the CIO unions now began to organize Negro workers on an equal basis with whites. To accomplish this end, Negro organizers were sent among the steel, maritime, and auto workers, and, when the permanent Congress of Industrial Organizations was formed in 1938, a clause in the constitution prohibited any constituent union from discriminating on grounds of race. The startling improvement in the Negro's position in the thirties could not help but redound to the benefit of the party in power.

By 1940, the capturing of the Negro vote by the Democrats was an accomplished fact, and the party platform of that year, using the word "Negro" for the first time, boasted of its friendship for the black man. "Our Negro citizens," the platform proclaimed, "have participated actively in the economic and social advances launched by this Administration." It would not have been an exaggeration, for once in the history of political platforms, if it had been noted that this was about the first time since the 1870's that any party could truthfully say half as much.

REVOLUTION IN LABOR

The change wrought in the political affiliations of Negroes by the depression was as nothing compared with the catalytic and subversive effect it worked upon the labor movement. And, analogous to the change in the preference of the Negro voter, the alteration in the position and power of labor was indebted to the action of the Roosevelt administration, the Democratic Congress, and the new social atmosphere of the depression era.

During the prosperity of the twenties the labor movement had gone into a decline rare in the history of unionization. The usual tendency had been for membership to rise in prosperous times and to decline in bad. But whereas in 1920 organized labor could claim its largest membership to date — some five million workers — by 1929 barely three million could be counted. Thus labor entered the depression under the handicap of declining membership. But instead of killing off many unions, as depressions had done earlier, the depression of the thirties seemed to stimulate a new and aggressive organizing spirit among the workers. In the light of the later tremendous expansion of union membership, it might be said that the depression created a class consciousness among American workingmen for the first time sufficient to permit large-scale unionization. . . .

The enormous expansion of unionization in the last years of the depression was not solely attributable to the novel spirit among the unions and the workers. Much of the impetus came from the new attitude of the government. We have already seen the catalytic effect the NRA had on the rush toward unionization, and it would be difficult to exaggerate that effect. When that act was declared unconstitutional in 1935, its place was taken by the National Labor Relations Act (the Wagner Act), in itself perhaps the most revolutionary single measure in American labor history.

The Wagner Act started from the same premise as section 7a of the NRA — that is, that workers should be free to choose their own unions and employers must abstain from interfering in this choice. It also required that employers accept duly constituted unions as legitimate representatives of their employees and bargain with them. The act also set up a board — the National Labor Relations Board — whose duty it was to supervise elections for the certification of unions as representatives of a majority of the workers in a plant, and to hear complaints against employers for having interfered with union organizing. The Board was also empowered to hear complaints against employers for refusing to bargain with a certified union.

In two different ways, the act threw the enormous prestige and power of the government behind the drive for organizing workers. In the first place, it flatly declared unionization to be a desirable thing for the national economy, forbidding employers to interfere in the process of organization. Five so-called unfair labor practices were listed, all of them acts which only an employer could commit; the act listed no "unfair" practices of labor. (Actually, the courts had built up such a large body of common-law interpretations of unfair labor practices by unions that it was hardly necessary to add to them in the act.) Moreover, as an additional indication of its belief in the labor movement, the law virtually outlawed the company union — that is, the labor organization sponsored by the employer. In the second place, once a union was formed, and it had been certified by the Board as speaking for a majority of the workers, the employer, under the act, had no alternative but to recognize it as the representative of his employees. Though it is true that many employers refused to accept the constitutionality of the law — usually on the advice of their lawyers — until after the Supreme Court decision of 1937 in the Jones and Laughlin Steel case, this placing of the government on the side of unionization was of central importance in the success of many an organizational drive of the C.I.O., notably those against Ford and Little Steel.[8]

The passage of this controversial act marked, insofar as labor was concerned, an acceptance of governmental assistance which would have made old Sam Gompers apoplectic. All during his leadership of the A.F. of L., labor had consistently refused to accept (except for the war emergency) government intervention at the bargaining table of labor and business. But by accepting governmental assistance, the American labor movement not only departed from its own traditions, but from those of European labor as well. Although well aware of the benefits to be derived from such government support as the American movement received, labor in England and on the Continent has not abandoned its historic independence of the state. European labor unions have preferred to remain untouched by the quasi-governmental status in which the American labor movement has permitted itself to be clothed. Labor's bête noire, the Taft-Hartley Act, is an obvious confirmation of the truism that dependence on government is a knife which cuts both ways. . . .

Enormous as was the assistance which labor received from government in the form of the NLRA, there was still another piece of legislation which offered a boost to labor. This was the Wages and Hours Act of 1938, which set minimum wages and maximum hours for workers in industries engaged in interstate commerce. Since its example has been followed by several industrial states like New York, the principle of a legislative floor under wages and a ceiling on hours has been extended beyond the constitutional limits of the federal government's power. Because the minimum set by law was well below the going industrial wage, the act did not affect most workers, but it helped considerably to pull up wages in certain unorganized industries. Furthermore, it helped to narrow the wage differences between northern and southern industries. During the first two years of the act, nearly a million workers received increased wages under its provisions and over three million had their hours shortened. Subsequent to that time, the minimum wage has been progressively increased from the original 40 cents an hour to the present (1968) $1.60, thereby putting a rising floor under the nation's industrial wage scale. Furthermore, in abolishing child labor in all industries involved in interstate commerce, the act achieved a long-sought goal of the labor and liberal movements in the United States. And once again, it is worth noticing, it was accomplished through the powerful intervention of an active federal government.

Seen against a broader canvas, the depression, together with government support, profoundly altered the position of labor in American society. Girded with its new-found power and protections, Big Labor now took its place beside Big Business and Big Government to complete a triumvirate of economic power. And when it is recognized that through the so-called farm bloc in Congress agriculture also has attained a sort of veto power on the operations of the economic system, it is not difficult to appreciate the aptness of John Galbraith's description of modern American capitalism as a system of "countervailing power." Instead of competition being the regulator of the economic system, Professor Galbraith persuasively argues, we now have a system of economic checks and balances — Big Labor, Big Business, Big Agriculture, and so forth — no one of which is big enough or powerful enough to control the total economy. Though Galbraith's argument is not totally convincing, his conception of the American economy is much closer to reality than is the old competitive model. And insofar as Professor Galbraith's analysis is correct, it is clear that this system of countervailing power came into being during the depression, with the rise of Big Government, Organized Agriculture, and Big Labor.

WAS IT A NEW OR OLD DEAL?

One of the most enduring monuments to the Great Depression was that congeries of contradictions, naïveté, humanitarianism, realistic politics, and economic horse sense called the New Deal of Franklin D. Roosevelt. As the governmental agent which recast American thinking on the responsibilities of government, the New Deal was clearly the offspring of the depression. As we have seen, it was also more than that: it was a revitalization of the Democratic party; it was the political manifestation of that new spirit of reform which was stirring among the ranks of labor and the Negro people.

In their own time and since, the New Deal and Franklin Roosevelt have had a polarizing effect upon Americans. Probably at no time before Roosevelt has the leader of a great democratic nation come to symbolize as he did the hopes and the fears of so many people.[9] Not even Jackson, in whom Roosevelt himself recognized a President of his own popularity- and hatred-producing caliber, could rival him. Two decades after Roosevelt's death, the mention of his name can still evoke emotions, betrayed by the wistful look in the eye or in the hard set of the jaw.

For the Democratic party, Roosevelt was like a lightning rod, drawing to himself all the venom and hatred of the opposition, only to discharge it harmlessly; nothing, it seemed, could weaken his personal hold on the affections of the majority of Americans. That something more was involved than sheer popularity is shown by the example of Dwight Eisenhower. Though held in even greater popular esteem, Eisenhower was unable to invest his party with his own vote-getting power; Republicans lost while Eisenhower won. The difference between FDR and Ike is that one stood for a program, a hope, and a future, while the other stood for himself as a good, well-intentioned man whom all instinctively trusted and perhaps even admired. The one was a leader of a nation, the other a popular hero. Roosevelt is already a member of that tiny pantheon of great leaders of Americans in which Washington, Jackson, Lincoln, and Wilson are included; it is difficult to believe that Eisenhower will be included. His monument is more likely to be inscribed: "The best-liked man ever to be President."

In the thirties, as now, the place of the New Deal in the broad stream of American development has been a matter of controversy. Historians and commentators on the American scene have not yet reached a firm agreement — if they ever will — as to whether the New Deal was conservative or radical in character. Certainly if one searches the writings and utterances of Franklin Roosevelt, his own consciousness of conservative aims is quickly apparent. "The New Deal is an old deal — as old as the earliest aspirations of humanity for liberty and justice and the good life," he declared in 1934. "It was this administration," he told a Chicago audience in 1936, "which saved the system of private profit and free enterprise after it had been dragged to the brink of ruin. . . ."

But men making a revolution among a profoundly conservative people do not advertise their activity, and above all Franklin Roosevelt understood the temper of his people.[10] Nor should such a statement be interpreted as an insinuation of high conspiracy — far from it. Roosevelt was at heart a conservative, as his lifelong interest in history, among other things, suggests. But he was without dogma in his conservatism, which was heavily interlaced with genuine concern for people.[11] He did not shy away from new means and new approaches to problems when circumstances demanded it. His willingness to experiment, to listen to his university-bred Brains Trust, to accept a measure like the TVA, reveal the flexibility in his thought. Both his lack of theoretical presuppositions and his flexibility are to be seen in the way he came to support novel measures like social security and the Wagner Act. Response to popular demand was the major reason. "The Congress can't stand the pressure of the Townsend Plan unless we have a real old-age insurance system," he complained to Frances Perkins, "nor can I face the country without having . . . a solid plan which will give some assurance to old people of systematic assistance upon retirement." In like manner, the revolutionary NLRA was adopted as a part of his otherwise sketchy and rule-of-thumb philosophy of society. Though ultimately Roosevelt championed the Wagner bill in the House, it was a belated conversion dictated by the foreshadowed success of the measure and the recent invalidation of the NRA. In his pragmatic and common-sense reactions to the exigencies of the depression, Roosevelt, the easy-going conservative, ironically enough became the embodiment of a new era and a new social philosophy for the American people.

"This election," Herbert Hoover presciently said in 1932, "is not a mere shift from the ins to the outs. It means deciding the direction our nation will take over a century to come." The election of Franklin Roosevelt, he predicted, would result in "a radical departure from the foundations of 150 years which have made this the greatest nation in the world." Though Hoover may be charged with nothing more than campaign flourishing, it is nevertheless a fact that his speech was made just after Roosevelt's revealing Commonwealth Club address of September. Only in this single utterance, it should be remembered, did Roosevelt disclose in clear outline the philosophy and program which was later to be the New Deal. "Every man has a right to life," he had said, "and this means that he has also a right to make a comfortable living. . . . Our government, formal and informal, political and economic," he went on, "owes to everyone an avenue to possess himself of a portion of that plenty [from our industrial society] sufficient for his needs, through his own work." Here were the intimations of those new goals which the New Deal set for America.

Accent as heavily as one wishes the continuity between the reforms of the Progressive era and the New Deal, yet the wide difference between the goals of the two periods still remains. The Progressive impulse was narrowly reformist: it limited business, it assisted agriculture, it freed labor from some of the shackles imposed by the courts, but it continued to conceive of the state as policeman or judge and nothing more. The New Deal, on the other hand, was more than a regulator — though it was that too, as shown by the SEC and the reinvigoration of the antitrust division of the Justice Department. To the old goals for America set forth and fought for by the Jeffersonians and the Progressives the New Deal appended new ones. Its primary and general innovation was the guaranteeing of a minimum standard of welfare for the people of the nation. WPA and the whole series of relief agencies which were a part of it, wages and hours legislation, AAA, bank deposit insurance, and social security,[12] each illustrates this new conception of the federal government. A resolution offered by New Deal Senator Walsh in 1935 clearly enunciated the new obligations of government. The resolution took notice of the disastrous effects of the depression "upon the lives of young men and women . . ." and then went on to say that "it is the duty of the Federal Government to use every possible means of opening up opportunities" for the youth of the nation "so that they may be rehabilitated and restored to a *decent standard of living* and ensured proper development of their talents. . . ."

But the guarantor state as it developed under the New Deal was more active and positive than this. It was a vigorous and dynamic force in the society, energizing and, if necessary, supplanting private enterprise when the general welfare required it. With the Wagner Act, for example, the government served notice that it would actively participate in securing the unionization of the American worker; the state was no longer to be an impartial policeman merely keeping order; it now declared for the side of labor. When social and economic problems like the rehabilitation of the Valley of the Tennessee were ignored or shirked by private enterprise, then the federal government undertook to do the job. Did private enterprise fail to provide adequate and sufficient housing for a minimum standard of welfare for the people, then the government would build houses. As a result, boasted Nathan Straus, head of the U.S. Housing Authority, "for the first time in a hundred years the slums of America ceased growing and began to shrink."

Few areas of American life were beyond the touch of the experimenting fingers of the New Deal; even the once sacrosanct domain of prices and the valuation of money felt the tinkering. The devaluation of the dollar, the gold-purchase program, the departure from the gold standard — in short, the whole monetary policy undertaken by FDR as a means to stimulate recovery through a price rise — constituted an unprecedented repudiation of orthodox public finance. To achieve that minimum standard of well-being which the depression had taught the American people to expect of their government, nothing was out of bounds.[13]

But it is not the variety of change which stamps the New Deal as the creator of a new America; its significance lies in the permanence of its program. For, novel as the New Deal program was, it has, significantly, not been repudiated by the Eisenhower administration, the first Republican government since the reforms were instituted. Verbally, it is true, the Republican administration has had to minimize its actual commitments to the New Deal philosophy, and it tended to trust private business more than the New Dealers did — witness, for example, its elimination of the minor governmental manufacturing enterprises which competed with private firms. But despite this, the administration's firm commitment to the guaranteeing of prosperity and averting depression at all costs is an accurate reflection of the American people's agreement with the New Deal's diagnosis of the depression. Nor has the Republican party dared to repeal or even emasculate the legislation which made up the vitals of the New Deal: TVA, banking and currency, SEC, social security, the Wagner Act, and fair treatment of the Negro. The New Deal Revolution has become so much a part of the American Way that no political party which aspires to high office dares now to repudiate it.

It may or may not be significant in this regard (for apothegms are more slippery than precise) but it is nonetheless interesting that Roosevelt and Eisenhower have both been impressed with the same single sentence from Lincoln regarding the role of government. "The legitimate object of Government," wrote Lincoln, "is to do for a community of people whatever they need to have done but cannot do at all or cannot do so well for themselves in their separate or individual capacities." Twice, in 1934 and again in 1936, FDR in public addresses used this expression to epitomize his own New Deal, and Robert Donovan in his officially inspired book on the Eisenhower administration writes that this same "fragment of Lincoln's writing . . . Eisenhower uses time and again in describing his own philosophy of government." Between Lincoln and Eisenhower there was no Republican President, except perhaps Theodore Roosevelt, who would have been willing to subscribe to such a free-wheeling description of the federal power; in this can be measured the impact of the New Deal and the depression.

The conclusion seems inescapable that, traditional as the words may have been in which the New Deal expressed itself, in actuality it was truly a revolution in ideas, institutions and practices, when one compares it with the political and social world that preceded it. In its long history, America has passed through two revolutions since the first one in 1776, but only the last two, the Civil War and the depression, were of such force as to change the direction of the relatively smooth flow of its progress. The Civil War rendered a final and irrevocable decision in the long debate over the nature of the Union and the position of the Negro in American society. From that revolutionary experience, America emerged a strong national state and dedicated by the words of its most hallowed document to the inclusion of the black man in a democratic culture. The searing ordeal of the Great Depression purged the American people of their belief in the limited powers of the federal government and convinced them of the necessity of the guarantor state. And as the Civil War constituted a watershed in American thought, so the depression and its New Deal marked the crossing of a divide from which, it would seem, there could be no turning back.

Sources of the New Deal

ARTHUR M. SCHLESINGER, JR.

This essay is important for two clearly stated ideas. The first is that many changes associated with the New Deal, especially those in which new social groups rapidly expanded their political power and secured greater access to America's economic opportunities, would have occurred even without a depression. This is a useful perspective, and one which few will want to dispute. The second idea raises a more fundamental issue and is considerably more controversial. As Schlesinger, Albert Schweitzer Professor at The City University of New York, sees it, history offered western societies three choices in the interwar period: totalitarianisms of either right or left and reform-oriented liberal democracy. The economic crisis forced many nations to abandon political democracy for systems which, whatever their other deficiencies, would at least bring economic security. In the United States, Roosevelt and the New Dealers proved that a democratic government, despite its ponderous parliamentary forms, could act with energy and decisiveness and even measurable economic success. They found a middle way between totalitarianisms, and their example helped democracy through the spiritual and economic crisis between the wars.

After reading such an essay, democrats might think that they have no choice but to approve of the New Deal. This would be true if history offered only three choices. Such is Schlesinger's brilliant argument, but it is one that need not be acquiesced in. One might argue, with all due respect to Roosevelt, that the

*middle way was a wide channel with many alternative courses
and speeds, and the man who earned our gratitude for plotting a
course in that channel might merit our criticism for not having
edged much farther left (or right). This perspective revives the
critical faculties, which are likely to be dulled by Schlesinger's
compelling summary of the historical alternatives.*

In the background of any historical episode lies all previous history.
The strands which a historian may select as vital to an understanding of the
particular episode will vary widely according to his interest, his tempera-
ment, his faith and his time. Each man must unravel the seamless web in his
own way. I do not propose here any definite assessment of the sources of the
New Deal. I doubt whether a final assessment is possible. I want rather to call
attention to certain possible sources which may not have figured extensively
in the conventional accounts, including my own — to the relation of the New
Deal to the ebb and flow of American national politics and then its relation
to the international dilemma of free society in this century.

Such relationships are speculative; nonetheless, an attempt to see
them may perhaps cast light on some of the less discussed impulses behind
the New Deal itself. To begin — and in order to make a sharp issue — let me
ask this question: would there have been a New Deal if there had been no
depression? Without a depression, would we have had nothing but a placid
continuation, so long as prosperity itself continued, of the New Era of the
Twenties?

I would answer that there would very likely have been some sort of
New Deal in the Thirties even without the Depression. I think perhaps our
contemporary thinking has come too unreflectively to assume depression as
the necessary preliminary for any era of reform. Students of American history
know better. The fight against depression was, to be sure, the heart of the
New Deal, but it has not been the central issue of traditional American reform: it was not the heart of Jeffersonian democracy nor of Jacksonian democracy nor of the anti-slavery movement nor of the Progressive movement.

What preceded these other epochs of reform was an accumulation
of disquietudes and discontents in American society, often non-economic in
character, and producing a general susceptibility to appeals for change — this
and the existence within society of able men or groups who felt themselves

From Arthur M. Schlesinger, Jr., "Sources of the New Deal: Reflections
on the Temper of a Time." Reprinted from the *Columbia Forum*, Fall
1959, Volume II, Number 4. Copyright 1959 by the Trustees of Columbia University in the City of New York.

cramped by the status quo and who were capable of exploiting mounting dissatisfaction to advance policies and purposes of their own. This combination
of outsiders striving for status and power and a people wearying of the existing leadership and the existing ideals has been the real archetype of American reform.

The official order in the Twenties presented perhaps the nearest we
ever came in our history to the identification of the national interest with the
interests, values and goals of a specific class — in this case, of course, the American business community. During the generation before Harding, the political
leaders who had commanded the loyalties and the energies of the American
people — Theodore Roosevelt and Woodrow Wilson — expressed strains in
American life distinct from and often opposed to the dominant values of
business. They represented a fusion of patrician and intellectual attitudes
which saw in public policy an outlet for creative energy — in Lippmann's
phrase, they stood for mastery as against drift. In the service of this conception,
they led the people into great national efforts of various sorts, culminating in
the convulsive and terrible experience of war. Two decades of this — two decades under the glittering eyes of such leaders as Roosevelt and Wilson, Bryan
and La Follette — left the nation in a state of exhaustion.

By 1920 the nation was tired of public crisis. It was tired of discipline
and sacrifice. It was tired of abstract and intangible objectives. It could gird
itself no longer for heroic moral or intellectual effort. Its instinct for idealism
was spent. "It is only once in a generation," Wilson himself had said, "that a
people can be lifted above material things. That is why conservative government is in the saddle two-thirds of the time." And the junior official to whom
he made this remark, the young Assistant Secretary of the Navy, also noted
soon after his unsuccessful try for the Vice-Presidency in 1920, "Every war
brings after it a period of materialism and conservatism; people tire quickly
of ideals and we are now repeating history." John W. Davis, the Democratic
candidate in 1924, said a few years later: "The people usually know what
they want at a particular time . . . In 1924 when I was a candidate what
they wanted was repose."

A nation fatigued with ideals and longing for repose was ready for
"normalcy." As popular attention receded from public policy, as values and
aspirations became private again, people stopped caring about politics, which
meant that political power inevitably gravitated to society's powerful economic interests — the government of the exhausted nation quite naturally
fell to the businessmen. And for nearly a decade the business government
reigned over a prosperous and expanding country.

Yet, for all the material contentment of the Twenties, the decade
was also marked by mounting spiritual and psychological discontent. One
could detect abundant and multiplying symptoms of what Josiah Royce,

after Hegel, used to call a self-estranged social order. The official creed began to encounter growing skepticism, and even opposition and ridicule, in the community at large. Able and ambitious groups, denied what they considered fitting recognition or opportunity, began to turn against the Establishment.

If the economic crash of 1929 astonished the experts, a spiritual crash was diagnosed well in advance. "By 1927," reported Scott Fitzgerald, "a widespread neurosis began to be evident, faintly signalled, like a nervous beating of the feet, by the popularity of crossword puzzles." In the same year Walter Lippmann pointed more soberly to the growing discrepancy between the nominal political issues of the day and the actual emotions of the people. If politics took up these real issues, Lippmann said, it would revolutionize the existing party system. "It is not surprising, then, that our political leaders are greatly occupied in dampening down interest, in obscuring issues, and in attempting to distract attention from the realities of American life."

What was wrong with the New Era was not (as yet) evidence of incompetence or stupidity in public policy. Rather, there was a profound discontent with the monopoly of power and prestige by a single class and the resulting indifference of the national government to deeper tension. Those excluded from the magic circle suffered boredom, resentment, irritation and eventually indignation over what seemed the intolerable pretensions and irrelevances of their masters. Now it is the gravest error to underrate the power of boredom as a factor in social change. Our political scientists have pointed out convincingly how the human tendency toward inertia sets limits on liberalism; I wish they would spend equal time showing how the human capacity for boredom sets limits on conservatism. The dominant official society — the Establishment — of the Twenties was an exceedingly boring one, neither bright nor witty nor picturesque nor even handsome, and this prodded the human impulse to redress the balance by kicking up heels in back streets.

All this encouraged the defection of specific groups from a social order which ignored their needs and snubbed their ambitions. Within the business community itself there were dissident individuals, especially in the underdeveloped areas of the country, who considered that opportunities for local growth were unduly restrained by Wall Street's control of the money market. The farmers felt themselves shut out from the prevailing prosperity. Elements in the labor movement resented their evident second-class citizenship. Members of foreign nationality groups, especially the newer immigration and its children, chafed under the prevalent assumption that the real America was Anglo-Saxon, Protestant, middle-class and white. In time some of the younger people of the nation began to grow restless before the ideals held out to them; while others, in accepting these ideals, acquired a smug mediocrity which even depressed some of their elders.

Gravest among the symptoms was the defection of the intellectuals:

writers, educators, newspapermen, editors — those who manned the machinery of opinion and who transmitted ideas. The fact of their particular estrangement and discontent guaranteed the articulation, and thus, to a degree, the coordination of the larger unrest. The intellectuals put the ruling class in its place by substituting for its own admiring picture of itself a set of disrespectful images, which an increasing number of people found delightful and persuasive; the insiders, who had before been seen in the reverent terms of Bruce Barton and the *American Magazine,* were now to be seen less reverently through the eyes of H. L. Mencken and Sinclair Lewis. Satire liberated people from the illusion of business infallibility and opened their minds to other visions of American possibility. The next function of the intellectuals was precisely to explore and substantiate those other visions. They did so with zest and ingenuity; and the result was that, beneath the official crust, the Twenties billowed with agitation, criticism and hope. Dewey affirmed man's capability for social invention and management; Beard argued that intelligent national planning was the irresistible next phase in history; Parrington insisted that Jeffersonian idealism had a sound basis in the American past, and indeed expressed a truer Americanism than did materialism. Together the satirists and the prophets drew a new portrait of America — both of the American present and of the American promise — and the increasingly visible discrepancy between what was and what might be in America armed the spreading discontent.

The well of idealism was rising again; energies were being replenished, batteries recharged. Outsiders were preparing to hammer on the gates of the citadel. The 1928 election, in which an Irish Catholic challenged Yankee Protestant supremacy, illustrated the gathering revolt against the Establishment. And, though Hoover won the election, Samuel Lubell has pointed out that "Smith split not only the Solid South but the Republican North as well." Smith carried counties which had long been traditionally Republican; he smashed the Republican hold on the cities; he mobilized the new immigrants. In losing, he polled nearly as many votes as Calvin Coolidge had polled in winning four years before. He stood for the vital new tendencies of politics; and it is likely that the prolongation of these tendencies would have assured a national Democratic victory, without a depression, in 1932 or certainly by 1936. And such a Democratic victory would surely have meant the discharge into public life of able and ambitious people denied preference under a business administration — much the same sort of people, indeed, who eventually came to power with the New Deal; and it would have meant new opportunities for groups that had seen the door slammed in their faces in the Twenties — labor, the farmers, the ethnic minorities, the intellectuals.

The suspicion that a political overturn was due even without a depression is fortified, I think, by the calculations of my father in his essay of some years back "The Tides of National Politics." In this essay he proposed that liberal and conservative periods in our national life succeed themselves at intervals of about fifteen or sixteen years; this alternation takes place, he wrote, without any apparent correlation with economic circumstances or, indeed, with anything else, except the ebb and flow of national political psychology. By this argument, a liberal epoch was due in America around 1934 or 1935, depression or no.

In short, the New Deal was, among other things, an expression of what would seem — to use a currently unfashionable concept — an inherent cyclical rhythm in American politics. The Depression did not cause the cycle: what the Depression did was to increase its intensity and deepen its impact by superimposing on the normal cycle the peculiar and unprecedented urgencies arising from economic despair. One might even argue — though I do not think I would — that the Depression coming at another stage in the cycle would not necessarily have produced a New Deal. It is certainly true, as I said, that depressions did not induce epochs of reform in 1873 or in 1893. I think myself, however, that the magnitude of the shock made a political recoil almost certain after 1929. Still, the fact that this recoil took a liberal rather than a reactionary turn may well be due to the accident that the economic shock coincided with a liberal turn in the political cycle.

In any event, the fact remains that the historical New Deal, whether or not something like it might have come along anyway, was after all brought into being by the Depression. It assumed its particular character as it sought to respond to the challenge of economic collapse. And, in confronting this challenge, it was confronting a good deal more than merely an American problem. Mass unemployment touched the very roots of free institutions everywhere. "This problem of unemployment," as Winston Churchill said in England in 1930, "is the most torturing that can be presented to civilized society." The problem was more than torturing; it was something civilized society had to solve if it were to survive. And the issue presented with particular urgency was whether representative democracy could ever deal effectively with it.

Churchill, in the same Romanes lecture at Oxford in 1930, questioned whether it could: democratic governments, he said, drifted along the lines of least resistance, took short views, smoothed their path with platitudes, and paid their way with sops and doles. Parliaments, he suggested, could deal with political problems, but not with economic. "One may even be pardoned," Churchill said, "for doubting whether institutions based on adult suffrage could possibly arrive at the right decisions upon the intricate propositions of modern business and finance." These were delicate problems requiring specialist treatment. "You cannot cure cancer by a majority. What is wanted is a remedy."

The drift of discussion in the United States as well as in Britain in the early Thirties revealed an increasingly dour sense of existing alternatives; on the one hand, it seemed, was parliamentary democracy with economic chaos; on the other, economic authoritarianism with political tyranny. Even more dour was the sense that history had already made the choice — that the democratic impulse was drained of vitality, that liberalism was spent as a means of organizing human action. Consider a selection of statements from American writers at the time, and their mortuary resonance:

> The rejection of democracy is nowadays regarded as evidence of superior wisdom. (Ralph Barton Perry)
> The moral and intellectual bankruptcy of liberalism in our time needs no demonstration. It is as obvious as rain and as taken for granted. (Nathaniel Peffer)
> To attempt a defense of democracy these days is a little like defending paganism in 313 or the divine right of kings in 1793. It is taken for granted that democracy is bad and that it is dying. (George Boas)
> "Liberalism is dead." So many people who seem to agree upon nothing else have agreed to accept these three sweeping words. (Joseph Wood Krutch)
> Modern Western civilization is a failure. That theory is now generally accepted. (Louise Maunsell Fields)
> Why is it that democracy has fallen so rapidly from the high prestige which it had at the Armistice? . . . Why is it that in America itself — in the very temple and citadel of democracy — self-government has been held up to every ridicule, and many observers count it already dead? (Will Durant)

Only the most venerable among us can remember the creeping fear of a quarter of a century ago that the free system itself had run out of energy, that we had reached, in a phrase Reinhold Niebuhr used as a part of the title of a book in 1934, the "end of an era." What this pessimism implied for the realm of public policy was that democracy had exhausted its intellectual and moral resources, its bag of tricks was played out, and salvation now lay in moving over to a system of total control.

In affirming that there was no alternative between laissez-faire and tyranny, the pessimists were endorsing a passionate conviction held both by the proponents of individualism and the proponents of collectivism. Ogden Mills spoke with precision for American conservatives: "We can have a free country or a socialistic one. We cannot have both. Our economic system cannot be half free and half socialistic. . . . There is no middle ground between governing and being governed, between absolute sovereignty and liberty, between tyranny and freedom." Herbert Hoover was equally vehement: "Even

partial regimentation cannot be made to work and still maintain live democratic institutions." In such sentiments, Hoover and Mills would have commanded the enthusiastic assent of Stalin and Mussolini. The critical question
was whether a middle way was possible — a mixed system which might give
the state more power than conservatives would like, enough power, indeed,
to assure economic and social security, but still not so much as to create dicta-
torship. To this question the Hoovers, no less than the Stalins and Musso-
linis, had long since returned categorical answers. They all agreed on this, if
on nothing else: no.

As I have said, economic planning was not just an American problem. Great Britain, for example, was confronting mass unemployment and
economic stagnation; moreover, she had had since 1929 a Labor government.
In a sense, it would have been hard to select a better place to test the possibilities of a tranquil advance from laissez-faire capitalism to a managed
society. Here was a Labor leadership, sustained by a faith in the "inevitability
of gradualness," ruling a nation committed by tradition and instinct to the
acceptance of empirical change. How did the British Labor government visu-
alize its problem and opportunity?

The central figures in the Labor government of 1929 were Ramsay
MacDonald, now Prime Minister for the second time, and Philip Snowden,
his sharp and dominating Chancellor of the Exchequer. Both were classical
Socialists who saw in the nationalization of basic industry the answer to all
economic riddles. Yet in the existing political situation, with a slim Labor
majority, nationalization was out of the question. With socialism excluded,
MacDonald and Snowden — indeed, nearly all the Labor party leaders —
could see no alternative to all-out socialism but nearly all-out laissez-faire. A
capitalist order had to be operated on capitalist principles. The economic
policy of the Labor government was thus consecrated as faithfully as that of
Herbert Hoover's Republican administration in the United States to the balanced budget and the gold standard — and, far more faithfully than American Republicanism, to free trade.

Socialism across the Channel was hardly more resourceful. As the
German Social Democrat Fritz Naphtali put it in 1930, "I don't believe that
we can do very much, nor anything very decisive, from the point of view of
economic policy, to overcome the crisis until it has run its course." In this
spirit of impotence, the democratic Socialists of Europe (until Léon Blum
came to power some years later) denied the possibility of a middle way and
concluded that, short of full socialization, they had no alternative but to
accept the logic of laissez-faire.

The assumption that there were two absolutely distinct economic
orders, socialism and capitalism, expressed, of course, an unconscious Platonism — a conviction that the true reality lay in the theoretical essences of

which any working economy, with its compromises and confusions, could only be an imperfect copy. If in the realm of essences socialism and capitalism were separate phenomena based on separate principles, then they must be kept rigorously apart on earth. Nor was this use of Platonism — this curious belief that the abstraction was somehow more real than the reality, which Whitehead so well called the "fallacy of misplaced concreteness" — confined to doctrinaire capitalists and doctrinaire socialists. The eminent Liberal economist Sir William Beveridge, director of the London School of Economics, braintruster for the Lloyd George welfare reforms before the First World War, spoke for enlightened economic opinion when he identified the "inescapable fatal danger" confronting public policy in the Depression as "the danger of mixing freedom and control. We have to decide either to let production be guided by the free play of prices or to plan it socialistically from beginning to end . . . Control and freedom do not mix." Beveridge, encountering Donald Richberg in Washington in the glowing days of 1933, asked a bit patronizingly whether Richberg really believed that there was "a halfway between Wall Street and Moscow." As for Britain, "there is not much that anyone can do now to help us," Beveridge said. "We must plan to avoid another crisis later. We shall not by conscious effort escape this one."

So dogma denied the possibility of a managed capitalism. But could dogma hold out in Britain against the urgencies of depression? Some Englishmen dissented from the either/or philosophy. In the general election of 1929, for example, John Maynard Keynes and Hubert Henderson had provided the Liberal party with the rudiments of an expansionist policy, based on national spending and public works. As unemployment increased in 1930, so too did the pressure for positive government action. That year Sir Oswald Mosley, a member of the Labor government, proposed to a cabinet committee on unemployment an active program of government spending, accompanied by controls over banking, industry and foreign trade. But he could make no impression on the capitalist orthodoxy of the Socialists leaders; Snowden rejected the Mosley memorandum. Another minister suggested leaving the gold standard; Snowden covered him with scorn. To the party conference of 1930, MacDonald said, "I appeal to you to go back to your Socialist faith. Do not mix that up with pettifogging patching, either of a Poor Law kind or Relief Work kind." In other words, socialism meant all or — in this case — nothing!

As economic pressure increased, more and more had to be sacrificed to the balancing of the budget; and the implacable retrenchment meant more governmental economy, reduction in salaries, reduction in normal public works, until, in time, the frenzy for economy threatened the social services and especially the system of unemployment payments on which many British workers relied to keep alive. The summer crisis of 1931, after the failure of

Kreditanstalt, [Vienna's leading bank, whose failure set off a financial panic in central Europe — Ed.] weakened the pound; and to Snowden and the Labor government nothing now seemed more essential than staying on the gold standard. To keep Britain on gold required American loans; American loans would not be forthcoming unless satisfactory evidence existed of a determination to balance the budget; and the evidence most likely to satisfy J. P. Morgan and Company, which was arranging the American credit, was a cut in unemployment benefits.

In August 1931, MacDonald and Snowden confronted the cabinet with this dismal logic. Arthur Henderson made it clear that the whole cabinet absolutely accepted Snowden's economic theory: "We ought to do everything in our power to balance the Budget." But MacDonald's proposal for a cut in the dole seemed downright wrong; the Labor government fell. MacDonald soon returned to office as head of a National government. The new government, slightly more adventurous than its predecessors, took Britain off gold in a few weeks. Sidney Webb, Labor's senior intellectual, provided the Labor government its obituary: "No one ever told *us* we could do that!"

The Labor government having immobilized itself by its intellectual conviction that there was no room for maneuver, no middle way, now succeeded through its collapse in documenting its major premise. Then the experience of 1931 displayed the Right as too hardboiled ever to acquiesce in even the most gradual democratic change. "The attempt to give a social bias to capitalism, while leaving it master of the house," wrote R. H. Tawney, "appears to have failed."

If piecemeal reforms were beyond the power of the Labor government, as they were beyond the desire of a Tory government, then the only hope lay in the rapid achievement of full socialism; the only way socialism could be achieved seemed to be through ruthlessness on the Left as great as that on the Right. Such reasoning was responsible for the lust for catastrophic change that suffused the British Left and infected a part of the American Left in the early Thirties. No one drew more facile and sweeping conclusions than Harold Laski. The fate of the MacDonald government, Laski wrote, was "tantamount to an insistence that if socialists wish to secure a state built upon the principles of their faith, they can only do so by revolutionary means."

From this perspective Laski and those like him quite naturally looked with derision on the advocate of the middle way. In December 1934, for the perhaps somewhat baffled readers of *Redbook* magazine, Laski debated with Maynard Keynes whether America could spend its way to recovery. Public spending, Laski said with horror, would lead to inflation or heavy taxation or waste; it would mean, he solemnly wrote, "an unbalanced budget with the disturbance of confidence (an essential condition of recovery) which this implies": it would bequeath a "bill of staggering dimensions" to future generations. "Government spending as anything more than a temporary and limited expedient," he concluded, "will necessarily do harm in a capitalist society." This was, of course, not only the argument of Ramsay MacDonald but of Herbert Hoover; Laski's novelty was to use it to defend, not a balanced budget and the gold standard, but — socialist revolution.

One way or another, the British Left began to vote against liberal democracy. Sir Oswald Mosley, who had championed the most constructive economic program considered within the MacDonald government, indicated the new direction when, with John Strachey and others, he founded the authoritarian-minded New Party in 1931. Mosley's excesses soon led him toward fascism and discredit; but plenty of others were reaching similar conclusions about the impossibility of reform under capitalism. Sidney and Beatrice Webb abandoned Fabianism for the mirage of a new civilization in the Soviet Union. All peaceful roads to progress seemed blocked. After a visit with Roosevelt in Washington, Cripps wrote, "My whole impression is of an honest anxious man faced by an impossible task — humanizing capitalism and making it work. The one thing that is not inevitable now," said Cripps, "is gradualness."

Both Right and Left — Hoover and Stalin, John W. Davis and Mussolini, Ogden Mills and Stafford Cripps — thus rejected the notion of a socially directed and managed capitalism, of a mixed economy, of something in between classical free enterprise and classical socialism. And the either/or demonstration commanded considerable respect in the United States — self-evidently on the American Right; and to some degree on the American Left. So Laski had made clear in *Democracy in Crisis* that the American ruling class would be as tough and hopeless as any other:

> What evidence is there, among the class which controls the destiny of America, of a will to make the necessary concessions? Is not the execution of Sacco and Vanzetti, the long indefensible imprisonment of Mooney, the grim history of American strikes, the root of the answer to that question?

In 1932 both Right and Left thus stood with fierce intransigence on the solid ground of dogma. In so doing, they were challenging an essential part of the American liberal tradition. When Professor Rexford G. Tugwell of the Columbia University economics department, on leave in Washington, revisited his campus in 1933, he rashly bragged of the New Deal's freedom from "blind doctrine," and the *Columbia Spectator*, then edited by a brilliant young undergraduate named James Wechsler, seized on this boast as the fatal weakness of Tugwell's argument and of the whole New Deal. "This is the crux of the problem," the *Spectator* said; "the blind stumbling in the most chaotic fashion — experimenting from day to day — without any anchor except a few idealistic phrases — is worthless. It is merely political pragmatism."

Merely political pragmatism — to ideologists, whether of Right or of Left, this seemed conclusive evidence of intellectual bankruptcy. As the conservatives had said that any attempt to modify the capitalist system must mean socialism, so the radicals now said that any attempt to maintain the capitalist system must mean fascism. "Roosevelt's policies can be welded into a consistent whole," wrote I. F. Stone, "only on the basis of one hypothesis . . . that Mr. Roosevelt intends to move toward fascism." "The essential logic of the New Deal," wrote Max Lerner, "is increasingly the naked fist of the capitalist state."

Convinced of the fragility of the system, the radicals saw themselves as the forerunners of apocalypse. "American commercial agriculture is doomed," wrote Louis Hacker; capitalism was doomed, too, and the party system, and the traditional American way of life. In 1934 Sidney Hook, James Burnham, Louis Budenz, V. F. Calverton, James Rorty and others addressed "An Open Letter to American Intellectuals." "We cannot by some clever Rooseveltian trick," the letter warned,

> evade the unfolding of basic economic and political developments under capitalism . . . Let us not deceive ourselves that we shall not have to face here also the choice between reaction, on the one hand, and a truly scientific economy under a genuine workers' democracy on the other.

In 1935 *The New Republic* stated with magisterial simplicity the argument of the radicals against the New Dealers, of New York against Washington, of the Marxists against the pragmatists.

> Either the nation must put up with the confusions and miseries of an essentially unregulated capitalism, or it must prepare to supersede capitalism with socialism. *There is no longer a feasible middle course.*

Both radicalism and conservatism thus ended in the domain of either/or. The contradictions of actuality, which so stimulated the pragmatists of Washington, only violated the proprieties and offended the illusions of the ideologists. While they all saw themselves as hardheaded realists, in fact they were Platonists, preferring essence to existence and considering abstractions the only reality.

The great central source of the New Deal, in my judgment, lay precisely in the instinctive response of practical, energetic, and compassionate

people to those dogmatic absolutes. This passion to sacrifice reality to doctrine presented a profound challenge to the pragmatic nerve. Many Americans, refusing to be intimidated by abstractions or to be overawed by ideology, responded by doing things. The whole point of the New Deal lay in its
belief in activism, its faith in gradualness, its rejection of catastrophism, its
indifference to ideology, its conviction that a managed and modified capitalist order achieved by piecemeal experiment could combine personal freedom
and economic growth. "In a world in which revolutions just now are coming easily," said Adolf Berle, "the New Deal chose the more difficult course of
moderation and rebuilding." "The course that the new Administration did
take," said Harold Ickes, "was the hardest course. It conformed to no theory,
but it did fit into the American system — a system of taking action step by
step, a system of regulation only to meet concrete needs, a system of coura-
geous recognition of change." Tugwell, rejecting laissez-faire and communism, spoke of the "third course."

Roosevelt himself, of course, was the liberal pragmatist *par excellence.* His aim was to steer between the extremes of chaos and tyranny by
moving always, in his phrase, "slightly to the left of center." "Unrestrained
individualism" he wrote, had proved a failure; yet "any paternalistic system
which tries to provide for security for everyone from above only calls for an
impossible task and a regimentation utterly uncongenial to the spirit of our
people." He constantly repeated Macaulay's injunction to reform if you
wished to preserve.

Roosevelt had no illusions about revolution. Mussolini and Stalin
seemed to him, in his phrase, "not mere distant relatives" but "blood brothers." When Emil Ludwig asked him his "political motive," he replied, "My
desire is to obviate revolution . . . I work in a contrary sense to Rome and
Moscow." He said during the 1932 campaign:

> Say that civilization is a tree which, as it grows, continually produces
> rot and dead wood. The radical says: "Cut it down." The conservative says:
> "Don't touch it." The liberal compromises: "Let's prune, so that we lose
> neither the old trunk nor the new branches." This campaign is waged to
> teach the country to march upon its appointed course, the way of change,
> in an orderly march, avoiding alike the revolution of radicalism and the
> revolution of conservatism.

I think it would be a mistake to underestimate the extent to which
this pragmatic attitude was itself a major source of New Deal vitality. The
exaltation of the middle way seems banal and obvious enough today. Yet the
tyranny of dogma was such in the early years of the Great Depression that
infatuation with ideology blocked and smothered the instinctive efforts of

free men to work their own salvation. In a world intoxicated with abstractions, Roosevelt and the New Dealers stood almost alone in a stubborn faith in rational experiment, in trial and error. No one understood this more keenly than the great English critic of absolutes; Keynes, in an open letter to Roosevelt at the end of 1933, stated the hopes generated by the New Deal with precision and eloquence. "You have made yourself," Keynes told Roosevelt,

> the trustee for those in every country who seek to mend the evils of our condition by reasoned experiment within the framework of the existing social system. If you fail, rational choice will be gravely prejudiced throughout the world, leaving orthodoxy and revolution to fight it out. But, if you succeed, new and bolder methods will be tried everywhere, and we may date the first chapter of a new economic era from your accession to office.

The question remains: why did the New Deal itself have the pragmatic commitment? Why, under the impact of depression, was it not overborne by dogma as were most other governments and leaders in the world? The answer to this lies, I suspect, in the point I proposed earlier — in the suggestion that the New Deal represented, not just a response to depression, but also a response to pent-up frustration and needs in American society — frustrations and needs which would have operated had there been no depression at all. The periodic demand for forward motion in American politics, the periodic breakthrough of new leadership — these were already in the works before the Depression. Depression, therefore, instead of catching a nation wholly unprepared, merely accelerated tendencies toward change already visible in the national community. The response to depression, in short, was controlled and tempered by the values of traditional American experimentalism, rather than those of rigid ideology. The New Deal was thus able to approach the agony of mass unemployment and depression in the pragmatic spirit, in the spirit which guaranteed the survival rather than the extinction of freedom, in the spirit which in time rekindled hope across the world that free men could manage their own economic destiny.

THE HALFWAY REVOLUTION

The Roosevelt Reconstruction:
Retrospect

WILLIAM E. LEUCHTENBURG

William E. Leuchtenburg's Franklin D. Roosevelt and the New Deal *is acknowledged by historians as the best one-volume survey of the New Deal. Its style captures the life and vibrancy of the 1930s, as well as its suffering; its judgments rest on impressive research. Leuchtenburg, who teaches history at Columbia University, discovers inadequacies throughout the New Deal, both in ideas and in administration. Where there was an important gap between appearance and reality in a particular New Deal program, Leuchtenburg exposes it. He is sharply critical of the record in taxation, in social insurance, and in agriculture; he underscores Roosevelt's deep caution and mental fuzziness in pursuing economic recovery; and he admits to defects in the "broker state" approach to policy-making. No liberal author has dealt so extensively with the disappointing side of the New Deal. Even so, Leuchtenburg gives full attention to the New Deal's better moments: its revival of faith in American institutions, its energy and imagination, its stimulus to national unity, its unfeigned sympathy for economic and even racial underdogs. In his summary, Leuchtenburg reviews the long-run changes effected by the New Deal — the new role for government, the strengthened Presidency, the inclusion of new groups into positions of political importance — and judges the New Deal at the very least a halfway revolution.*

By 1934, the pattern of the early New Deal was beginning to emerge. Its distinguishing characteristic was the attempt to redress the imbalances of the old order by creating a new equilibrium in which a variety of groups and classes would be represented. The New Dealers sought to effect a truce similar to that of wartime, when class and sectional animosities abated and the claims of partisan or private economic interest were sacrificed to the demands of national unity. Roosevelt presented himself not as the paladin of liberalism but as father to all the people, not as the representative of a single class but as the conductor of a concert of interests. A man above the political battle, the President aimed to serve as the unifier of interests and the harmonizer of divergent ideologies. In March, 1934, he declined to take part in Jefferson Day celebrations, and even suggested it would be a "fine thing" if nonpartisan Jefferson dinners were held with as many Republicans as Democrats on the banquet committee. "Much as we love Thomas Jefferson we should not celebrate him in a partisan way," the President wrote.[1]*

Roosevelt incorporated a wide spectrum of views in the government and tolerated deep divisions within his administration over which policies he should sponsor. At the head of one faction, Rexford Tugwell, the debonair Assistant Secretary of Agriculture, advocated extensive government planning, heavy spending for relief and public works, and curbs on profiteers. He rued the failure to take advantage of the banking crisis to set up a national bank and take over "large blocks of paralyzed industries."[2] Tugwell spoke for the ardent New Deal reformers and for congressional progressives like Bob La Follette. At the head of the opposing faction, Budget Director Lewis Douglas, Roosevelt's "Minister of Deflation," opposed government spending, abhorred currency tinkering, and believed that prosperity would come by balancing the budget and leaving capital investment to private industry. "The condition precedent to the establishment of a communistic or fascistic order of society," Douglas warned the President, "is the destruction of the middle class by paper inflation or unbearable taxation." Around Douglas gathered the "Treasury crowd," business-oriented New Dealers such as Raymond Moley and Donald Richberg, and the conservative southern Democrats, many of whom felt a halt should be called to further reforms.[3]

Roosevelt spurned the opportunity to be broken on the rocks of factional warfare. At heart a man of orthodox fiscal ideas who dreaded unbalanced budgets, he wanted Douglas around to check the spenders. Douglas, the President confided, was "in many ways the greatest 'find' of the adminis-

From pp. 84–89, 326–327, 331–333, 335, 346–348 in *Franklin D. Roosevelt and the New Deal 1932–1940*, by William E. Leuchtenburg. Copyright © 1963 by William E. Leuchtenburg.
* [See pp. 186–188 for notes to this article. — Ed.]

tration." At the same time, he recognized that relief appropriations would be necessary during the emergency, and, while he nodded reassuringly to Douglas, he went ahead with plans which upset the budget. Although he shunned massive deficit spending, the President refused to restrict expenditures to estimated receipts. He favored a middle course of providing for the needy, even at the cost of an unbalanced budget, convinced that in the near future the economy, partly in response to different New Deal enterprises, would take an upward turn and the budget could be balanced out of tomorrow's surpluses.[4]

The Roosevelt administration spun an intricate web of procedures to permit the will of different interest groups to be expressed. Millions of farmers voted in AAA crop referendums, including thousands of southern Negroes who had never before cast a ballot, and the Triple A administered the farm law through production-control associations manned by more than 100,000 committeemen.[5] The Taylor Grazing Act of 1934, which provided for the segregation of up to eighty million acres of public grasslands, stipulated that the Secretary of the Interior co-operate with local associations of stockmen in administering the grazing districts. At a powwow in the Black Hills, Commissioner John Collier, speaking through his Sioux interpreter, Young Red Tomahawk, explained the New Deal for the Indians to Blackfeet from Montana, Winnebagoes from Iowa, and Arapahoes from Wyoming. In the Tennessee Valley, the TVA raised the principle of local participation to a fine art. By the end of the thirties, the New Deal had extended the idea of popular involvement to a host of different agencies. Millions of workmen cast ballots in Labor Board collective bargaining elections; district boards of operators and miners set quotas for bituminous coal; local advisory committees were consulted in the national youth and arts projects; and farmers balloted to create soil conservation districts. As the Mescalero Apaches prepared to vote under the authority of the Indian Reorganization Act of 1934, their tribal leaders presented plays to illustrate each section of the proposed constitution.[6]

TVA Director David Lilienthal hailed these procedures as "grassroots democracy," Congressman Taylor spoke of "home rule on the range," and Henry Wallace wrote of "a hierarchy of New England town meetings." [7] Lilienthal claimed that they resolved the dilemma of how to achieve effective government without creating a leviathan state that would destroy democracy, for they combined national power with local "grassroots" administration. While such sentiments were sincerely expressed, they obscured the fact that "grassroots democracy" frequently meant a surrender of the national interest to local power groups. The AAA, by vesting authority in county production associations, turned the power of decision over to the Farm Bureau Federation, the Extension Service, and the land-grant colleges — in short, the larger landholders.[8] Conservationists objected that the Taylor Act gave stockmen an opportunity to exploit the domain for their advantage. "If they really believe the Taylor Grazing Act is a blow at 'special privilege,'" one editor observed, "then Heaven help democracy." [9] Lilienthal's mystical prose about "democracy on the march" glossed over the political bargain he had struck with TVA Director Harcourt Morgan. He had neutralized opposition to public power at the high cost of acquiescence to Morgan's administration of the TVA's farm program in the interests of the more prosperous white planters.[10] Fifteen years later Rexford Tugwell penned the biting verdict: "TVA is more an example of democracy in retreat than democracy on the march." [11]

Interest-group democracy had the tactical advantage of weakening opposition by incorporating potential opponents within the administration, but it also served to make the Roosevelt administration the prisoner of its own interest groups.[12] The President often shied away from decisions that might antagonize one or another of the elements in the coalition. Government sanction greatly enhanced the power of such groups as the Farm Bureau Federation and the trade associations. Like the mercantilists, the New Dealers protected vested interests with the authority of the state. "What Colbert did under Louis XIV," wrote Walter Lippmann, "was precisely what General Johnson and Secretary Wallace did under President Roosevelt." By 1942, the farm bloc would be able to impose a demand for 110 per cent of parity; it had developed, observed A. Whitney Griswold, "from a ward of charity into a political force capable of pursuing its own interests even to the point of defying the head of the nation in wartime." As early as 1934, the Harvard political scientist E. Pendleton Herring inquired: "Can the presidential system continue as a game of touch and go between the Chief Executive and congressional *blocs* played by procedural dodges and with bread and circuses for forfeit?" [13]

Roosevelt's predilection for balanced government often meant that the privileges granted by the New Deal were in precise proportion to the strength of the pressure groups which demanded them. "Because NRA policy formulation involved the pitting of private economic groups against each other, the outcome could never be too different from the parties' estimate of their chances of winning in a direct conflict in the economic arena," one scholar has observed. "Unions won important gains in NRA codes only where they were economically strong." [14] Conversely, causes which were not sustained by powerful interest groups frequently made little headway. Those which relied on a mythical "consumer interest" fared poorly, as the history of the NRA Consumers' Advisory Board and the sad saga of Tugwell's futile attempt to get an effective pure food and drugs bill amply demonstrated.[15]

If the state was to be no more than "a parallelogram of pressures," any attempt at reform which required a direct challenge to vested interests was doomed. Joseph Eastman had little success in co-ordinating the railroads because the railroads would not let him. When carriers and unions withdrew their support, the program died. Advocates of slum clearance made only superficial progress because the administration would not tackle those elements — the real estate bloc, insurance companies, and building trades unions — which blocked large-scale public housing. NRA policy, noted Arthur R. Burns, "was directed to considerations no more far reaching than an estimate of what representatives of industry would accept without protest. Essential reform must necessarily involve from time to time the imposition of policies distasteful to the class that is most highly organized and articulate." [16] An early commentator on the New Deal advanced a view which later historians have adopted: "Roosevelt is essentially a broker. He has neither the will nor the power to move against the political currents of the day. He does not and cannot invent his policies." [17]

Critics have been quicker to see the limitations than the benefits of "broker state" government. It marked an important advance from the "single interest" administrations of the 1920's. It gave to such interests as the farm groups a voice in government that had been largely denied them in the twenties. If industrial unionists were disadvantaged in the early New Deal years, they also had new forums for expressing their grievances and champions like Senator Wagner who argued that interest-group government implied public encouragement of unionization. "In order that the strong may not take advantage of the weak," Wagner reasoned, "every group must be equally strong." [18] Moreover, the New Deal was never simply a broker state. The need to create overnight a new civil service brought to power men who had not been routinized by years in a bureaucracy and who were not easily disciplined; instead of viewing themselves simply as agents of the President, they often pushed programs of their own which the President was compelled to accept. Finally, Roosevelt himself insisted that there was a public interest paramount to that of any private group. He scolded bankers in 1934: "The old fallacious notion of the bankers on one side and the Government on the other side as being more or less equal and independent units, has passed away. Government by the necessity of things must be the leader, must be the judge of the conflicting interests of all groups in the community, including bankers." [19] . . .

In eight years, Roosevelt and the New Dealers had almost revolutionized the agenda of American politics. "Mr. Roosevelt may have given the wrong answers to many of his problems," concluded the editors of *The Economist*. "But he is at least the first President of modern America who has asked the right questions." In 1932, men of acumen were absorbed to an astonishing degree with such questions as prohibition, war debts, and law enforcement. By 1936, they were debating social security, the Wagner Act, valley authorities, and public housing. The thirties witnessed a rebirth of issues politics, and parties split more sharply on ideological lines than they had in many years past. "I incline to think that for years up to the present juncture thinking Democrats and thinking Republicans had been divided by an imaginary line," reflected a Massachusetts congressman in 1934. "Now for the first time since the period before the Civil War we find vital principles at stake." Much of this change resulted simply from the depression trauma, but much too came from the force of Roosevelt's personality and his use of his office as both pulpit and lectern. "Of course you have fallen into some errors — that is human," former Supreme Court Justice John Clarke wrote the President, "but you have put a new face upon the social and political life of our country." [20]

Franklin Roosevelt re-created the modern Presidency. He took an office which had lost much of its prestige and power in the previous twelve years and gave it an importance which went well beyond what even Theodore Roosevelt and Woodrow Wilson had done. Clinton Rossiter has observed: "Only Washington, who made the office, and Jackson, who remade it, did more than [Roosevelt] to raise it to its present condition of strength, dignity, and independence." [21] Under Roosevelt, the White House became the focus of all government — the fountainhead of ideas, the initiator of action, the representative of the national interest. . . .

For the first time for many Americans, the federal government became an institution that was directly experienced. More than state and local governments, it came to be *the* government, an agency directly concerned with their welfare. It was the source of their relief payments; it taxed them directly for old age pensions; it even gave their children hot lunches in school. As the role of the state changed from that of neutral arbiter to a "powerful promoter of society's welfare," people felt an interest in affairs in Washington they had never had before.[22]

Franklin Roosevelt personified the state as protector. It became commonplace to say that people felt toward the President the kind of trust they would normally express for a warm and understanding father who comforted them in their grief or safeguarded them from harm. An insurance man reported: "My mother looks upon the President as someone so immediately concerned with her problems and difficulties that she would not be greatly surprised were he to come to her house some evening and stay to dinner." From his first hours in office, Roosevelt gave people the feeling that they could confide in him directly. As late as the Presidency of Herbert Hoover, one man, Ira Smith, had sufficed to take care of all the mail the White House received. Under Roosevelt, Smith had to acquire a staff of fifty people to handle the thousands of letters written to the President each week. Roosevelt gave people a sense of membership in the national community. Justice Douglas has written: "He was in a very special sense the people's President, because he made them feel that with him in the White House they shared the Presidency. The sense of sharing the Presidency gave even the most humble citizen a lively sense of belonging." [23]

When Roosevelt took office, the country, to a very large degree, responded to the will of a single element: the white, Anglo-Saxon, Protestant property-holding class. Under the New Deal, new groups took their place in the sun. It was not merely that they received benefits they had not had before but that they were "recognized" as having a place in the commonwealth. At the beginning of the Roosevelt era, charity organizations ignored labor when seeking "community" representation; at the end of the period, no fund-raising committee was complete without a union representative. While Theodore Roosevelt had founded a lily-white Progressive party in the South and Woodrow Wilson had introduced segregation into the federal government, Franklin Roosevelt had quietly brought the Negro into the New Deal coalition. When the distinguished Negro contralto Marian Anderson was denied a concert hall in Washington, Secretary Ickes arranged for her to perform from the steps of Lincoln Memorial. Equal representation for religious groups became so well accepted that, as one priest wryly complained, one never saw a picture of a priest in a newspaper unless he was flanked on either side by a minister and a rabbi.

The devotion Roosevelt aroused owed much to the fact that the New Deal assumed the responsibility for guaranteeing every American a minimum standard of subsistence. Its relief programs represented an advance over the barbaric predepression practices that constituted a difference not in degree but in kind. One analyst wrote: "During the ten years between 1929 and 1939 more progress was made in public welfare and relief than in the three hundred years after this country was first settled." The Roosevelt administration gave such assistance not as a matter of charity but of right. This system of social rights was written into the Social Security Act. Other New Deal legislation abolished child labor in interstate commerce and, by putting a floor under wages and a ceiling on hours, all but wiped out the sweatshop.[24]

Roosevelt and his aides fashioned a government which consciously sought to make the industrial system more humane and to protect workers and their families from exploitation. In his acceptance speech in June, 1936, the President stated: "Governments can err, Presidents do make mistakes, but the immortal Dante tells us that divine justice weighs the sins of the cold-blooded and the sins of the warm-hearted in different scales.

"Better the occasional faults of a Government that lives in a spirit of charity than the constant omission of a Government frozen in the ice of its own indifference." Nearly everyone in the Roosevelt government was caught up to some degree by a sense of participation in something larger than themselves. A few days after he took office, one of the more conservative New Deal administrators wrote in his diary: "This should be a Gov't of humanity." [25]

The federal government expanded enormously in the Roosevelt years. The crisis of the depression dissipated the distrust of the state inherited from the eighteenth century and reinforced in diverse ways by the Jeffersonians and the Spencerians. Roosevelt himself believed that liberty in America was imperiled more by the agglomerations of private business than by the state. The New Dealers were convinced that the depression was the result not simply of an economic breakdown but of a political collapse; hence, they sought new political instrumentalities. The reformers of the 1930's accepted almost unquestioningly the use of coercion by the state to achieve reforms.[26] Even Republicans who protested that Roosevelt's policies were snuffing out liberty voted overwhelmingly in favor of coercive measures.[27] . . .

Under the New Deal, the federal government greatly extended its power over the economy. By the end of the Roosevelt years, few questioned the right of the government to pay the farmer millions in subsidies not to grow crops, to enter plants to conduct union elections, to regulate business enterprises from utility companies to air lines, or even to compete directly with business by generating and distributing hydroelectric power. All of these powers had been ratified by the Supreme Court, which had even held that a man growing grain solely for his own use was affecting interstate commerce and hence subject to federal penalties.[28] The President, too, was well on his way to becoming "the chief economic engineer," although this was not finally established until the Full Employment Act of 1946. In 1931, Hoover had hooted that some people thought "that by some legerdemain we can legislate ourselves out of a world-wide depression." In the Roosevelt era, the conviction that government both should and could act to forestall future breakdowns gained general acceptance. The New Deal left a large legacy of antidepression controls — securities regulation, banking reforms, unemployment compensation — even if it could not guarantee that a subsequent administration would use them.[29] . . .

The New Deal left many problems unsolved and even created some perplexing new ones. It never demonstrated that it could achieve prosperity in peacetime. As late as 1941, the unemployed still numbered six million, and not until the war year of 1943 did the army of the jobless finally disappear. It enhanced the power of interest groups who claimed to speak for millions, but sometimes represented only a small minority.[30] It did not evolve a way to protect people who had no such spokesmen, nor an acceptable method for disciplining the interest groups. In 1946, President Truman would resort to a threat to draft railway workers into the Army to avert a strike. The New Deal achieved a more just society by recognizing groups which had been largely unrepresented — staple farmers, industrial workers, particular ethnic groups, and the new intellectual-administrative class. Yet this was still a halfway revolution; it swelled the ranks of the bourgeoisie but left many Americans — sharecroppers, slum dwellers, most Negroes — outside of the new equilibrium.

Some of these omissions were to be promptly remedied. Subsequent Congresses extended social security, authorized slum clearance projects, and raised minimum-wage standards to keep step with the rising price level. Other shortcomings are understandable. The havoc that had been done before Roosevelt took office was so great that even the unprecedented measures of the New Deal did not suffice to repair the damage. Moreover, much was still to be learned, and it was in the Roosevelt years that the country was schooled in how to avert another major depression. Although it was war which freed the government from the taboos of a balanced budget and revealed the potentialities of spending, it is conceivable that New Deal measures would have led the country into a new cycle of prosperity even if there had been no war. Marked gains had been made before the war spending had any appreciable effect. When recovery did come, it was much more soundly based because of the adoption of the New Deal program.

Roosevelt and the New Dealers understood, perhaps better than their critics, that they had come only part of the way. Henry Wallace remarked: "We are children of the transition — we have left Egypt but we have not yet arrived at the Promised Land." Only five years separated Roosevelt's inauguration in 1933 and the adoption of the last of the New Deal measures, the Fair Labor Standards Act, in 1938. The New Dealers perceived that they had done more in those years than had been done in any comparable period in American history, but they also saw that there was much still to be done, much, too, that continued to baffle them. "I believe in the things that have been done," Mrs. Roosevelt told the American Youth Congress in February, 1939. "They helped but they did not solve the fundamental problems. . . . I never believed the Federal government could solve the whole problem. It bought us time to think." She closed not with a solution but with a challenge: "Is it going to be worth while?" [31]

"This generation of Americans is living in a tremendous moment of history," President Roosevelt stated in his final national address of the 1940 campaign.

"The surge of events abroad has made some few doubters among us ask: Is this the end of a story that has been told? Is the book of democracy now to be closed and placed away upon the dusty shelves of time?

"My answer is this: All we have known of the glories of democracy — its freedom, its efficiency as a mode of living, its ability to meet the aspirations of the common man — all these are merely an introduction to the greater story of a more glorious future.

"We Americans of today — all of us — we are characters in the living book of democracy.

"But we are also its author. It falls upon us now to say whether the chapters that are to come will tell a story of retreat or a story of continued advance." [32]

THE CONSERVATIVE
NEW DEAL

New Deal Thought

HOWARD ZINN

Howard Zinn, who teaches at Boston University and is the author of a biography of Fiorello LaGuardia, published in 1966 an essay that was to be one of the most widely read revisionist writings on the New Deal. It deserves a large audience; the essay is literate, incisive, stimulating. Zinn candidly professes to study the past only to make it "speak wisely to present needs," to "affect the world around us." No one can doubt that the past may be made to do so after reading Zinn's critique of New Deal thought. By juxtaposing the ideas of New Deal mainstream liberals, especially Roosevelt, against the bolder thought of some radical intellectuals of the 1930s, Zinn clearly shows how limited was the liberals' thinking. Since he says nothing to mitigate the liberals, the essay diminishes our respect for them. The intended effect, though, was probably to diminish our respect for Lyndon Johnson, Hubert Humphrey, and the liberals of the "present," which is Zinn's real interest.

In forcing the past to speak to present needs, one risks distorting the past to elicit the answers one wants. The present requires that liberalism be discredited. The past may assist us. We lift from its data bank the ideas of its most advanced thinkers and display them against the more drab, blunt notions of its politicians. An interesting study in political philosophy, but is it good history? Good written history leaves out no part of the past that is essential to our understanding. Zinn has left out the social and political ideas of average Americans whose influence is decisive — congressmen, clergymen, university presidents, bankers,

*industrialists. At once, were these elements added, the thought
of the New Dealers might appear in a different light. But allowing the past's full context to come into view might jeopardize
Zinn's hard-earned achievement so useful for the present — a sharp
condemnation of liberalism. And so the context is omitted, and at
the insignificant price of failing to answer such lingering questions as "I wonder why the New Dealers were so incredibly conservative?" we receive the sharp, clear moral our era requires.
It is the least the past can do for us.*

When we compel the past to speak, we want neither the gibberish
of total recall nor the nostalgia of fond memories; we would like the past to
speak wisely to our present needs. And so we have a good reason for trying
to recapture some of the lost dialogue of the New Deal years — that which
was carried on, with varying degrees of tension, inside and outside the
Roosevelt circle.

The New Dealers themselves were articulate, humane, and on occasion profound. Among them were the "brains trust" [1]* (Adolf A. Berle,
Raymond Moley, Rexford Guy Tugwell), the cabinet members (Henry Wallace, Frances Perkins, Harold Ickes, and others), the administrators of the
alphabetic agencies (Harry Hopkins, David Lilienthal, and others), the Congressional spokesmen (Robert F. Wagner, Hugo Black, and others). And
above them all was Franklin D. Roosevelt himself. They had no clearly defined set of goals, beyond that of extricating the nation from the depression
of 1929–1932. In the course of easing the crisis, however, they found themselves — pushed partly by the cries of alarm on all sides, partly by inner
humanitarian impulses — creating new laws and institutions like the Tennessee Valley Authority, the social security system, farm subsidies, minimum
wage standards, the National Labor Relations Board, and public housing.

These accomplishments were considerable enough to give many
Americans the feeling they were going through a revolution, while they successfully evaded any one of a number of totalitarian abysses into which they
might have fallen. So it is not surprising that the New Deal left a glow of enthusiasm, even adoration, in the nation at large.

Yet, when it was over, the fundamental problem remained — and
still remains — unsolved: how to bring the blessings of immense natural

From *New Deal Thought,* edited by Howard Zinn, copyright © 1966,
by The Bobbs-Merrill Company, Inc., reprinted by permission of the
publisher.
* [See pp. 188–189 for notes to this article. — Ed.]

wealth and staggering productive potential to every person in the land. Also unsolved was the political corollary of that problem; how to organize ordinary people to convey to national leadership something more subtle than the wail of crisis (which speaks for itself); how to communicate the day-to-day pains felt, between emergencies, in garbage-strewn slums, crowded schools, grimy bus stations, inadequate hospital wards, Negro ghettos, and rural shacks — the environment of millions of Americans clawing for subsistence in the richest country in the world.

When the reform energies of the New Deal began to wane around 1939 and the depression was over, the nation was back to its normal state: a permanent army of unemployed; twenty or thirty million poverty-ridden people effectively blocked from public view by a huge, prosperous, and fervently consuming middle class; a tremendously efficient yet wasteful productive apparatus that was efficient because it could produce limitless supplies of what it decided to produce, and wasteful because what it decided to produce was not based on what was most needed by society but on what was most profitable to business.[2]

What the New Deal did was to refurbish middle-class America, which had taken a dizzying fall in the depression, to restore jobs to half the jobless, and to give just enough to the lowest classes (a layer of public housing, a minimum of social security) to create an aura of good will. Through it all, the New Dealers moved in an atmosphere thick with suggestions, but they accepted only enough of these to get the traditional social mechanism moving again, plus just enough more to give a taste of what a truly far-reaching reconstruction might be.

This harsh estimate of New Deal achievements derives from the belief that the historian discussing the past is always commenting — whether he realizes it or not — on the present; and that because he is part of a morally responsible public, his commentary should consider present needs at the expense, if necessary, of old attachments. It is fruitless today to debate "interpretations" of the New Deal. We can no longer vote for or against Roosevelt. We can only affect the world around us. And although this is the 1960's, not the 1930's, some among us live very high, and some live very low, and a chronic malaise of lost opportunities and wasted wealth pervades the economic air.[3]

It is for today, then, that we turn to the thinking of the New Deal period. Although the New Deal gave us only fragments of solutions, it did leave us — perhaps because those were desperate years, and desperation stimulates innovation — with a public discussion more intense and more sweeping than any we have had before or since. People outside the New Deal entourage, invited or not, joined that discussion and extended the boundaries of political and economic imagination beyond those of the New Dealers —

sometimes to the left, sometimes to the right, sometimes in directions hard to plot.

Among these were philosophers, writers, critics, lawyers, poets, college professors, journalists, dissident politicians, or commentators without special portfolio. Their names are still known today: John Dewey, Charles Beard, Reinhold Niebuhr, Paul Douglas, Stuart Chase, John Maynard Keynes, Norman Thomas, Oswald Garrison Villard, Heywood Broun, Max Lerner, Morris Cohen, Walter White, Edmund Wilson, Felix Frankfurter, John Steinbeck, John L. Lewis, Upton Sinclair.

Their thinking does not give us facile solutions, but if history has uses beyond that of reminiscence, one of them is to nourish lean ideological times with the nectars of other years. And although the present shape of the world was hardly discernible in 1939, certain crucial social issues persist in both eras. Somehow, in the interaction between the ideas of the New Dealers themselves and those of social critics who gathered in various stances and at various distances around the Roosevelt fire, we may find suggestions or approaches that are relevant today.

The word "pragmatic" has been used, more often perhaps than any other, to describe the thinking of the New Dealers.[4] It refers to the experimental method of the Roosevelt administration, the improvisation from one step to the next, the lack of system or long-range program or theoretical commitment. Richard Hofstadter, in fact, says that the only important contribution to political theory to come out of the Roosevelt administration was made by Thurman Arnold, particularly in his two books, *The Symbols of Government* and *The Folklore of Capitalism*. Hofstadter described Arnold's writing as "the theoretical equivalent of FDR's opportunistic virtuosity in practical politics — a theory that attacks theories." [5] As the chief expression of Roosevelt's "ideology," Arnold's work deserves some attention.

All through both his books, in a style of cool irony, Arnold cuts away at "preconceived faiths," "preconceived principles," "theories and symbols of government," "high-sounding prejudices," "traditional ideals," "moral ideals," "permanent cures." In the last paragraphs of *The Symbols of Government,* he writes:

> So long as the public hold preconceived faiths about the fundamental principles of government, they will persecute and denounce new ideas in that science, and orators will prevail over technicians. So long as preconceived principles are considered more important than practical results, the practical alleviation of human distress and the distribution of available comforts will be paralyzed. . . . The writer has faith that a new public attitude toward the ideals of law and economics is slowly appearing to create an atmosphere where the fanatical alignments between

opposing political principles may disappear and a competent, practical,
opportunistic governing class may rise to power. . . .[6]

Because the Roosevelt administration did, in fact, experiment and
improve without a total plan, FDR's "pragmatism" has come, for many, to
be the most important statement about the thinking of the New Dealers.
This emphasis on the method rather than on the substance of that thinking
tends to obscure what may be its greatest significance.[7]

Most statesmen experiment: Tsar Nicholas instituted a Duma, Lenin
encouraged private enterprise for several years, Bismarck sponsored social
welfare measures, Mao Tse-tung introduced back-yard steel furnaces, and
George Washington supported a national bank. These examples show that
experimentation can be linked to a variety of social ideals. Some statesmen
engage in more experiments than others, and in a time of crisis one who is
willing to undertake a vast number of them deserves commendation, as
Roosevelt does. The truly important question that can be asked about the
thinking of any government is: in what direction, and how far, is it willing to
experiment? What goals, what ideals, what expectations direct that experimentation?

Thurman Arnold himself contributed to this misplaced emphasis on
method rather than substance. He was so anxious to demolish old myths that
stood in the way of the welfare measures of the New Deal that mythology itself became his chief concern. He was so intent on sweeping away old debris,
that he became obsessed, ironically, with a folklore of his own, in which the
idea of debris-clearing crowded out the concept of what he wanted to plant
in the cleared area.

Examining Arnold's *The Symbols of Government,* one sees that what
started him on a crusade against myths was that he sought to expose the
symbolism that stood in the way of bringing cheap electric power to people
and of instituting relief, public works, social security.[8] His strongest expression on social justice was his statement that: "Those who rule our great
industrial feudalism still believe inalterably the old axioms that man works
efficiently only for personal profit; that humanitarian ideals are unworkable
as the principal aim of government or business organization; that control of
national resources, elimination of waste, and a planned distribution of goods
would destroy both freedom and efficiency." [9]

As was true of his associate, Thurman Arnold, FDR's experimentalism and iconoclasm were not devoid of standards and ideals. They had a certain direction, which was toward governmental intervention in the economy
to prevent depression, to help the poor, and to curb ruthless practices in big
business. Roosevelt's speeches had the flavor of a moral crusade. Accepting
the nomination at the Democratic Convention of 1932, he said that "the

Federal Government has always had and still has a continuing responsibility for the broader public welfare," and pledged "a new deal for the American people." In a campaign speech that year at the Commonwealth Club in San Francisco, he said: "Our government . . . owes to every one an avenue to possess himself of a portion of that plenty sufficient for his needs, through his own work." In his 1936 speech accepting the nomination, he spoke of the power of the "economic royalists" and said: "Our allegiance to American institutions requires the overthrow of this kind of power."

But FDR's ideas did not have enough clarity to avoid stumbling from one approach to another: from constant promises to balance the budget, to large-scale spending in emergencies; from an attempt to reconcile big business interests and labor interests (as in the National Recovery Act), to belated support for a pro-labor National Labor Relations Act; from special concern for the tenant farmer (in the Resettlement Administration), to a stress on generous price supports for the large commercial farmer (in the Agricultural Adjustment Act of 1938).

His ideas on political leadership showed the same indecision, the same constriction of boundaries, as did his ideas about economic reform. Roosevelt was cautious about supporting the kind of candidates in 1934 (Socialist Upton Sinclair in California, Progressive Gifford Pinchot in Pennsylvania) who represented bold approaches to economic and social change; and when he did decide to take vigorous action against conservative Congressional candidates in 1938, he did so too late and too timorously. He often attempted to lead Congress in a forceful way to support his economic program; yet his leadership was confined to working with the existing Congressional leadership, including many Southern conservatives who ruled important committees. Roosevelt's political daring did not extend to building new political forces among the poor, the unemployed, the tenant farmers, and other disadvantaged groups, with whose support he might have given the country a bolder economic program.

The circle of men around Roosevelt, the cabinet members and administrators, was an odd mixture of liberals and conservatives who often worked at cross-purposes, Rexford Guy Tugwell, a bold advocate of national planning to help the lower-income groups, was close to Roosevelt for several years; but so was Raymond Moley, who believed in a kind of planning more beneficial to business interests. Even the liberal New Dealers, with rare exceptions, hesitated to carry their general concern for the underprivileged too far. Frances Perkins, the Secretary of Labor, had the humanitarian instincts of a first-rate social worker, but she seemed often to be trailing behind the labor movement, rather than helping to give it direction. (The most advanced piece of New Deal labor legislation was the Wagner Act, but Secretary Perkins wrote later: "I myself, had very little sympathy with the bill.")

Progressive Secretary of the Interior Harold Ickes was offset by conservative Secretary of Commerce Daniel Roper. And although Roper was succeeded in 1939 by Harry Hopkins, there remained in the cabinet a powerful force for fiscal conservatism and budget-balancing — Secretary of the Treasury Henry Morgenthau.

The experimentalism of the New Deal, in short, had its limits: up to these limits, Roosevelt's social concern was genuinely warm, his political courage huge, his humanitarian spirit unfailing; beyond them, his driving force weakened. Thus, by 1938, with the nation out of the worst of the depression, with a skeletal structure of social reform in the statute books, and with that year's Congressional elections showing a sudden waning of political approbation, the Roosevelt program began to bog down. As it slid to its close, it left behind a mountain of accomplishment, and ahead, mountains still unclimbed. Many millions — businessmen, professionals, unionized workingmen, commercial farmers — had been given substantial help. Many millions more — sharecroppers, slum-dwellers, Negroes of North and South, the unemployed — still awaited a genuine "new deal."

Why did the New Deal sputter out around 1938–1939? One important factor seems to be that the urgency of 1933–1935 was gone. By 1939, although there were still nine million unemployed, the sense of panic was over. After all, unemployment was normal in America. Harry Hopkins had said in 1937 that even in prosperity it was "reasonable to expect a probable minimum of 4,000,000 to 5,000,000 unemployed." [10] The American nation had developed over the years a set of expectations as to what constituted "normal" times; and by 1938 it was approaching these.

Hopkins' statement and the administration's inaction indicate that the ideals of the New Dealers did not extend very far beyond the traditional structure of the American economy. They had wanted to get out of the terrible economic despair of 1932 and 1933 and to establish certain moderate reforms. These aims had been accomplished. True, some of the New Dealers, including FDR himself, did speak of what still remained to be done. But once the nation was restored to close to the old balance — even if income was still distributed with gross inequality, even if rural and urban slums crisscrossed the land, even if most workingmen were still unorganized and underpaid, and a third of the nation still, in FDR's words "ill-nourished, ill-clad, ill-housed" — the driving force of the New Deal was gone.

Why were the expectations and ideals of the New Deal (its folklore, its symbols, according to Thurman Arnold) so limited? Why did the New Dealers not declare that the government would continue spending, experimenting, and expanding governmental enterprises — until no one was unemployed, and all slums were gone from the cities, until no family received

below-subsistence incomes and adequate medical care was available to everyone, until anyone who wanted a college education could get one? True, there
were political obstacles to realizing such objectives, but to state them as *goals*
would itself have constituted the first step toward overcoming those obstacles.
For this might have enabled FDR to do what political scientist James Mac-
Gregor Burns asserts was not done: to build "a solid, organized mass base"
among labor and other underprivileged groups.[11]

Humanitarianism pure and simple can go only so far, and self-
interest must carry it further. Beyond the solicitude felt by the New Dealers
for the distressed, beyond the occasionally bold rhetoric, there was not
enough motive power to create a radically new economic equilibrium; this
would have to be supplied by the groups concerned themselves; by the tenant
farmers, the aged, the unemployed, the lowest-paid workers in the economy.
Those who *did* organize — the larger farm operators, the several million industrial workers who joined the CIO — improved their position significantly.
But as Paul Douglas, then an economics professor at the University of Chicago and now a United States Senator, wrote in 1933:

> Along with the Rooseveltian program must go . . . the organization
> of those who are at present weak and who need to acquire that which
> the world respects, namely, power. . . . Unless these things are done, we
> are likely to find the permanent benefits of Rooseveltian liberalism to be
> as illusory as were those of the Wilsonian era.[12]

Many organized movements sprang up in the 1930's, spurred by
need and encouraged by the new atmosphere of innovation. The Townsend
Movement sought $200 a month pensions for the aged. FatherCharles Cough-
lin's panacea of "Social Justice" was heard by millions of radio listeners.
Huey Long, the Louisiana Senator, excited many others with his "Share the
Wealth" plan. The National Negro Congress, the Farmers Union, and the
American Youth Congress all represented special needs and all hurled their
energies into the boiling political pot in Washington.

But there was no political program around which these disparate
groups could effectively unite. And many of them began to lose their thrust
when their demands were partially met. Even the Congress of Industrial
Organizations, the largest and most successful of those mass movements born
in the depression and stimulated by New Deal legislation, came eventually
to represent a special interest of its own.

The Madisonian argument that political stability would be assured
in a federal republic of many states, because an uprising in one would die
for lack of support, applied also in the economic sphere, where no single
economic interest, fierce as it might be in its own domain, ever developed a

concern wide enough to embrace society at large. Perhaps one reason is that in the United States every little rebellion, every crisis, has been met with enough concessions to keep general resentment below the combustible level, while isolated aggrieved groups fought their way up to the point of complacency.[13]

But if — as Paul Douglas forecasts — the underprivileged are the only ones who can supply the driving force for a sharp change in their condition, then it is probably the intellectuals of society who will furnish the theories, state the ideals, define the expectations. And so it is from those thinkers who clustered, half-friendly, half-reproachful, around the New Deal, their ideological reach less restrained, perhaps, by the holding of power, that our generation may find suggestions.

Almost immediately, with John Dewey, we are brought face to face with the proof that it is not the fact of experimentalism, but the definition of its boundaries, that is of supreme significance. He was one of the fathers of American pragmatism, the theoretician par excellence of the experimental method. In an article of 1918, he expressed the view of pragmatic experimentation that he held to the end of his life in 1952.

> The question is whether society . . . will learn to utilize the intelligence, the insight and foresight which are available, in order to take hold of the problem and to go at it, step by step, on the basis of an intelligent program — a program which is not too rigid, which is not a program in the sense of having every item definitely scheduled in advance, but which represents an outlook on the future of things which most immediately require doing, trusting to the experience which is got in doing them to reveal the next things needed and the next steps to be taken.[14]

Roosevelt and Dewey were both experimentalists and they both operated within a range of ideals; but that range, for John Dewey, involved goals that went well beyond Roosevelt's farthest bounds. Roosevelt wrote to newspaper publisher Roy Howard on September 2, 1935, that his legislation was "remedial," described the New Deal program as involving "modifications in the conditions and rules of economic enterprise" and said that: "This basic program, however, has now reached substantial completion." Undoubtedly he was bending over backward to satisfy an anxious and influential citizen. And his program did go on to embrace a minimum wage law, public housing, and other measures. But that was largely because of the momentum already created for reform and because of pressures among the public. The Roosevelt vision had been stretched almost to its limits.

In Dewey's 1935 lectures at the University of Virginia, he said:

> The only form of enduring social organization that is now possible
> is one in which the new forces of productivity are cooperatively controlled
> and used in the interest of the effective liberty and the cultural develop-
> ment of the individuals that constitute society. Such a social order can-
> not be established by an unplanned and external convergence of the
> actions of separate individuals, each of whom is bent on personal private
> advantage. . . . Organized social planning, put into effect for the creation
> of an order in which industry and finance are socially directed . . . is
> now the sole method of social action by which liberalism can realize its
> professed aims.[15]

Both Roosevelt and Dewey believed in moving step by step. But
FDR wanted to preserve the profit system; Dewey was willing to reshape it
drastically. Because Dewey's aim was larger, his steps were longer ones, taken
two or three at a time, and were less haphazard. "In short," he said, "liberalism must now become radical. . . . For the gulf between what the actual
situation makes possible and the actual state itself is so great that it cannot be
bridged by piecemeal policies undertaken *ad hoc.*" [16] Dewey was very conscious of the dangers of totalitarianism, but he believed that the spirit of free
expression could remain alive, even while liberalism went on to "socialize
the forces of production." [17] Among pragmatists, apparently, crucial distinctions exist.

Part of Roosevelt's "pragmatism" was his rejection of doctrinaire
ideas of the left.[18] Marxism was in the air all around him. Many intellectuals
were enthusiastic about the Five Year Plans of Soviet Russia. British Marxists
were influential: Harold J. Laski lectured and wrote extensively in the
United States; John Strachey popularized the concepts of socialism in *The
Nature of Capitalist Crisis* (1935) and other works. Some in depression-ridden
America were attracted to Marxism's claims that society could be analyzed
"scientifically": that economic crisis was inevitable where production was
complex and gigantic, yet unplanned; that exploitation of working people
was built into a system where private profit was the chief motive; that the
state was not neutral but an instrument of those who held economic power;
that only the working class could be depended on to take over society and
move it towards a classless, strifeless commonwealth. A true pragmatist might
at least have explored some of the suggestions of Marxist thought. Roosevelt's thinking, however, remained in a kind of airtight chamber that allowed him to regulate what currents he would permit inside — and Marxism
was not one of them.

Nevertheless, to steer clear of the theories of the Marxists, as of the

Hooverian folklore of "free enterprise," "thrift," and "laissez-faire," left a vast middle ground of which Roosevelt explored only one sector. Edmund Wilson, for instance, a social critic and essayist, also rejected Marxian dialectics; yet he tried to extract from it some truths. He wrote with apparent warmth of the idea that (as he put it, in an imaginary restatement of a more acceptable Marxism): ". . . if society is to survive at all, it must be reorganized on new principles of equality." [19] Others, not Marxists, but more demanding in their notion of reform than was the New Deal, reconnoitered beyond its ideological fences.

Reinhold Niebuhr, a theologian and social philosopher who carried the Social Gospel to new borders in the 1930's, urged that "private ownership of the productive processes" be abandoned,[20] yet he hoped that through an alliance among farmers, industrial workers, and the lower income classes, the transition to a new order could be accomplished without violence. Stuart Chase, an economist who wrote a series of widely selling books in the 1930's, suggested that old alternatives had been swept aside by the onrush of technology, that the choice was no longer between capitalism and socialism; there was a need, he said, for some uncategorizable collectivist society whose "general objective will be the distribution of the surplus, rather than a wrangling over the ownership of a productive plant which has lost its scarcity position." [21]

William Ernest Hocking, a Harvard philosopher, asked for "collectivism of a sort," but neither the collectivism of a "headless Liberalism" or of a "heady" Communism or Fascism. He wrote: "What the State has to do with production is to drive into economic practice the truth that there is little or no capital whose use is not 'affected by a public interest.' " Hocking said: "Economic processes constitute a single and healthy organism only when the totality of persons in a community who have a right to consume *determine what is produced.* . . ." [22] Hocking was setting goals quite beyond the Rooseveltian ones.

Upton Sinclair, a muckraker since the early part of the century, preached a non-Marxist, home-grown socialism that attracted enough adherents to bring him very close to winning the gubernatorial election in California in 1934.[23] Sinclair prophesied that "in a cooperative society every man, woman, and child would have the equivalent of $5000 a year income from labor of the able-bodied young men for three or four hours per day." [24] This prophesy was certainly utopian in 1933, but such vision, even if it were going to be bent and modified in practice, might carry a program of social reform much further — and perhaps win more powerful blocs of electoral support — than did the more moderate goals of the New Deal.

A program may be pragmatic in its willingness to explore various means, yet be certain of its goals; it may be limited in how far it is willing to go, and yet be clear about the direction of its thrust. There is a difference between experimentation and vacillation. Robert MacIver, a distinguished social scientist, was impressed in 1934 by the variety of new institutions created under Roosevelt, but wondered if they meant "the inauguration of a period of social and cultural reformation." He asked: "The new institutions are here, but the essential point is — Who shall control them?" [25] There was uncertainty about the New Deal, particularly in its first two years, when the National Recovery Act set out to create large planning organizations for industry in which big business seemed to be making the important decisions. It led some liberals and radicals to see in it possible Fascist aims,[26] led some important businessmen to support it,[27] and kept political loyalties crisscrossed in a happy chaos.

After 1935 (although ambiguity remained in specific areas like trustbusting), the over-all direction of the New Deal became clear: it was sympathetic to the underprivileged, and to organized labor, and it was pervaded by a general spirit of liberal, humanitarian reform. But also the scope of the New Deal became clear. This limitation is shown in a number of issues that the New Deal faced, or sometimes tried to avoid facing, between 1933 and 1939: the problem of planning; the question of how to deal with monopolistic business; the controversy over deficit financing and the extension of public enterprise; the creation of an adequate system of social security.

When Roosevelt told students at Oglethorpe University during his 1932 campaign that he was in favor of "a larger measure of social planning," it was not clear how large this measure was. Was he willing to go as far as his own advisor, Columbia professor Rexford Guy Tugwell? Tugwell attacked the profit motive, said that "planning for production means planning for consumption too," declared that "profits must be limited and their uses controlled," and said he meant by planning "something not unlike an integrated group of enterprises run for its consumers rather than for its owners." The statement, he said, that "business will logically be required to disappear" is "literally meant" because: "Planning implies guidance of capital uses. . . . Planning also implies adjustment of production to consumption; and there is no way of accomplishing this except through a control of prices and of profit margins." To limit business in all these ways, he said, meant in effect "to destroy it as business and to make of it something else." [28]

Raymond Moley, who played a direct role in shaping Roosevelt's early legislation, also deplored the lack of planning in the New Deal. But Moley was interested in planning for quite different groups. Tugwell was concerned with the lower classes' lack of purchasing power. Moley, although he too was moved by a measure of genuine concern for deprived people, was most worried about "the narrow margin of profit" and "business confidence." [29] In the end, Roosevelt rejected both ideas. Whatever planning he would do would try to help the lower classes, for example, the Tennessee Valley Authority. On the other hand, the planning would not be national; nor would it interfere with the fundamental character of the American economy, based as it was on corporate profit; nor would it attempt any fundamental redistribution of wealth in the nation. And the TVA embodied these too because it represented *piecemeal* planning.

David Lilienthal's defense of this method, in his book on the TVA, comes closest to the New Deal approach. "We move step by step — from where we are," wrote Lilienthal.[30] Not only was any notion of national economic planning never seriously considered, but after the TVA, the moving "step by step" did not carry very far. Housing developments and several planned communities were inspiring, but came nowhere near matching the enormity of the national need.

Ambiguity persisted longest in the policy towards monopoly and oligopoly. The NRA was a frank recognition of the usefulness — or at least, the inevitability — of large enterprise, when ordered by codes. The Securities Exchange Commission and the Public Utilities Holding Company Act moved back (but weakly, as William O. Douglas recognized at the time) [31] to the Brandeis idea of trying to curb the size and strength of large enterprises. Roosevelt's basic policy towards giantism in business, although he vigorously attacked "economic royalists" in 1936, remained undetermined until 1938, when he asked Congress for a sweeping investigation of monopoly. And although he was clearly returning to the idea of restraining the power of big business, one sentence in his message to Congress reveals his continuing uncertainty: "The power of the few to manage the economic life of the Nation must be diffused among the many or be transferred to the public and its democratically responsible government."

The first alternative was an obviously romantic notion; the second was really much farther than either Congress or FDR was prepared to go. Hence, the Temporary National Economic Committee, after hearing enough testimony to fill thirty-one volumes and forty-three monographs, was unwilling, as William Leuchtenburg writes, "to tackle the more difficult problems or to make recommendations which might disturb vested interests." [32] Roosevelt had come close to expressing, but he still did not possess, nor did he communicate to the nation, a clear, resolute goal of transferring giant and irresponsible economic power "to the public and its democratically responsible government." The restraints on the New Dealers' thinking is shown best perhaps by Adolf A. Berle, who said that prosperity depended on either a gigantic expansion of private activity or nationalization of key industries. Yet, knowing private industry was not going to fill the need, he did not advocate nationalization — nor did any other New Dealer.

Roosevelt was experimental, shifting, and opportunistic in his espousal of public enterprise and the spending that had to accompany such governmental activity. As James MacGregor Burns says: "Roosevelt had tried rigid economy, then heavy spending, then restriction of spending again. He had shifted back and forth from spending on direct relief to spending on public works." [33] The significant measure, however, was not the swings of the pendulum, but the width of the arcs. When FDR went all-out for spending, it was still only a fraction of what the British economist John Maynard Keynes was urging as a way of bringing recovery. An American Keynesian, Professor Alvin Hansen, was arguing that the economy was "mature" and therefore required much more continuous and powerful injections of governmental spending than was being given.[34]

Roosevelt himself had introduced into public discussion the idea of a "yardstick," which the Tennessee Valley Authority represented — a public enterprise that would, by competing with private producers, force them to bend more towards the needs of the consumer. (Later FDR tried, unsuccessfully, to get Congress to introduce "seven little TVA's" in other river valleys.) But the vast implications of the concept were left unexplored. When political scientist Max Lerner called for government-owned radio stations and government-subsidized newspapers to break into the growing monopolization of public opinion by giant chains, there was no response.[35] TVA, a brief golden period of federal theater, a thin spread of public housing, and a public works program called into play only at times of desperation, represented the New Deal's ideological and emotional limits in the creation of public enterprise.

It is one thing to experiment to discover the best means of achieving a certain objective; it is quite another thing to fail to recognize that objective. The Social Security System, as set up, was not an experiment to find the best type of system. Roosevelt knew from the beginning that it was not the most effective way to handle the problems of poverty for the aged, the unemployed, and the helpless. Behind the basic political problem of getting the bill passed lay fundamental narrowness of vision. Social security expert Abraham Epstein pointed this out at the time,[36] and it was noted on the floor of Congress.[37] Henry E. Sigerist, a physician and student of welfare medicine in other countries, wrote patiently and clearly about the need for socialized medicine, answered the arguments against it, and explained how it might operate.[38]

Thus, if the concept of New Deal thought is widened to include a large circle of thinkers — some close to the administration itself, others at varying distance from it — we get not panaceas or infallible schemes but larger commitments, bolder goals, and greater expectations of what "equality" and "justice" and "security" meant.

For our view of the New Deal as a particularly energetic gyroscopic motion putting the traditional structure aright again, we have what the natural scientists might call a set of "controls" — a way of checking up on the hypothesis — one in the area of race relations, another in the experience of war.

In the field of racial equality, where there was no crisis as in economics, where the gyroscope did not confront a sharply titled mechanism, there was no "new deal." The special encumbrances of the depression were lifted for Negroes as for many other Americans, but the *permanent* caste structure remained unaltered by the kind of innovations that at least threatened the traditional edifice in economics. The white South was left, as it had been since the Compromise of 1877, to deal with Negroes as it chose — by murder, by beatings, by ruthless exclusion from political and economic life; the Fourteenth Amendment waited as fruitlessly for executive enforcement as it had in all earlier administrations since Grant. Washington, D.C., itself remained a tightly segregated city. And the Harlems of the North continued as great symbols of national failure.

The warm belief in equal rights held by Eleanor Roosevelt, as well as by FDR himself, the appointments of Mary McLeod Bethune, Robert Weaver, and others to important secondary posts in the government, even the wide distribution of relief and WPA jobs, were not enough to alter the fundamental injustice attached to being a Negro in the United States. The disposition of the New Deal to experiment could have led to important accomplishments, but the clear goal of ending segregation, as with comparable objectives in economics, was never established.

With the coming of World War II, economic and social experimentation blossomed under Roosevelt's leadership and involved a good measure of national planning, jobs for everyone, and a vast system of postwar educational benefits to eighteen million veterans. There was little inhibition; new, radically different national goals were not required for the traditional objective of winning at war. With such an aim, policy could be fearless and far-reaching.

Some coming generation perhaps, while paying proper respects to the spirit of the New Deal, may find, as William James put it, "the moral equivalent of war" — in new social goals, new expectations, with imaginative, undoctrinaire experimentation to attain them. If, in such an adventure, the thought of the past can help, it should be put to work.

The Conservative Achievements
of Liberal Reform

BARTON J. BERNSTEIN

Barton J. Bernstein, who teaches at Stanford University, is another young historian who describes the New Deal as a conservative political movement, at least in its outcome, and a great disappointment to the advocates of substantial social reform. Bernstein, who writes primarily on the Truman period, has written what is certainly the best documented essay on the New Deal by any radical, New Left historian. Other recent critical efforts from the radical left are less substantial or less compact than the essays of Zinn and Bernstein.

Radical criticism of the New Deal, it should be noted, is not new. Intellectuals in the 1930s, men such as John Dewey, Mauritz Hallgren, George Soule, and Stuart Chase, thought the New Deal had substantially failed. Even Eleanor Roosevelt, summing up in 1940, thought the most the New Dealers had accomplished was to "buy ourselves time to think," and Rexford G. Tugwell agreed with her. The sense of defeat was strong at the end of the 1930s; it was not invented in the 1960s.

But Bernstein is not simply reviving an old argument. The structure and emphasis of the criticism are his own, and he writes after completing extensive research in original sources and recent monographs. As I argue in the Conclusion to this book, he and Zinn are very persuasive in part of their argument, and become more so with every run of the university presses. Roosevelt was personally conservative, and the New Deal, too, was truly conservative in its outcome. The New Deal either backed away from or, more often, never seriously contemplated basically reforming the American political mechanism, the profit system, the biracial order. The final essay in this book raises numerous questions about interpretations of the New Deal that place such stress on the unassailable truth that the New Deal was not socialism.

Writing from a liberal democratic consensus, many American historians in the past two decades have praised the Roosevelt administration for its nonideological flexibility and for its far-ranging reforms. To many historians, particularly those who reached intellectual maturity during the depression,[1]* the government's accomplishments, as well as the drama and passion, marked the decade as a watershed, as a dividing line in the American past.

Enamored of Franklin D. Roosevelt and recalling the bitter opposition to welfare measures and restraints upon business, many liberal historians have emphasized the New Deal's discontinuity with the immediate past. For them there was a "Roosevelt Revolution," or at the very least a dramatic achievement of a beneficent liberalism which had developed in fits and spurts during the preceding three decades.[2] Rejecting earlier interpretations which viewed the New Deal as socialism [3] or state capitalism,[4] they have also disregarded theories of syndicalism [5] or of corporate liberalism.[6] The New Deal has generally commanded their approval for such laws or institutions as minimum wages, public housing, farm assistance, the Tennessee Valley Authority, the Wagner Act, more progressive taxation, and social security. For most liberal historians the New Deal meant the replenishment of democracy, the rescuing of the federal government from the clutches of big business, the significant redistribution of political power. Breaking with laissez faire, the new administration, according to these interpretations, marked the end of the passive or impartial state and the beginning of positive government, of the interventionist state acting to offset concentrations of private power, and affirming the rights and responding to the needs of the unprivileged.

From the perspective of the late 1960s these themes no longer seem adequate to characterize the New Deal. The liberal reforms of the New Deal did not transform the American system; they conserved and protected American corporate capitalism, occasionally by absorbing parts of threatening programs. There was no significant redistribution of power in American society, only limited recognition of other organized groups, seldom of unorganized people. Neither the bolder programs advanced by New Dealers nor the final legislation greatly extended the beneficence of government beyond the middle classes or drew upon the wealth of the few for the needs of the many. Designed to maintain the American system, liberal activity was directed toward essentially conservative goals. Experimentalism was most frequently limited to means; seldom did it extend to ends. Never questioning private enterprise, it operated within safe channels, far short of Marxism or even of native

From *Towards a New Past*, edited by Barton J. Bernstein. Copyright ©
1967, 1968 by Random House, Inc. Reprinted by permission of Pantheon Books, a Division of Random House, Inc.
* [See pp. 189–193 for notes to this article. — Ed.]

American radicalisms that offered structural critiques and structural solutions.

All of this is not to deny the changes wrought by the New Deal — the extension of welfare programs, the growth of federal power, the strengthening of the executive, even the narrowing of property rights. But it is to assert that the elements of continuity are stronger, that the magnitude of change has been exaggerated. The New Deal failed to solve the problem of depression, it failed to raise the impoverished, it failed to redistribute income, it failed to extend equality and generally countenanced racial discrimination and segregation. It failed generally to make business more responsible to the social welfare or to threaten business's pre-eminent political power. In this sense, the New Deal, despite the shifts in tone and spirit from the earlier decade, was profoundly conservative and continuous with the 1920s.

Rather than understanding the 1920s as a "return to normalcy," the period is more properly interpreted by focusing on the continuation of progressive impulses, demands often frustrated by the rivalry of interest groups, sometimes blocked by the resistance of Harding and Coolidge, and occasionally by Hoover.[7] Through these years while agriculture and labor struggled to secure advantages from the federal government, big business flourished. Praised for creating American prosperity, business leaders easily convinced the nation that they were socially responsible, that they were fulfilling the needs of the public.[8] Benefitting from earlier legislation that had promoted economic rationalization and stability, they were opponents of federal benefits to other groups but seldom proponents of laissez faire.[9]

In no way did the election of Herbert Hoover in 1928 seem to challenge the New Era. An heir of Wilson, Hoover promised an even closer relationship with big business and moved beyond Harding and Coolidge by affirming federal responsibility for prosperity. As Secretary of Commerce, Hoover had opposed unbridled competition and had transformed his department into a vigorous friend of business. Sponsoring trade associations, he promoted industrial self-regulation and the increased rationalization of business. He had also expanded foreign trade, endorsed the regulation of new forms of communications, encouraged relief in disasters, and recommended public works to offset economic decline.[10]

By training and experience, few men in American political life seemed better prepared than Hoover to cope with the depression. Responding promptly to the crisis, he acted to stabilize the economy and secured the agreement of businessmen to maintain production and wage rates. Unwilling to let the economy "go through the wringer," the President requested easier money, self-liquidating public works, lower personal and corporate income taxes, and stronger commodity stabilization corporations.[11] In reviewing these unprecedented actions, Walter Lippmann wrote, "The national government undertook to make the whole economic order operate prosperously." [12]

But these efforts proved inadequate. The tax cut benefitted the wealthy and failed to raise effective demand. The public works were insufficient. The commodity stabilization corporations soon ran out of funds, and agricultural prices kept plummeting. Businessmen cut back production, dismissed employees, and finally cut wages. As unemployment grew, Hoover struggled to inspire confidence, but his words seemed hollow and his understanding of the depression limited. Blaming the collapse on European failures, he could not admit that American capitalism had failed. When prodded by Congress to increase public works, to provide direct relief, and to further unbalance the budget, he doggedly resisted. Additional deficits would destroy business confidence, he feared, and relief would erode the principles of individual and local responsibility.[13] Clinging to faith in voluntarism, Hoover also briefly rebuffed the efforts by financiers to secure the Reconstruction Finance Corporation (RFC). Finally endorsing the RFC,[14] he also supported expanded lending by Federal Land Banks, recommended home-loan banks, and even approved small federal loans (usually inadequate) to states needing funds for relief. In this burst of activity, the President had moved to the very limits of his ideology.

Restricted by his progressive background and insensitive to politics and public opinion, he stopped far short of the state corporatism urged by some businessmen and politicians. With capitalism crumbling he had acted vigorously to save it, but he would not yield to the representatives of business or disadvantaged groups who wished to alter the government.[15] He was reluctant to use the federal power to achieve through compulsion what could not be realized through voluntary means. Proclaiming a false independence, he did not understand that his government already represented business interests; hence, he rejected policies that would openly place the power of the state in the hands of business or that would permit the formation of a syndicalist state in which power might be exercised (in the words of William Appleman Williams) "by a relatively few leaders of each functional bloc formed and operating as an oligarchy." [16]

Even though constitutional scruples restricted his efforts, Hoover did more than any previous American president to combat depression. He "abandoned the principles of laissez faire in relation to the business cycle, established the conviction that prosperity and depression can be publicly controlled by political action, and drove out of the public consciousness the old idea that depressions must be overcome by private adjustment," wrote Walter Lippmann.[17] Rather than the last of the old presidents, Herbert Hoover was the first of the new.

A charismatic leader and a brilliant politician, his successor expanded federal activities on the basis of Hoover's efforts. Using the federal government to stabilize the economy and advance the interests of the groups, Franklin D. Roosevelt directed the campaign to save large-scale corporate capitalism. Though recognizing new political interests and extending benefits to them, his New Deal never effectively challenged big business or the organization of the economy. In providing assistance to the needy and by rescuing them from starvation, Roosevelt's humane efforts also protected the established system: he sapped organized radicalism of its waning strength and of its potential constituency among the unorganized and discontented. Sensitive to public opinion and fearful of radicalism, Roosevelt acted from a mixture of motives that rendered his liberalism cautious and limited, his experimentalism narrow. Despite the flurry of activity, his government was more vigorous and flexible about means than goals, and the goals were more conservative than historians usually acknowledge.[18]

Roosevelt's response to the banking crisis emphasizes the conservatism of his administration and its self-conscious avoidance of more radical means that might have transformed American capitalism. Entering the White House when banks were failing and Americans had lost faith in the financial system, the President could have nationalized it — "without a word of protest," judged Senator Bronson Cutting.[19] "If ever there was a moment when things hung in the balance," later wrote Raymond Moley, a member of the original "brain trust," "it was on March 5, 1933 — when unorthodoxy would have drained the last remaining strength of the capitalistic system." [20] To save the system, Roosevelt relied upon collaboration between bankers and Hoover's Treasury officials to prepare legislation extending federal assistance to banking. So great was the demand for action that House members, voting even without copies, passed it unanimously, and the Senate, despite objections by a few Progressives, approved it the same evening. "The President," remarked a cynical congressman, "drove the money-changers out of the Capitol on March 4th — and they were all back on the 9th." [21]

Undoubtedly the most dramatic example of Roosevelt's early conservative approach to recovery was the National Recovery Administration (NRA). It was based on the War Industries Board (WIB) which had provided the model for the campaign of Bernard Baruch, General Hugh Johnson, and other former WIB officials during the twenties to limit competition through industrial self-regulation under federal sanction. As trade associations flourished during the decade, the FTC encouraged "codes of fair competition" and some industries even tried to set prices and restrict production. Operating without the force of law, these agreements broke down. When the depression struck, industrial pleas for regulation increased.[22] After the Great Crash, important business leaders including Henry I. Harriman of the Chamber of Commerce and Gerard Swope of General Electric called for suspension of antitrust laws and federal organization of business collaboration.[23] Joining them were labor leaders, particularly those in "sick" industries — John L. Lewis of the United Mine Workers and Sidney Hillman of Amalgamated Clothing Workers.[24]

Designed largely for industrial recovery, the NRA legislation provided for minimum wages and maximum hours. It also made concessions to pro-labor congressmen and labor leaders who demanded some specific benefits for unions — recognition of the worker's right to organization and to collective bargaining. In practice, though, the much-heralded Section 7a was a disappointment to most friends of labor.[25] (For the shrewd Lewis, however, it became a mandate to organize: "The President wants you to join a union.") To many frustrated workers and their disgusted leaders, NRA became "National Run Around." The clause, unionists found (in the words of Brookings economists), "had the practical effect of placing NRA on the side of anti-union employers in their struggle against trade unions. . . . [It] thus threw its weight against labor in the balance of bargaining power."[26] And while some far-sighted industrialists feared radicalism and hoped to forestall it by incorporating unions into the economic system, most preferred to leave their workers unorganized or in company unions. To many businessmen, large and independent unions as such seemed a radical threat to the system of business control.[27]

Not only did the NRA provide fewer advantages than unionists had anticipated, but it also failed as a recovery measure. It probably even retarded recovery by supporting restrictionism and price increases, concluded a Brookings study.[28] Placing effective power for code-writing in big business, NRA injured small businesses and contributed to the concentration of American industry. It was not the government-business partnership as envisaged by Adolf A. Berle, Jr., nor government managed as Rexford Tugwell had hoped, but rather, business managed, as Raymond Moley had desired.[29] Calling NRA "industrial self-government," its director, General Hugh Johnson, had explained that "NRA is exactly what industry organized in trade associations makes it." Despite the annoyance of some big businessmen with Section 7a, the NRA reaffirmed and consolidated their power at a time when the public was critical of industrialists and financiers.

Viewing the economy as a "concert of organized interests,"[30] the New Deal also provided benefits for farmers — the Agricultural Adjustment Act. Reflecting the political power of larger commercial farmers and accepting restrictionist economics, the measure assumed that the agricultural problem was overproduction, not underconsumption. Financed by a processing tax designed to raise prices to parity, payments encouraged restricted production and cutbacks in farm labor. With benefits accruing chiefly to the larger owners, they frequently removed from production the lands of sharecroppers and tenant farmers, and "tractored" them and hired hands off the land. In assisting agriculture, the AAA, like the NRA, sacrificed the interests of the marginal and the unrecognized to the welfare of those with greater political and economic power.[31]

In large measure, the early New Deal of the NRA and AAA was a "broker state." Though the government served as a mediator of interests and sometimes imposed its will in divisive situations, it was generally the servant of powerful groups. "Like the mercantilists, the New Dealers protected vested interests with the authority of the state," acknowledges William Leuchtenburg. But it was some improvement over the 1920s when business was the only interest capable of imposing its will on the government.[32] While extending to other groups the benefits of the state, the New Deal, however, continued to recognize the pre-eminence of business interests.

The politics of the broker state also heralded the way of the future — of continued corporate dominance in a political structure where other groups agreed generally on corporate capitalism and squabbled only about the size of the shares. Delighted by this increased participation and the absorption of dissident groups, many liberals did not understand the dangers in the emerging organization of politics. They had too much faith in representative institutions and in associations to foresee the perils — of leaders not representing their constituents, of bureaucracy diffusing responsibility, of officials serving their own interests. Failing to perceive the dangers in the emerging structure, most liberals agreed with Senator Robert Wagner of New York: "In order that the strong may not take advantage of the weak, every group must be equally strong." [33] His advice then seemed appropriate for organizing labor, but it neglected the problems of unreprsentative leadership and of the many millions to be left beyond organization.[34]

In dealing with the organized interests, the President acted frequently as a broker, but his government did not simply express the vectors of external forces.[35] The New Deal state was too complex, too loose, and some of Roosevelt's subordinates were following their own inclinations and pushing the government in directions of their own design.[36] The President would also depart from his role as a broker and act to secure programs he desired. As a skilled politician, he could split coalitions, divert the interests of groups, or place the prestige of his office on the side of desired legislation.

In seeking to protect the stock market, for example, Roosevelt endorsed the Securities and Exchange measure (of 1934), despite the opposition of many in the New York financial community. His advisers split the opposition. Rallying to support the administration were the out-of-town exchanges,

representatives of the large commission houses, including James Forrestal of
Dillon, Read, and Robert Lovett of Brown Brothers, Harriman, and such
commission brokers as E. A. Pierce and Paul Shields. Opposed to the Wall
Street "old guard" and their companies, this group included those who
wished to avoid more radical legislation, as well as others who had wanted
earlier to place trading practices under federal legislation which they could
influence.[37]

Though the law restored confidence in the securities market and
protected capitalism, it alarmed some businessmen and contributed to the
false belief that the New Deal was threatening business. But it was not the disaffection of a portion of the business community, nor the creation of the
Liberty League, that menaced the broker state.[38] Rather it was the threat of
the Left — expressed, for example, in such overwrought statements as Minnesota Governor Floyd Olson's: "I am not a liberal . . . I am a radical. . . .
I am not satisfied with hanging a laurel wreath on burglars and thieves . . .
and calling them code authorities or something else." [39] While Olson, along
with some others who succumbed to the rhetoric of militancy, would back
down and soften their meaning, their words dramatized real grievances: the
failure of the early New Deal to end misery, to re-create prosperity. The New
Deal excluded too many. Its programs were inadequate. While Roosevelt
reluctantly endorsed relief and went beyond Hoover in support of public
works, he too preferred self-liquidating projects, desired a balance budget,
and resisted spending the huge sums required to lift the nation out of depression.

For millions suffering in a nation wracked by poverty, the promises
of the Left seemed attractive. Capitalizing on the misery, Huey Long offered
Americans a "Share Our Wealth" program — a welfare state with prosperity,
not subsistence, for the disadvantaged, those neglected by most politicians.
"Every Man a King": pensions for the elderly, college for the deserving,
homes and cars for families — that was the promise of American life. Also
proposing minimum wages, increased public works, shorter work weeks, and
a generous farm program, he demanded a "soak-the-rich" tax program. Despite the economic defects of his plan, Long was no hayseed, and his forays
into the East revealed support far beyond the bayous and hamlets of his native South.[40] In California discontent was so great that Upton Sinclair, food
faddist and former socialist, captured the Democratic nomination for governor on a platform of "production-for-use" — factories and farms for the
unemployed. "In a cooperative society," promised Sinclair, "every man,
woman, and child would have the equivalent of $5,000 a year income from
labor of the able-bodied young men for three or four hours per day." [41] More

challenging to Roosevelt was Francis Townsend's plan — monthly payments
of $200 to those past sixty who retired and promised to spend the stipend
within thirty days.[42] Another enemy of the New Deal was Father Coughlin,
the popular radio priest, who had broken with Roosevelt and formed a
National Union for Social Justice to lead the way to a corporate society beyond capitalism.

To a troubled nation offered "redemption" by the Left, there was
also painful evidence that the social fabric was tearing — law was breaking
down. When the truckers in Minneapolis struck, the police provoked an in-
cident and shot sixty-seven people, some in the back. Covering the tragedy,
Eric Sevareid, then a young reporter, wrote, "I understood deep in my bones
and blood what fascism was." [43] In San Francisco union leaders embittered
by police brutality led a general strike and aroused national fears of class
warfare. Elsewhere, in textile mills from Rhode Island to Georgia, in cities
like Des Moines and Toledo, New York and Philadelphia, there were brutality and violence, sometimes bayonets and tear gas.[44]

Challenged by the Left, and with the new Congress more liberal and
more willing to spend, Roosevelt turned to disarm the discontent. "Boys —
this is our hour," confided Harry Hopkins. "We've got to get everything we
want — a works program, social security, wages and hours, everything — now
or never. Get your minds to work on developing a complete ticket to provide
security for all the folks of this country up and down and across the board." [45]
Hopkins and the associates he addressed were not radicals: they did not seek
to transform the system, only to make it more humane. They, too, wished to
preserve large-scale corporate capitalism, but unlike Roosevelt or Moley,
they were prepared for more vigorous action. Their commitment to reform
was greater, their tolerance for injustice far less. Joining them in pushing the
New Deal left were the leaders of industrial unions, who, while also not wish-
ing to transform the system, sought for workingmen higher wages, better
conditions, stronger and larger unions, and for themselves a place closer to
the fulcrum of power.

The problems of organized labor, however, neither aroused Roosevelt's humanitarianism nor suggested possibilities of reshaping the political
coalition. When asked during the NRA about employee representation, he
had replied that workers could select anyone they wished — the Ahkoond of
Swat, a union, even the Royal Geographical Society.[46] As a paternalist, viewing himself (in the words of James MacGregor Burns) as a "partisan and
benefactor" of workers, he would not understand the objections to company
unions or to multiple unionism under NRA. Nor did he foresee the political
dividends that support of independent unions could yield to his party.[47]
Though presiding over the reshaping of politics (which would extend the

channels of power to some of the discontented and redirect their efforts to
competition within a limited framework), he was not its architect, and he
was unable clearly to see or understand the unfolding design.

When Senator Wagner submitted his labor relations bill, he received
no assistance from the President and even struggled to prevent Roosevelt from
joining the opposition. The President "never lifted a finger," recalls Miss
Perkins. ("I, myself, had very little sympathy with the bill," she wrote.[48]) But
after the measure easily passed the Senate and seemed likely to win the
House's endorsement, Roosevelt reversed himself. Three days before the Supreme Court invalidated the NRA, including the legal support for unionization, Roosevelt came out for the bill. Placing it on his "must" list, he may
have hoped to influence the final provisions and turn an administration defeat into victory.[49]

Responding to the threat from the left, Roosevelt also moved during
the Second Hundred Days to secure laws regulating banking, raising taxes,
dissolving utility-holding companies, and creating social security. Building
on the efforts of states during the Progressive Era, the Social Security Act
marked the movement toward the welfare state, but the core of the measure,
the old-age provision, was more important as a landmark than for its substance. While establishing a federal-state system of unemployment compensation, the government, by making workers contribute to their old age
insurance, denied its financial responsibility for the elderly. The act excluded
more than a fifth of the labor force leaving, among others, more than five
million farm laborers and domestics without coverage.[50]

Though Roosevelt criticized the tax laws for not preventing "an un-
just concentration of wealth and economic power," [51] his own tax measure
would not have significantly redistributed wealth. Yet his message provoked
an "amen" from Huey Long and protests from businessmen.[52] Retreating
from his promises, Roosevelt failed to support the bill, and it succumbed to
conservative forces. They removed the inheritance tax and greatly reduced
the proposed corporate and individual levies. The final law did not "soak the
rich." [53] But it did engender deep resentment among the wealthy for increasing taxes on gifts and estates, imposing an excess-profits tax (which Roosevelt
had not requested), and raising surtaxes. When combined with such regressive levies as social security and local taxes, however, the Wealth Tax of 1935
did not drain wealth from higher-income groups, and the top one per cent
even increased their shares during the New Deal years.[54]

Those historians who have characterized the events of 1935 as the
beginning of a second New Deal have imposed a pattern on those years which
most participants did not then discern.[55] In moving to social security, guarantees of collective bargaining, utility regulation, and progressive taxation,

the government did advance the nation toward greater liberalism, but the shift was exaggerated and most of the measures accomplished far less than either friends or foes suggested. Certainly, despite a mild bill authorizing destruction of utilities-holding companies, there was no effort to atomize business, no real threat to concentration.

Nor were so many powerful businessmen disaffected by the New Deal. Though the smaller businessmen who filled the ranks of the Chamber of Commerce resented the federal bureaucracy and the benefits to labor and thus criticized NRA,[56] representatives of big business found the agency useful and opposed a return to unrestricted competition. In 1935, members of the Business Advisory Council — including Henry Harriman, outgoing president of the Chamber, Thomas Watson of International Business Machines, Walter Gifford of American Telephone and Telegraph, Gerard Swope of General Electric, Winthrop Aldrich of the Chase National Bank, and W. Averell Harriman of Union Pacific — vigorously endorsed a two-year renewal of NRA.[57]

When the Supreme Court in 1935 declared the "hot" oil clause and then NRA unconstitutional, the administration moved to measures known as the "little NRA." Reestablishing regulations in bituminous coal and oil, the New Deal also checked wholesale price discrimination and legalized "fair trade" practices. Though Roosevelt never acted to revive the NRA, he periodically contemplated its restoration. In the so-called second New Deal, as in the "first," government remained largely the benefactor of big business, and some more advanced businessmen realized this.[58]

Roosevelt could attack the "economic royalists" and endorse the TNEC investigation of economic concentration, but he was unprepared to resist the basic demands of big business. While there was ambiguity in his treatment of oligopoly, it was more the confusion of means than of ends, for his tactics were never likely to impair concentration. Even the antitrust program under Thurman Arnold, concludes Frank Freidel, was "intended less to bust the trusts than to forestall too drastic legislation." Operating through consent degrees and designed to reduce prices to the consumer, the program frequently "allowed industries to function much as they had in NRA days." In effect, then, throughout its variations, the New Deal had sought to cooperate with business.[59]

Though vigorous in rhetoric and experimental in tone, the New Deal was narrow in its goals and wary of bold economic reform. Roosevelt's sense of what was politically desirable was frequently more restricted than others' views of what was possible and necessary. Roosevelt's limits were those of ideology; they were not inherent in experimentalism. For while the President explored the narrow center, and some New Dealers considered bolder possibilities, John Dewey, the philosopher of experimentalism, moved far beyond the New Deal and sought to reshape the system. Liberalism, he warned, "must now become radical. . . . For the gulf between what the actual situation makes possible and the actual state itself is so great that it cannot be bridged by piecemeal policies undertaken *ad hoc*." [60] The boundaries of New Deal experimentalism, as Howard Zinn has emphasized, could extend far beyond Roosevelt's cautious ventures. Operating within very safe channels, Roosevelt not only avoided Marxism and the socialization of property, but he also stopped far short of other possibilities — communal direction of production or the organized distribution of surplus. The President and many of his associates were doctrinaires of the center, and their maneuvers in social reform were limited to cautious excursions. [61]

Usually opportunistic and frequently shifting, the New Deal was restricted by its ideology. It ran out of fuel not because of the conservative opposition, [62] but because it ran out of ideas. [63] Acknowledging the end in 1939, Roosevelt proclaimed, "We have now passed the period of internal conflict in the launching of our program of social reform. Our full energies may now be released to invigorate the processes of recovery in order to preserve our reforms. . . ." [64]

The sad truth was that the heralded reforms were severely limited, that inequality continued, that efforts at recovery had failed. Millions had come to accept the depression as a way of life. A decade after the Great Crash, when millions were still unemployed, Fiorello LaGuardia recommended that "we accept the inevitable, that we are now in a new normal." [65] "It was reasonable to expect a probable minimum of 4,000,000 to 5,000,000 unemployed," Harry Hopkins had concluded. [66] Even that level was never reached, for business would not spend and Roosevelt refused to countenance the necessary expenditures. "It was in economics that our troubles lay," Tugwell wrote. "For their solution his [Roosevelt's] progressivism, his new deal was pathetically insufficient. . . ." [67]

Clinging to faith in fiscal orthodoxy even when engaged in deficit spending, Roosevelt had been unwilling to greatly unbalance the budget. Having pledged in his campaign to cut expenditures and to restore the balanced budget, the President had at first adopted recovery programs that would not drain government finances. Despite a burst of activity under the Civil Works Administration during the first winter, public works expenditures were frequently slow and cautious. Shifting from direct relief, which Roosevelt (like Hoover) considered "a narcotic, a subtle destroyer of the human spirit," the government moved to work relief. [68] ("It saves his skill. It gives him a chance to do something socially useful," said Hopkins. [69]) By 1937 the government had poured enough money into the economy to spur production to within 10 percent of 1929 levels, but unemployment still hovered over seven million. Yet so eager was the President to balance the budget that he cut expenditures for public works and relief, and plunged the economy into a greater depression. While renewing expenditures, Roosevelt remained cautious in his fiscal policy, and the nation still had almost nine million unemployed in 1939. After nearly six years of struggling with the depression, the Roosevelt administration could not lead the nation to recovery, but it had relieved suffering.[70] In most of America, starvation was no longer possible. Perhaps that was the most humane achievement of the New Deal.

Its efforts on behalf of humane *reform* were generally faltering and shallow, of more value to the middle classes, of less value to organized workers, of even less to the marginal men. In conception and in practice, seemingly humane efforts revealed the shortcomings of American liberalism. For example, public housing, praised as evidence of the federal government's concern for the poor, was limited in scope (to 180,000 units) and unfortunate in results.[71] It usually meant the consolidation of ghettos, the robbing of men of their dignity, the treatment of men as wards with few rights. And slum clearance came to mean "Negro clearance" and removal of the other poor. Of much of this liberal reformers were unaware, and some of the problems can be traced to the structure of bureaucracy and to the selection of government personnel and social workers who disliked the poor.[72] But the liberal conceptions, it can be argued, were also flawed for there was no willingness to consult the poor, nor to encourage their participation. Liberalism was elitist. Seeking to build America in their own image, liberals wanted to create an environment which they thought would restructure character and personality more appropriate to white, middle-class America.

While slum dwellers received little besides relief from the New Deal, and their needs were frequently misunderstood, Negroes as a group received even less assistance — less than they needed and sometimes even less than their proportion in the population would have justified. Under the NRA they were frequently dismissed and their wages were sometimes below the legal minimum. The Civilian Conservation Corps left them "forgotten" men — excluded, discriminated against, segregated. In general, what the Negroes gained — relief, WPA jobs, equal pay on some federal projects — was granted them as poor people, not as Negroes.[73] To many black men the distinction was unimportant, for no government had ever given them so much. "My friends, go home and turn Lincoln's picture to the wall," a Negro publisher told his race. "That debt has been payed in full." [74]

Bestowing recognition on some Negro leaders, the New Deal appointed them to agencies as advisers — the "black cabinet." Probably more dramatic was the advocacy of Negro rights by Eleanor Roosevelt. Some whites like Harold Ickes and Aubrey Williams even struggled cautiously to break down segregation. But segregation did not yield, and Washington itself remained a segregated city. The white South was never challenged, the Fourteenth Amendment never used to assist Negroes. Never would Roosevelt ex-

pend political capital in an assault upon the American caste system.[75] Despite
the efforts of the NAACP to dramatize the Negroes' plight as second-class citizens, subject to brutality and often without legal protection, Roosevelt would
not endorse the antilynching bill. ("No government pretending to be civilized can go on condoning such atrocities," H. L. Mencken testified. "Either
it must make every possible effort to put them down or it must suffer the
scorn and contempt of Christendom.") [76] Unwilling to risk schism with
Southerners ruling committees, Roosevelt capitulated to the forces of rac-
ism.[77]

Even less bold than in economic reform, the New Deal left intact
the race relations of America. Yet its belated and cautious recognition of the
black man was great enough to woo Negro leaders and even to court the
masses. One of the bitter ironies of these years is that a New Dealer could tell
the NAACP in 1936: "Under our new conception of democracy, the Negro
will be given the chance to which he is entitled. . . ." But it was true, Ickes
emphasized, that "The greatest advance [since Reconstruction] toward assur-
ing the Negro that degree of justice to which he is entitled and that equality of
opportunity under the law which is implicit in his American citizenship, has
been made since Franklin D. Roosevelt was sworn in as President. . . ." [78]

It was not in the cities and not among the Negroes but in rural
America that Roosevelt's administration made its (philosophically) boldest efforts: creation of the Tennessee Valley Authority and the later attempt to
construct seven little valley authorities. Though conservation was not a new
federal policy and government-owned utilities were sanctioned by municipal
experience, federal activity in this area constituted a challenge to corporate
enterprise and an expression of concern about the poor. A valuable example
of regional planning and a contribution to regional prosperity, TVA still fell
far short of expectations. The agency soon retreated from social planning.
("From 1936 on," wrote Tugwell, "the TVA should have been called the
Tennessee Valley Power Production and Flood Control Corporation.") Fearful of antagonizing the powerful interests, its agricultural program neglected
the tenants and the sharecroppers.[79]

To urban workingmen the New Deal offered some, but limited, material benefits. Though the government had instituted contributory social
security and unemployment insurance, its much-heralded Fair Labor Standards Act, while prohibiting child labor, was a greater disappointment. It
exempted millions from its wages-and-hours provisions. So unsatisfactory was
the measure that one congressman cynically suggested, "Within 90 days after
appointment of the administrator, she should report to Congress whether
anyone is subject to this bill." [80] Requiring a minimum of twenty-five cents
an hour ($11 a week for 44 hours), it raised the wages of only about a half-
million at a time when nearly twelve million workers in interstate commerce
were earning less than forty cents an hour.[81]

More important than these limited measures was the administration's support, albeit belated, of the organization of labor and the right of collective bargaining. Slightly increasing organized workers' share of the national income,[82] the new industrial unions extended job security to millions who were previously subject to the whim of management. Unionization freed them from the perils of a free market.

By assisting labor, as well as agriculture, the New Deal started the institutionalization of larger interest groups into a new political economy. Joining business as tentative junior partners, they shared the consensus on the value of large-scale corporate capitalism, and were permitted to participate in the competition for the division of shares. While failing to redistribute income, the New Deal modified the political structure at the price of excluding many from the process of decision making. To many what was offered in fact was symbolic representation, formal representation. It was not the industrial workers necessarily who were recognized, but their unions and leaders; it was not even the farmers, but their organizations and leaders. While this was not a conscious design, it was the predictable result of conscious policies. It could not have been easily avoided, for it was part of the price paid by a large society unwilling to consider radical new designs for the distribution of power and wealth.

In the deepest sense, this new form of representation was rooted in the liberal's failure to endorse a meaningful egalitarianism which would provide actual equality of opportunity. It was also the limited concern with equality and justice that accounted for the shallow efforts of the New Deal and left so many Americans behind. The New Deal was neither a "third American Revolution," as Carl Degler suggests, nor even a "half-way revolution," as William Leuchtenburg concludes. Not only was the extension of representation to new groups less than full-fledged partnership, but the New Deal neglected many Americans — sharecroppers, tenant farmers, migratory workers and farm laborers, slum dwellers, unskilled workers, and the unemployed Negroes. They were left outside the new order.[83] As Roosevelt asserted in 1937 (in a classic understatement), one third of the nation was "ill-nourished, ill-clad, ill-housed." [84]

Yet, by the power of rhetoric and through the appeals of political organization, the Roosevelt government managed to win or retain the allegiance of these peoples. Perhaps this is one of the crueller ironies of liberal politics, that the marginal men trapped in hopelessness were seduced by rhetoric, by the style and movement, by the symbolism of efforts seldom reaching beyond words. In acting to protect the institution of private property and in advancing the interests of corporate capitalism, the New Deal assisted the middle and upper sectors of society. It protected them, sometimes, even at the cost of injuring the lower sectors. Seldom did it bestow much of substance upon the lower classes. Never did the New Deal seek to organize these groups into independent political forces. Seldom did it risk antagonizing established interests. For some this would constitute a puzzling defect of liberalism; for some, the failure to achieve true liberalism. To others it would emphasize the inherent shortcomings of American liberal democracy. As the nation prepared for war, liberalism, by accepting private property and federal assistance to corporate capitalism, was not prepared effectively to reduce inequities, to redistribute political power, or to extend equality from promise to reality.

The Conservative Welfare State

PAUL CONKIN

Paul Conkin, who teaches at the University of Wisconsin, in The New Deal *(1967) adds brilliantly to the critical literature on the Roosevelt period. The book irritates some scholars by its considerable ambiguity as to whether the New Deal deserves censure because it squandered its opportunities, or whether the entire culture bears the blame for the sad failures of reform. The book is short, and Conkin does not seriously explore the shifting, complex relation between historical opportunities and historical obstacles. At places he seems angry with the men of the 1930s (especially, in his first chapter, with Franklin Roosevelt) for their mistakes and weaknesses. But the book is permeated by a sadness that the reader associates with tragedy, not folly, and in the closing passages Conkin seems to decide that the culture prevented real reform in the 1930s.*

In Roosevelt's terms, every New Deal "reform" was a generous act by good men of power against bad men of power. In fact, it was usually a confused compromise by an indistinguishable mixture of good and bad men of

From Paul Conkin, *The New Deal*, pp. 72–73, 51–52, 73–81. Copyright © 1967 by the Thomas Y. Crowell Company.

power, with Roosevelt (abetted by many historians) generally finding most
Republican politicians, conservative Southern Democrats, and at least four
Supreme Court judges to be bad men of power, allied to numerous bad men
throughout the country. But neither bad men nor good men saw much beyond the evident selfishness of their opponents. Thus, instead of recognizing
real devils, or contemplating major but almost impossible changes in American institutions or in the real power structure (not the party structure), the
good men either tried some mild detergent in futile efforts to clean up the
existing system or tried to appease and care for those who were suffering
because of its inadequacies. The good men of power were as much a part of
the system as the bad men of power. They could not see that monopoly was a
natural and not always harmful end result of a private market system, that
negative regulations in behalf of competition would not, could not, and
probably should not work, and that more biting, more stringent positive controls would be truly revolutionary, that is, would force a shift of economic
and political control, and thus often threaten their own privileged positions.
Even when Roosevelt, conventional in beliefs but pleasingly archaic in his
gentlemanly *noblesse oblige,* or his academic advisers (presumably good men
without power) framed legislation that had some bite, such as a pure food
and drugs act or a tax reform bill, it rarely survived Congress. When an
ambiguous, potentially radical program did survive, or was sneaked in by
executive order, it was usually neutralized by administrators, nullified by the
courts, endlessly frustrated in its day-by-day operations, or eventually destroyed or emasculated for political reasons.

The story of most New Deal frustration remains untold. The thirties was indeed a reform decade, a period when sensitivity to injustice, to vast
structures of privilege, to the terribly empty life of most people, prevailed as
never before. Much of the concern remained outside government, in critics
of the New Deal, in radical political movements, in artists of varied mediums,
in a few philosophers. But many reformers worked in or with New Deal agencies, particularly the relief agencies. They were always in the minority and
had to fight an unending battle within their own agencies. . . .

The best of the New Deal was not at the level of political visibility
but hidden in the agencies and subagencies. Roosevelt's very failure to
pursue one coherent program allowed a greater variety of fascinating people
to enter the government service. Among them were the social workers and
do-gooders, a few from the academies but most from labor unions, welfare
agencies, newspapers, and architectural firms. They were the glory of the
New Deal, molded more in the humane image of Eleanor Roosevelt than that
of her politician husband. Some were dreamers, even utopian dreamers. They
were often as unconventional as Roosevelt was conventional, as dogmatic in

outlook as he was flexible, as cocksure of their own plans as he was unclear about his. They worked on the Consumer Advisory Council of the N.R.A., carried out research for the National Resources Committee, designed homesteads in Appalachia, or planned minimal budgets for the F.E.R.A. A more sophisticated group formed a radical coterie in the A.A.A., concerned more for tenant farmers and migratory workers than for the welfare of the Farm Bureau. Others tried to organize miners, felt that Negroes should share equally in New Deal policies, organized community centers and applauded folk art, raved about town meetings, rarely talked for two minutes without mentioning co-operation, and made social concern a mark of acceptability and conservatism a mark of Cain. With an assumed air of worldly aplomb, or a carefully cultivated cynicism, many of them tried to hide their idealism and moralism behind their frequent sneers at Puritanism, by self-conscious boozing, or, like Harry Hopkins, by conspicuous larks at the races.

These rebels gathered in a hundred corridors to talk and plan and plot their ongoing revolution, their new world a making. In darker corners, some found their Communist cells and added an apocalyptic urgency to their profound concern. The New Deal went no one place, tried no one thing. But the individual agencies often developed clear plans and tried to achieve them. The New Deal, as a vast and complex whole, denied the idea of experimentation — clear hypotheses and controlled verification. But a dozen agencies were perfect social laboratories and remained so as long as they could hide from the compromises necessitated by politics. These reformers made the New Deal a humane undertaking, in spite of all the callous elements, the conflicting interests, that clashed at the top. Often overly paternalistic, often wonderfully naive, not yet corrupted by any brand of "realism," they worked out the lineaments of a new democracy, but never came close to achieving it. Instead, they had to quit or learn compromise, many to find a niche in something so mild, so basically conservative, as an embryonic welfare state. . . .

But the outside battle was the main one. As they struggled to carry out their programs, dealing directly with the exploited people who loved Roosevelt, they often found their task impossible. The economic and social institutions of a Democratic South, as an example, presented one tremendous source of frustration. Blocked at every turn, they learned anew the ever-relevant lesson of Lincoln Steffens. Those who effectively frustrated their efforts also loved Roosevelt and were on the side of the angels. They were also powerful. The devils could be dealt with, but not the angels. Mrs. Roosevelt knew their plight, and they loved her for knowing. On occasion, F.D.R. knew also and, when political realities permitted, tried to help his loyal good men without power. But there was nothing in his leadership capable of transforming the desires of these loyal reformers into a new structure of political power. It may have been impossible, even had he tried. Master of politics, he was also captive to politics. Thus the story of the New Deal is a sad story, the ever recurring story of what might have been. Perhaps only Tugwell among major historians has shown a vague appreciation of this sadness, but even he quickly returned to the charisma of an adored leader.

Since the New Deal failed to fulfill even the minimal dream of most reformers, why did all the evil men of power, plus millions of Republican dupes, oppose it? To Roosevelt, the answer was simple: they were evil. Economic royalists, with a monopoly of power, they were not content with a repaired and honest capitalism. Instead, they wanted to drive on with their plutocracy and bring down upon the heads of the good men of power the inevitable revolution. Then good bankers would suffer and good businessmen might lose the management of their corporations. But this answer, although in part true, was too simple. The opponents of Roosevelt misconstrued the direction of the New Deal. Many believed Roosevelt's class rhetoric. They really thought America was losing its "free" capitalist soul to some type of socialism. In their praise of freedom lurked some valuable criticism of the New Deal. Also, many Americans, perhaps particularly the monied classes, never trusted Roosevelt, much less some of his advisers. The New Deal was indeed a mixed company, a type of political bohemia, frequented by many of the better sort, but still dangerous. Roosevelt was a puzzling creature. Even when he served conservative causes, he preached an alien gospel. Let us have anything but a righteous gentleman in Washington. Even a Marxist would have made more sense to them. Finally, almost no one thought in terms of vast economic expansion, and thus no one could see welfare as other than a permanent liability, somehow drawn from the ledger of profits or high incomes, either directly by taxes or indirectly by government deficits and inflation. The threat to earnings, the inhibition to investment, seemed the central issue, more important than declining fears of revolution, humane concern, or an occasional recognition of the importance of purchasing power.

But the supreme irony is here. The enemies of the New Deal were wrong. They should have been friends. Security was a prime concern of the insecure thirties. It cut across all classes. Businessmen, by their policies, desperately sought it in lowered corporate debts and tried to get the government to practice the same austerity. Even when ragged and ill-housed, workers opened savings accounts. The New Deal, by its policies, underwrote a vast apparatus of security. But the meager benefits of Social Security were insignificant in comparison to the building system of security for large, established businesses. But like stingy laborers, the frightened businessmen did not use and enjoy this security and thus increase it. The New Deal tried to frame institutions to protect capitalism from major business cycles and began in an unclear sort of way to underwrite continuous economic growth and sustained profits. Although some tax bills were aimed at high profits, there was no attack on fair profits or even on large profits. During the thirties, as all the way up to the sixties, there was no significant leveling by taxes. The proportionate distribution of wealth remained. Because of tax policies, even relief expenditures were disguised subsidies to corporations, since they were in large part paid by future taxes on individual salaries or on consumer goods. Thus, instead of higher wages creating a market, at the short-term expense of profits, the government subsidized the businessman, without taking the cost out of his hide as he expected and feared.

Even at the local level there was no significant shift of the economic and social structure. Negroes, politically purchased by relief or by the occasional concern of bureaucrats or Mrs. Roosevelt, remained a submerged and neglected caste. Service and farm labor, including migratory, received slight succor. Millions continued in desultory enslavement to immediate needs. Thus the people of power gained added security and lost only two commodities: undisciplined freedom and a degree of popular respect. The last they regained quickly. Most of all, the individual farmer lost some entrepreneurial freedom and accepted a degree of central planning, albeit through democratic procedures. Even manufacturing industries had to accept new procedural limitations — labor laws, added regulatory agencies, new taxes, and minimum wage and maximum hours. But these were necessary for security and for ordered growth. Even without government action, many restraints were developing within large corporations, even in the twenties, and some were simply part of a rationalizing process in business. Security demanded procedural rules, a degree of uniformity in practice, and even a formalized relationship with organized labor. Only small, aggressive adventurers or promoters suffered from the new procedural limitations. The only leveling, and the only real bite, hit the middle income groups and some small businesses. Perhaps the Chambers of Commerce were correct in condemning Roosevelt in 1935. The National Association of Manufacturers was not.

Government spending in behalf of multiplied private spending, the strongest weapon of Eccles and Keynes, was to be the final and most complete insurance policy for American capitalism. After 1937, even Roosevelt reluctantly swallowed this pill. Keynes was the last great classical economist, in the tradition of Adam Smith, Ricardo, the Mills, Marx, and Marshall. A British Liberal, formal, analytical, he tried to devise the minimal government devices necessary to maintain most of the free aspects of a market system. At the beginning of this greatest economic tradition, Adam Smith tried to get the freedom. At the end, Keynes tried to keep as much as possible. He wanted to set up safeguards to prevent serious depressions, to maintain full employment, and at the same time provide all the welfare measures required by human concern. He wanted to avoid socialist ownership and bureaucratic management on one hand and the severe controls of a corporate state on the other. His complex arguments had small influence on the New Deal, but his general prescription eventually prevailed.

The magic in Keynes, at least for an interval, was the magic of growth itself, which springs from new knowledge but is implemented through political economy. Growth can raise a whole society, with rising profits matching rising wages and rising government income supporting rising welfare measures. Business, so fearful of new welfare, never realized that it could be paid for by government credit and that public debts could be maintained (or repaid) without extra tax rates and without a significant redistribution of income or wealth. Roosevelt wanted some redistribution. Like Keynes, he had social as well as economic goals. But he rarely achieved these — witness again the congressional compromises and the frustrated bureaucrats on the moral battlefield. During World War II, when massive spending purchased unbelievable growth, Roosevelt had to suspend social goals and let the public subsidize plant expansion, profits, and, above all, future profits. By then he had no political alternative. Full employment, plus overtime, reduced the welfare burden, while growth and temporarily high taxes helped pay the cost of war. Some temporary leveling actually occurred. After the war the large government subsidy to business continued — in huge defense purchases, in contracts awarded in behalf of corporate survival, in research, in tax relief, in a flexible use of antitrust laws, in enough welfare increases to soothe the discontented, in a tacit acceptance of administered prices, and increasingly even in an unwillingness to antagonize the business community (even Democrats learned the old Hoover bit about confidence).

The battle between economic leaders and the New Deal was never complete. Some businessmen and many large farmers (historians generally call them enlightened) supported Roosevelt throughout the thirties. Many more, if they had understood Roosevelt's purposes, would surely have backed him. In the same sense, Roosevelt, considering his objectives, his willingness to retain and strengthen a private economy, should have worked more at understanding and communicating with businessmen, for their choices had more to do with the success of the New Deal than anything else. Yet, there was a real issue dividing the two. Simply, it was a matter of power. Roosevelt was powerful and could not be controlled by anyone or by any group. In this sense he was incorruptible, perhaps as much so as any President in American history. For two years even intense lobbying could not block his control over the legislative process. As Tugwell always believed, there was the potentiality of a major shift in the government of the country, with Roosevelt responding to academic advisers and effecting policies which would seriously invade the managerial prerogatives of major private interests. Instead of a limited socialization of product via welfare, Roosevelt could have socialized management or even the plant. He never did this; seemingly, he never wanted to, but until 1937 he seemed to have the political power and never gave enough assurances to convince businessmen that he might not. For a while, normal channels of power in the federal government were circumvented, particularly in 1933–34. This is why the courts became the heroes of conservative groups. But even as Roosevelt secured great political power, and thus potential economic power, the power of economic decision making remained perilously in private hands, less secure and less potent than ever before. The tense situation could not endure.

The shift to welfare policies and then to Keynesian recovery policies took away most of the threat and left private interests shaken but more secure than ever. Nationalization and economic planning became dead issues. Through banking and budgetary policies the government's resources were to be used to protect, support, and occasionally discipline private producers. This meant a helping hand for private industry, but with too many obligations, too many secure guarantees, and too many restrictions for many old-fashioned industrialists. Security does reduce freedom.

But the government had, more clearly than ever in the past, committed itself to national economic goals. This was one of the enduring achievements of the New Deal. Since it rejected planning (except to a degree in agriculture) and refused to do its own producing, it had no alternative but to rely on the major corporations and to subsidize them if necessary to insure its goals of rapid growth, high levels of employment, and low welfare needs. Even a slight increase in private economic activity can do more to benefit the country than vast welfare programs. Precluded from direct economic action, the government had to use indirect controls and incentives, plus persuasion, bribes, or, if politically possbile, threats and punitive measures. In this situation, high profits rightfully became desirable public policy, since they increased the total economic activity and the level of national prosperity. In spite of all the ridicule, nothing was now truer than the quip: "What is good for General Motors is good for the country." Under the emerging system, the welfare of both were inseparable.

The dependence was mutual. The large corporations, protected by a generous government against the insecurity of the past (when politicians could safely allow depressions) and also against their own worst mistakes and abuses, were tied to government policies. The national budget was almost as important as their corporate budgets. The action of the Federal Reserve Board, or even random pronouncements by government officials, could wreck their best-laid plans. Welfare spending became a small but marginally vital part of the total market for goods, forcing some business acquiescence even here. In a few areas, such as low-rent housing, welfare programs became the major support for very profitable businesses. Later, defense spending would completely support large companies and provide the margin of profit for hundreds. Increasingly, business and government were linked in more subtle ways, particularly by a common economic orthodoxy and a common need for certain skills. Bureaucrats moved from Ivy League campuses to corporations and on to Washington. The situation invited, in fact necessitated, co-operation, or a truly joint enterprise. Roosevelt cleared the way for such co-operation, but he never desired it or achieved it and probably never perceived its inescapable logic. Unlike most politicians, he was never a good businessman, nor could he share power easily.

The old, individualistic capitalist did not fit the new picture. Mavericks were taboo. But neither did reformers fit. The new partnership, with greater government participation and greater benefits (the welfare state for business), left room for tension, even bitter conflict, as between mutually dependent husband and wife. Always, one or the other partner could try to gain too much power and upset the partnership. There was an overlapping but never identical constituency. Generally, with time and enough advice from Keynesian counselors, the two settled into almost blissful matrimony. Lyndon Johnson finally illustrated what a beautiful and happy home is possible when both sides can sit down and reason together. What about the constituency? For business, the shareholders have profited. Dividends have been large and capital accumulation even larger. For government, the larger constituency presents a much more variegated pattern. But most able and fortunate people, if they have been loyal, have received well in material returns and have profited from the general benevolence and good will of both the private and government bureaucrats who look out for them.

But the economic magic of sustained growth and the political magic of welfare can be irrelevant to moral and religious vision, which may also demand a just community. For the more sensitive New Dealers, or outside critics, Keynes provided a technique for priming the economic pump but no means of purifying the water. They thirsted after the pure product. Growth could simply intoxicate the affluent minority (or majority), blunt their sensitivity, and leave them in satiated lethargy, full but unfulfilled. Welfare could do the same for the poor. Growth could lead to vast production, to an enormous gross national product, but also to ugliness and spiritual poverty everywhere. It might even lead to full employment and undreamed-of security (goals not attained because of too small a government investment), yet to a society bereft of meaningful work, of personal involvement, even of democratic participation. It might suggest the blessing of leisure but bring only the curse of idleness. Finally, it would surely conceal injustice and leave the exploited to the tender and prejudiced mercy of local conscience. During the war the disturbing reformers dropped from view and did not emerge again until the sixties. Then, to the profound surprise of all good men of power, the one-third ill-fed and ill-housed, and the two-thirds alienated and desperate, still existed. In spite of the New Deal and in spite of all that welfare!

CONCLUSION

New Deal Historiography:
Retrospect and Prospect

Otis L. Graham, Jr.

Are the radical historians correct about the New Deal? If this means their argument that the New Deal did not bring either much recovery or reform, even those who think the argument overstated must find it basically persuasive. Significant political changes did occur in the 1930s, along with increased security for some American workers, improvement in the economic level of many farmers, and a better conservation record than any previous administration. But these examples of movement did not touch the fundamentals. Social power and wealth were basically in the same hands at the end of the New Deal as they had been at the beginning. Even so, are the radical historians right when they say that the New Deal performance could and should have been better, and that the principal reason it was not better lay in intellectual deficiencies within liberalism? The answer must be: Not yet. We do not have much radical history written on the New Deal, and what has been written has not conclusively defined how much more was possible and where lies the responsibility for the remarkable persistence of the old habits and social arrangements.

Edward Freeman is supposed to have said that history is "past politics." Certainly that is one variety of history, but a poor variety, even though it has sold rather well over the years. Another popular but poor variety of history is history as present politics: a scholar is so influenced by contemporary political pressures, including those within himself, that he distorts the past for present purposes. None of us escapes these pressures

Copyright © 1971, by Otis L. Graham, Jr.

171

entirely. In elementary and high schools they are intense. History is expected to glorify the nation, reinforce patriotism and national pride. Professional historians have struggled to free themselves from the utilitarian standards forced on writers of elementary textbooks, but they nonetheless have serious problems contending with contemporary pressures, despite their relative institutional freedom. Pressure is especially acute in writing recent history, where there is much continuity with current problems, issues, even personalities. Historians with the rarest exceptions deplore the deliberate use of the past to serve contemporary ends, especially when it is done by academics from the socialist bloc. We are right to condemn it everywhere. Presentism is a vice.

Those historians interested in the New Deal must give this problem especially thoughtful attention. The simplest solution, to refuse to allow the present to influence us, is apparently not available. New Deal issues still agitate the contemporary mind. Baptism, the doctrine of the real presence, and the Immaculate Conception may be discussed without passion, but men display emotion at the first mention of federal economic policy, agricultural subsidies, public housing, conservation — even, still, at the name Franklin Delano Roosevelt. What scholar could be so ascetic as to have no opinions on such issues, so cloistered as to be unaware of their bearing upon his future and his society's future? Further, even if the issues of the 1930s were not so dangerously charged with contemporary significance, philosophers of history such as Charles Beard, Carl Becker, and Benedetto Croce tell us that the ideal of objectivity is unattainable.

Resourceful historians, recognizing all of this, have argued that some virtue may be distilled from our subjectivity. The present sharpens our sensitivity to new issues in what we thought was a familiar past and reveals new perspectives when the older ones are no longer productive. The present also will often tell us which men, groups, and tendencies won and lost in the long run; this too is possibly of some help. In this view, if we try to eliminate contemporary concerns from our minds we not only fail to do so, but we block ourselves from the invigoration of new perspectives and narrow the range of our probing of the past.

These reflections have much to recommend them, but they can lull us into forgetting how much truth there was in the fear of present-mindedness. The present is, after all, more important than the past, and will have a tendency to dominate it in any healthy mind. Men will entertain the hope, as they struggle as citizens with urgent private and public problems, that the past may be forced to yield up the lessons required for our immediate salvation. In this understandable frame of mind it is not long before the needs of the present become stronger than respect for the past, and we begin to manipulate the past, hearing some of its voices and dimming out others, carrying confidently out of its confusions the clear lessons we wish our peers and political leaders to adopt. This tendency caused men to devise the ideal of objectivity. Too many scholars go to the past as a Hanging Judge, in Acton's phrase, and flawed history is almost invariably the result. The concerns of the present, while they may make us receptive to more data, often wind up making us receptive to less.

The damaging effects of contemporary concerns mark the history of New Deal scholarship. Conservative writers, more interested in repealing the New Deal than in understanding it, credited the public policies of the 1930s with having accomplished a centralization of power in Washington that stifled capitalist initiative and granted political and economic power to obscure intellectuals and the indolent masses. This was nonsense. Power in the country did shift slightly toward Washington, yet long after the New Deal it was being used for the same general purposes as before. But this conservative view of what American government had become, however distorted, did seem to threaten the welfare measures of the 1930s and did influence liberal writers after the war. Their writing was adversely affected. They responded to the political environment by describing the public policies of the 1930s as having instituted a massive federal intervention, right enough, but one with the most benign purpose and beneficial effects. This view was not much closer to the truth than the exaggerations of the conservatives. The New Deal had been a short-term political success, but many nonliberal constituencies shared in its favors; its long-range political goals had been at least half-frustrated; and its economic goals, from recovery through security to a more equitable distribution of wealth and income, were substantially defeated. When this became clear in the 1960s it tended to discredit all earlier interpretive writing, even though both conservatives and liberals had occasionally written with insight and narrative skill.

Conservative hostility and liberal indulgence resulted from a virulent combination of ideological commitments and situational political pressures. These influences led them to write history that had less lasting value than their native talents, especially those of the liberals (the conservative writers had been politicians and journalists for the most part, with little scholarly potential to spoil), might have otherwise produced. The conservatives and liberals too frequently argued over whether the vast changes brought by the New Deal were good or bad for America. They put off addressing themselves to a more productive question: why have we had such stability in our basic social arrangements and institutions, even during the deepest economic crisis in our history?

Interestingly enough, those suspect influences, contemporary sociopolitical pressures and the ideology of the author himself, provided the perspective in the 1960s that undercut the emphasis upon "revolutionary" change. The writing of younger, radical historians has helped clarify how much more modest than we thought were New Deal attainments in income redistribution, in power restructuring — industrial and even political — and in relief of suffering. It is largely their writing that has alerted us to the considerable gains of the "business community," supposedly routed by Roosevelt's government. All these things had been pointed out by leftist critics in the 1930s, but the New Left critics of the 1960s supported these views with more and better evidence.

Having conferred its advantage, the present delivered its nemesis. It led the New Left interpreters, despite their valuable insights, to tell as one-sided, selective, and probably dated a story as did earlier politicized historians who wrote in the shadow of FDR's divisive memory.

Today's radical criticizes the American political economy and is convinced that liberalism not only helped produce the social crisis in which we find ourselves but cannot possibly lead us out of it. He believes that the state in a capitalist society cannot really respond to noncapitalistic groups, cannot really bring sufficient justice and rationality to capitalism to make it economically viable and ethically acceptable. He sees continuing liberalism in the 1970s as the conservatives' formula for co-optation, designed to deflect the forces of genuine change by a combination of idealistic rhetoric and minimal economic concessions.

Whether such views of contemporary America are valid is not the issue here. The issue is how they affect the scholarship of men who hold them. I have earlier paid my respects to the insights produced by the radical perspective. Now let us consider its potential defects. How would one prove, to advance today's struggle against a discredited liberalism, that the liberalism of the 1930s was defective? First, one would demonstrate that New Deal achievements for the poor and the general public were disappointing, even to some candid New Dealers themselves. This has been done, or is largely accomplished. But readers with unusual logical powers will see that the New Deal achievement, scanty as it was, may have been the most that was possible. So the radical scholar who is determined to employ his scholarship to save his country in the 1960s and 1970s must, for those readers, argue that opportunities were squandered, and he must lay the blame for that squandering on the ideology he strives to discredit. The liberals of the 1930s must be made to appear indefensibly cautious, insensitive to misery and injustice, in fact just another variety of conservative.

This interpretation would be greatly strengthened by a selective handling of the evidence. The forces of movement would be maximized in number and in resolution — and here one thinks of Huey Long, Father Coughlin, Governor Floyd Olson, Upton Sinclair, and other mass leaders with angry constituencies; the progressive bloc in Congress; the third party movement in Wisconsin; the pervasive radicalism of the intellectual classes.

The forces of resistance would be minimized — the Supreme Court; southern congressional leadership and antiquated congressional rules; the national media with its subserviency to large advertisers; the lack of trained people and adequate statistics for economic management; the public ignorance; the depth of the commitment to individualism; the political apathy and impotence of the under classes. This is fundamental. The possibilities of the situation may be manipulated like an accordion, narrowed or expanded by the relative emphasis given to the forces of movement and the forces of resistance. If one wished to write antiliberal history, the forces of movement would come to the foreground, and the only obstacle worth extensive mention would be liberal ideology, with its fatal cautions and blind spots.

Withdrawing any suggestion that they were consciously adopted, these are the perspectives that characterize New Left writing on the New Deal.[1]* The New Left conclusion, that in the 1930s opportunities for extensive change were inexcusably lost, that New Dealers always compromised too soon, may conceivably be valid. But one must question the route taken to that conclusion. To know where there was room for greater change, we must scrupulously reconstruct the full circumstances. We must make clear what ideas were heretical and what ideas were intelligible and acceptable to men of power, what institutions blocked reform and which ones could have been bent to its service, what was the weight of the past, what was the position and magnitude of revolutionary sentiment and the confidence and resolve of the moneyed classes.

Actually, few general interpreters of the New Deal have studied the relation between opportunities and obstacles in the 1930s with any real dedication. Every author forms his own impressions in this matter, believing it to be crucial. But few consider the pressures with meticulous care. One good reason for this is that a reasonably complete account of what happened does not compress easily into one volume (or even three, as with Schlesinger). To explore what could have happened as well as what did happen has been more than authors attempting synthesis could manage. So authors have relied upon quick calculations and instinct, the conservatives seeing Roosevelt pushing where there was no mandate or need, the liberals seeing barriers of exonerating dimensions, the radicals describing inviting vistas to the left.

The evidence suggests that an indignant tone toward the small steps taken by the New Dealers is not quite appropriate. To be sure, there seem to be occasions when the forces of movement had the advantage and failed to exploit it even reasonably well. To take one example, in their recent books on the Social Security Act, Dan Nelson and Roy Lubove strongly imply that concessions were made to conservative opinion in financing and in standards

* See pp. 193–194 for notes to this article.

that were not politically necessary. Other instances may exist where even the most diligent research fails to discover any substantial reasons why the President or his administration settled for less than they asked for. But one usually discovers formidable institutional and intellectual difficulties.

The New Deal story is heavy with barriers, resistance, dilution of the reform purpose. Recent studies reaffirm this impression. One learns in Robert Lekachman's *The Age of Keynes* (1967) and in Herbert Stein's recent *The Fiscal Revolution in America* (1969) how little economists of the 1930s understood the forces they sought to control, and how they lacked reliable statistical evidence on which to base their primitive prescriptions. Ellis Hawley's *The New Deal and the Problem of Monopoly* (1966) offers a most persuasive description of America's deep commitment to the mutually contradictory goals of economic individualism and of concentration and argues that in such a setting the New Deal could not have escaped the economic incoherence that helped defer recovery. Those who sense unlimited reform opportunities in the Hundred Days would receive some chastening in Raymond Moley's *The First New Deal* (1967), for example, where he makes a strong case that a more radical banking policy during the March collapse was completely ruled out by the absence of competent personnel who might have framed a nationalization measure. More significantly, William E. Leuchtenburg's essay "The New Deal and the Analogue of War" (1964) helps to explain the general atmosphere of "cooperation" with business that blunted the measures of the Hundred Days. The only relevant past, in the crisis of 1933, was the World War I planning experiment, and under the heavy influence of that memory with its stress on cooperation and unity the New Dealers understandably frittered away the golden months of conservative demoralization with schemes based on the cooperative ideal, which actually involved no fundamental reforms. Leuchtenburg, in another essay, "The Constitutional Revolution of 1937" (1969), explains very clearly the dampening influence on legislative draftsmanship and tactics exerted by the omnipresent threat of unconstitutionality. James T. Patterson has stretched out before us for the first time, in *The New Deal and The States* (1969), one of the most formidable labyrinths of all — the reactionary and unrepresentative state governments, where more New Deal measures were obstructed than even in Congress.

One could easily continue listing studies that enlarge our awareness of the defenses of existing arrangements in the 1930s. Those noted already appeared in the 1960s, and the shelves were full of such studies long before the 1960s arrived. Any interpretation of the New Deal must meet this evidence squarely. The writers on the left, old and new, have not done so. Just as the liberal centrist historians have had a tendency to lack a strong interest in the spaces to the left of Roosevelt, the New Left historians have systematically, even brilliantly, underrated the obstacles — with one impor- _ tant exception.

To speak in particular about the essays by Barton Bernstein and Howard Zinn that have attracted so much attention, radical historians focused on one major obstacle, an internal rather than an external one: the "ideology" of the liberals themselves. In Bernstein's words:

> The boundaries of New Deal experimentalism, as Howard Zinn has emphasized, could extend far beyond Roosevelt's cautious ventures. Operating within very safe channels, Roosevelt not only avoided Marxism and the socialization of property, but he also stopped far short of other possibilities — communal direction of production or the organized distribution of surplus. . . . Usually opportunistic and frequently shifting, the New Deal was restricted by its ideology. It ran out of fuel not because of the conservative opposition, but because it ran out of ideas.

Here is the heart of the New Left argument. There were possibilities for really radical change; a conservative set of New Deal liberals failed to explore them and blocked access to power for those who would.

Any student of the New Deal will sympathize initially with this argument. While no one has satisfactorily studied the ideas of the New Dealers (whatever may be meant by that label), we are familiar with many of their ideas, and who has not been exasperated by Morgenthau's fiscal conservatism, Hopkins' breezy superficiality, Moley's stubborn faith in businessmen, Wallace's confusing mysticism, Lilienthal's naive assumption that the Farm Bureau — Extension Service bureaucracy represented "grassroots democracy," Eleanor's unflagging innocence. They did not understand Keynes, they did not insist upon uncompromising racial justice, they actually believed that the federal regulatory bureaucracies could be made independent of business power. As for the President, commentators from Walter Lippmann through Richard Hofstadter and James M. Burns and Rex Tugwell to Paul Conkin have exposed the deficiencies of his simple, confused ideas and the many timidities of his leadership. With a little selective memory, they may be made to sound incredibly conservative and cautious. Recall and recite the occasions when they held back, remember their confusions; hold up their speeches against the brilliant essays of John Dewey and others with time to think and no political responsibilities; hold them up against our generation's broader social vision, three decades wiser and sadder. The result may be good contemporary politics, but as history it has serious drawbacks.

The full context has not been supplied. Let us add the total range of social and political ideas in America in the 1930s and before, and the New Dealers appear well toward the innovative and daring end of the spectrum, with stronger democratic instincts and a stronger commitment to racial justice and a more steady humanitarianism than all but a scant minority of their contemporaries. Then add the institutional barriers against which they worked. When these obstacles are restored to the picture in fair proportion to their contemporary massiveness, some defeats are going to be explained less by intellectual failings than by the sheer inertia of the existing network of social relations. Finally, restore to the picture the war, agent of the unravelling of so many liberal plans and the fortuitous strengthening of corporate capitalism. To those who know how many reformist initiatives and institutions were crippled by the war, only the most detailed and powerful argument will convince them that the America of 1945–1970 was designed and constructed by the New Dealers.

With these considerations in mind, it is not simple to answer the question: Why was there not more reform in the 1930s? How important in the final summation will be the inadequacies, preventable and inexcusable, of liberalism as an ideology? A safe guess is: not nearly as important as the New Left historians have said. Certainly there were times when Roosevelt and his lieutenants either failed to press an advantage or actually restrained more ardent champions of change. But I would judge that these occasions, if exploited, add up only to marginal gains and would not have made substantial inroads on the core of white, upper-class power. The answer to the question about social change in the 1930s is mostly structural, not ideological; the advantages of the defense, not the errors of the offense; a story justifying sadness more than indignation.

Some of my students, of well-matured radical views, are distressed by this argument. They do not like the sympathy it implies for liberals who held power and left so many unsolved problems. If we argue that the stress ought to be on the external rather than the internal impediments in the 1930s, are we not adopting a determinism that has its own ideological thrust — protecting American political leadership from serious criticism, when many of those leaders have been liberals? But I concede that there are periods in human affairs when men appear to have room to act, have the necessary ideas and power, and mismanage. Such periods would naturally be critically interpreted. Perhaps the New Deal was such a time. I have not insisted that it was not, but only expressed strong doubts that the inadequacies of American liberalism may be decisively demonstrated from the evidence of the 1930s. Too much evidence from that era testifies to inertia and resistance to reorganization, and the radical historians have not adequately argued for a more open situation. Conceivably, books rather than essays would secure Zinn's dream of a discredited liberalism based on a study of the New Deal. My unsolicited opinion is that this will be easier to manage for the postwar period, when the inadequacies of liberal policies gradually became more glaring.

But the 1930s should still attract the friends of a radically different, democratized America. History may not always allow us to condemn those we wish, since it is filled with mighty currents and confusions, and produces sympathy on occasion even for soldiers, hangmen, industrialists, and liberals. But good history seeks, among other things, to specify what it is that holds men back from realizing their best ideals. If it is man's nature that defeats him, this will not encourage the radical. But if, as I believe, men are held back by institutions and the superstructure of ideas they foster, to specify them and describe their deadening drag is to write the most radical history of all.

NOTES

Introduction

1 This is not to say that the right has no intellectual spokesmen worthy of attention. No one can ignore the so-called "Chicago school" of economists, led by Milton Friedman, who believe with such conviction in the power of the market to regulate human affairs better than any government. The prestige of the Chicago group is indeed on the rise, but it is the prestige of their argument that the supply of money is the crucial determinant of economic activity. This theory is now being tried out (apparently) by the Nixon Council of Economic Advisors and Federal Reserve Board and commands more respect generally than ever before. But it should be distinguished from the broader faith in the free market that often goes with it. Only the first is making any headway. While one must sympathize with Friedman's distaste for the performance of the federal regulatory bureaucracy and concur that taxation is often more effective than administrative regulation as a tool of social policy (see Friedman's *Capitalism and Freedom*), his faith in the free market is not justified and is even less persuasive now than similar ideas in the 1930s. Even in prosperity the market did not arrange a decent level of investment in human capital (health, education, etc.), in aesthetic advancement, in conservation, in recreation, or in basic research. Nor has the market ever shown much consideration for the feelings and the impaired talents of the old, the sick and disabled, the technologically unemployed, the nonwhite. To obtain a better performance in these areas will require reliance on intelligent management through democratically controlled institutions. Should a stray scholar be so bold as to argue that economic knowledge in the 1930s was so primitive that the New Deal should have been postponed pending better tools and recovery sought without recourse to large, blundering bureaucracies, he will have to argue this in a spirit of great sadness. For he will be advising that the men of the 1930s ought to have abandoned their efforts to narrow the income gap, provide employment opportunities for all, lessen urban squalor, succor the old and weak, rationalize transportation policies, stimulate the arts, and conserve natural resources — on the nauseating grounds that neither they nor their institutions were prepared to carry out the task efficiently. I doubt that we shall see such an argument, especially now, as we become aware in our recent past of the buried timebombs of overpopulation, pollution, and of national and international civil wars.

2 If there were not space limits, and if succinct accounts existed in all areas, materials on agriculture, banking, electric power, mortgage refunding, housing, transportation, conservation, antitrust, Constitutional law, monetary policy, and so on would also be included. Examination of these areas would have produced similar patterns to the five selected — some evidence that the New Deal brought great alterations, other evidence that it left power and money pretty much where they were.

Federalism in the Style of the 1930's, JAMES T. PATTERSON

1 For a guardedly favorable view of federalism in this period see Jane Perry Clark's *The Rise of a New Federalism*. Daniel J. Elazar is more optimistic in *The American Partnership: Intergovernmental Cooperation in Nineteenth Century United States*. He argues that "cooperative federalism was the rule in the nineteenth century as well as in the twentieth. . . . What has changed is the routinization of shared procedures." (337). See also Morton Grodzins, *The American System: A New View of Government in the United States* (Chicago 1966), ed., Elazar. Grodzins views the period 1913–1948 as the "triumph of cooperative federalism." 41–57.

2 David Sholtz (Fla.), *Proceedings of the 1935 Governors Conference*, 37. A sketchy study of Sholtz is Merlin G. Cox, "David Sholtz: New Deal Governor of Florida," *Florida Historical Quarterly*, XLIII (October 1964), 142–52.

3 Robert S. Allen, ed., *Our Sovereign State* (New York, 1949), XXIX.

4 John A. Perkins, "American Governors — 1930 to 1940," *National Municipal Review*, XXIX (March 1940), 178–84; Lynton K. Caldwell, "Perfecting State Administration," *Public Administration Review*, VII (Winter 1947), 25–36; and Leonard D. White and M. Harvey Sherman, "The Governors March On," *State Government*, XIII (October 1940), 195–97, 206 ff.

5 George C. Benson, *The New Centralization: A Study of Intergovernmental Relations in the United States* (New York, 1941), 117–21.

6 G. Lyle Belsley, "The Advance of the Merit System," *State Government*, XII (January 1939), 7–8, 18 ff.

7 *Proceedings of the 1935 Governors Conference*, 77.

8 Lester Milbrath, "Political Participation in the States," in Jacob and Vines, *Politics in the American States*, 38 ff. For the impact of national policy on voting trends in individual states see Fenton, *Politics in the Border States;* Gosnell, *Grass Roots Politics;* and Joseph P. Harris, *California Politics* (Stanford, 1955), 9 ff.

The End of the Turbulent Years, IRVING BERNSTEIN

1 George Korson, *Coal Dust on the Fiddle* (Philadelphia: University of Pennsylvania Press, 1943), 302–03, 444–46.

2 *Historical Statistics*, 93; Arthur M. Ross, *Trade Union Wage Policy* (Berkeley: University of California Press, 1948), ch. 6; Joseph W. Bloch, "Regional Wage Differentials: 1907–46," *MLR*, 66 (Apr. 1948), 371–77; Doris E. Pullman and L. Reed Tripp, "Collective Bargaining Developments," in *Labor and the New Deal*, 333–56; Neil W. Chamberlain, *The Union Challenge to Management Control* (New York: Harper, 1948), 77–80; Philip Taft, "Organized Labor and the New Deal," in *How Collective Bargaining Works* (New York: Twentieth Century Fund, 1945), 25–30. For the development and refinement of the concept of industrial democracy see Milton Derber, "The Idea of Industrial Democracy in America, 1898–1915," *Labor History*, 7 (Fall 1966), 259–86, and "The Idea of Industrial Democracy in America, 1915–1935," *Labor History*, 8 (Winter 1967), 3–29. The concept of industrial jurisprudence is set forth in Sumner H. Slichter, *Union Policies and Industrial Management* (Washington: Brookings Institution, 1941), ch. 1.

3 Bernstein, *New Deal Collective Bargaining*, ch. 10; R. W. Fleming, "The Significance of the Wagner Act," in *Labor and the New Deal*, 121–55; William M. Leiserson, *Right and Wrong in Labor Relations* (Berkeley: University of California Press, 1938), 24; Derber, "The Idea of Industrial Democracy in America, 1915–1935," 27. While the Wagner Act would not be changed to restrict unions until the passage of the Taft-Hartley amendments of 1947, this tendency was evident in the states before the war. Massachusetts, New York, Pennsylvania, Wisconsin, and Utah had adopted "little" Wagner Acts in 1937. But in 1939 Pennsylvania and Wisconsin amended their laws and Michigan and Minnesota enacted new statutes, all of the restrictive type. Harry A. Millis and Royal E. Montgomery, *Organized Labor* (New York: McGraw-Hill, 1945), 533–35.

4 *Roosevelt Press Conferences*, vol. 9, pp. 276–307.

The Economic Effects of Unionism, GEORGE H. HILDEBRAND

1 Harold M. Levinson, "Collective bargaining and income distribution," *American Economic Review*, Papers and Proceedings, XLIV:2, May 1954, 315–316.

2 Jesse Burkhead, "Changes in the functional distribution of income," *Journal of the American Statistical Association*, 48 (June, 1953); Levinson, "Collective bargaining and income distribution," *op. cit.;* Levinson, *Unionism, Wage Trends, and Income Distribution*, Michigan Business Studies, X:4 (Ann Arbor: University of Michigan Press, 1951); D. Gale Johnson, "The functional distribution of income in the United States, 1850–1952," *Review*

of *Economics and Statistics*, XXXVI:2, May 1954, 175–182; George J. Schuller, "The secular trend in income distribution by type, 1869–1948: A preliminary estimate," *Review of Economics and Statistics*, XXXV:4, November 1953, 302–324; Edward F. Denison, "Distribution of national income: Pattern of income shares since 1929," *Survey of Current Business*, 32:6, June 1952, 16–23; and E. H. Phelps Brown and P. E. Hart, "The share of wages in the national income," *Economic Journal*, LXII:246, June 1952, 253–277.

3 A similar conclusion is reached by Clark Kerr, "Trade Unionism and Distributive Shares," *American Economic Review*, Papers and Proceedings, 44 (May 1944), p. 289; Martin Bronfenbrenner, "The incidence of collective bargaining," *American Economic Review*, Papers and Proceedings, XLIV:2, May 1954, 307; William Fellner, *Trends and Cycles in Economic Activity: An Introduction to Problems of Economic Growth* (New York: Holt, 1956), p. 270; and George J. Stigler, *The Theory of Price* (rev. ed.; New York: Macmillan, 1952), p. 259.

4 Kerr, *op. cit.*, pp. 289–290.

5 Burkhead found that *before* corporate profits taxes, labor's share rose from 73.6 per cent of currently produced national income in 1929 to 76.2 per cent in 1950, a rise of 2.6 percentage points. *After* profits taxes, the gain was from 74.6 per cent to 82.3 per cent, or 7.7 percentage points. Net transfers in 1950 were $15.1 billion. Burkhead, *op. cit.*, pp. 203, 212–213.

6 Kerr, *op. cit.*, pp. 283–288, 291–292.

Was the New Deal a Social Revolution? DOUGLASS C. NORTH

1 E. C. Brown, "Fiscal Policy in the 'Thirties: A Reappraisal," *American Economic Review*, XLVI, No. 6 (December, 1956).

2 Labor's share of national income appears to have been increasing since about 1910, long before trade unions had any appreciable effect on the economy. A partial explanation is in the shift out of agriculture (self-employed entrepreneurial income) into wage status; but this is not a complete explanation. See Irving B. Kravis, "Relative Income Shares in Fact and Theory," *AER*, XLIX, No. 5 (Dec. 1959), 917–49.

3 The impact of trade unions upon wages has been the subject of extensive inquiry. A recent study by H. G. Lewis (*Unionism and Relative Wages in the United States: An Empirical Enquiry*. Chicago: Chicago Univ., 1963) summarizes previous studies along with the author's own investigations. The result is an indispensable study for those who wish enlightenment on this controversial issue.

Partial Planning for Business Under the New Deal, ELLIS W. HAWLEY

1 Paul T. Homan, in *Political Science Quarterly*, June 1936, pp. 169–72, 178–84; and in AEA, *Readings in the Social Control of Industry* (Philadelphia: Blakiston, 1942), 252–54; Merle Fainsod and Lincoln Gordon, *Government and the American Economy* (N.Y.: Norton, 1948), 621–54; Waldo E. Fisher and Charles M. James, *Minimum Price Fixing in the Bituminous Coal Industry* (Princeton: Princeton U. Press, 1955), 309–313.

2 Dwight E. Robinson, *Collective Bargaining and Market Control in the New York Coat and Suit Industry* (N.Y.: Columbia U. Press, 1949), 165–68; Constant Southworth, in *Plan Age*, Sept. 1937, pp. 180–87; *Newsweek*, Jan. 31, 1938, pp. 32, 34.

3 John H. Gray and Jack Levin, *The Valuation and Regulation of Public Utilities* (N.Y.: Harper, 1933), 1–5; Martin G. Glaeser, *Public Utilities in American Capitalism* (N.Y.: Macmillan, 1957), 8, 218–19, 414–16; Ford P. Hall, *The Concept of a Business Affected with a Public Interest* (Bloomington: Principia, 1940), 146–54; David Lynch, *The Concentration of Economic Power* (N.Y.: Columbia U. Press, 1946), 168–69; Horace M. Gray, in AEA, *Readings in the Social Control of Industry* (Philadelphia: Blakiston, 1942), 282–98; Ralph L. Dewey, in *AER*, March 1941, pp. 16–19; NRPB, *Transportation and National Policy* (1942), 10–11, 202–16, 355–56.

4 Thor Hultgren, *American Transportation in Prosperity and Depression* (N.Y.: National Bureau of Economic Research, 1948), 9–13; Harold G. Moulton et al., *The American Transportation Problem* (Washington: Brookings, 1933), 49–66, 87–90, 97–98, 173–77, 283–84, 289–91, 301, 471, 660–66, 714; NRPB, *Transportation*, 33–40; William N. Leonard, *Railroad Consolidation under the Transportation Act of 1920* (N.Y.: Columbia U. Press, 1946), 57–64; ICC, *Annual Report* (1930), 147; (1934), 99; and *Coordination of Motor Transportation* (1932), 4–5, 10–18; Ralph Sucher, in *Current History*, Dec. 1935, pp. 254–55; Julius H. Parmalee, in *Annals Am. Acad.*, Jan. 1934, pp. 155–58; *Fortune*, Aug. 1939, pp. 50–51.

5 Moulton et al., *Transportation Problem*, 56, 67–68, 377–78, 882–95; Earl Latham, *The Politics of Railroad Coordination, 1933–36* (Cambridge: Harvard U. Press, 1959), 8–15, 33–34; Arne C. Wiprud, *Justice in Transportation* (N.Y.: Ziff-Davis, 1945), 12–13, 48–56, 76–87; *Harvard Law Review*, Nov. 1933, pp. 18–20; NRPB, *Transportation*, 29–31; *Business Week*, Feb. 22, 1933, pp. 6–7; *New York Times*, Jan. 16, March 30, Nov. 16, 19, Dec. 2, 18, 1932, Jan. 10, 1933.

6 Donald V. Harper, *Economic Regulation of the Motor Trucking Industry by the States* (Urbana: U. of Ill. Press, 1959), 21–22, 27–31, 33–40; William J. Hudson and James A. Constantin, *Motor Transportation* (N.Y.: Ronald, 1958), 462–76; Moulton et al., *Transportation Problem*, 521–22; Latham, *Railroad Coordination*, 218–21, 226–31; ICC, *Coordination of Motor Transportation*, 2, 97–98, 102–3, 115–19; Senate Commerce Committee, *To Amend the Interstate Commerce Act* (74 Cong., 1 Sess., 1935), 1–37, 44–45, 97, 147–65, 241–43, 255–58, 263, 265, 271, 305–7, 403, 417–18, 433–35, 471, 484–506; *Congressional Record*, 74 Cong., 1 Sess., LXXIX, 1420, 5650–55,·5737; Federal Coordinator of Transportation, *Report* (House Doc. 89, 74 Cong., 1 Sess.), 14–18, 59–62; James C. Nelson, in *Journal of Political Economy*, Aug. 1936, pp. 464–70; Meyer H. Fishbein, in *Social Forces*, Dec. 1955, pp. 171–78; *Business Week*, March 17, 1934, p. 24; Aug. 10, 1935, pp. 11–12; C. H. Becker and D. H. O'Connell, "NRA Code History 287" (Trucking), 7, 100–110, CHF, NRA Records.

7 *Congressional Record*, 74 Cong., 1 Sess., LXXIX, 11813, 12196–12200, 12204–34, 1279, 12863; 49 *U.S. Statutes* 543, Public, No. 255, 74 Cong.; House Commerce Committee, *Amending Motor Carrier Act* (75 Cong., 3 Sess., 1938), 27–29; ICC, *Annual Report* (1936), 72–74, 82, 88; (1938), 83; Wiprud, *Justice in Transportation*, 32–37, 60; Hudson and Constantin, *Motor Transportation*, 466, 476–78; Ernest W. Williams, Jr., *The Regulation of Rail-Motor Rate Competition* (N.Y.: Harper, 1958), 205–6, 209–12, 220–23; NRPB, *Transportation*, 110–14, 217–30; Nelson, in *Journal of Political Economy*, Aug. 1936, pp. 470–94.

8 Charles Eliot, Memo. re Conference with Secretary of Agriculture, Feb. 15, 1937, Industrial Section File — CCF, NRPB Records; Henry A. Wallace, *Technology, Corporations, and the General Welfare* (Chapel Hill: U. of N.C. Press, 1937), 44–49.

9 See Paul T. Homan, in AEA, *Readings in the Social Control of Industry* (Philadelphia: Blakiston, 1942), 242–46, 252–54; and in *Political Science Quarterly*, June 1936, pp. 169–72, 178–84; Berle, in *Virginia Quarterly Review*, Summer 1938, pp. 330–31; Ernest Griffith, *Impasse of Democracy* (N.Y.: Harrison-Hilton, 1939), 231.

10 Homan, in *Political Science Quarterly*, June 1936, p. 181.

An Attempt to Revolutionize the American System of Life,
HERBERT C. HOOVER

1 H. G. Wells, one-half Socialist, one-half Communist, long an agitator of mass movements, visited Roosevelt several times at the White House. His summation *(Experiment in Autobiography*, pp. 681–682) is at least enlightening: "I do not say that the President has these revolutionary ideas in so elaborated and comprehensive a form as they have come to me; I do not think he has. I do not think he is consciously what I have called an Open Conspirator . . . But these ideas are sitting all around him now, and unless I misjudge him, they will presently possess him altogether. . . . My impression of both him and of Mrs. Roosevelt is that they are *unlimited* people . . . But as the vast problems about

them expose and play themselves into their minds, the goal of the Open Conspiracy becomes plainer ahead. Franklin Roosevelt does not embody and represent that goal, but he represents the way thither. He is being the most effective transmitting instrument possible for the coming of the new world order. . . . He is continuously revolutionary in the new way . . ."

2 The historian, Charles A. Beard, wrote a book bitterly exposing the difference between appearances and realities in Roosevelt's foreign policies during the year 1941. Although a disappointed isolationist, and thus inspired in pointing out these enormous divergencies, Beard had been a New Dealer and had published a series of books eulogizing the New Deal without a single remark on the same extraordinary divergence in appearance and reality — and with much misrepresentation of its opponents.

3 Rexford G. Tugwell and Howard C. Hill, *Our Economic Society and Its Problems.* (Harcourt, Brace & Co., New York, 1934). Italics mine.

4 *American Economic Review*, March, 1932.

5 *The Public Papers and Addresses of Franklin D. Roosevelt*, 1937 volume, p. 373.

The Third American Revolution, CARL N. DEGLER

1 A complementary and highly suggestive way of viewing this trend away from laissez faire, of which the events of the 1930's are a culmination, is that taken in K. William Kapp, *The Social Costs of Private Enterprise* (Cambridge, Mass., 1950). Kapp observes that for a long time private enterprise had shifted the social costs of production — like industrially polluted water, industrial injuries, smoke nuisances and hazards, unemployment, and the like — onto society. The decline of laissez faire has, in this view, actually been a movement to compel industry to pay for those social costs of production which it has hitherto shirked.

2 On the day that the first AAA was declared unconstitutional, a Gallup poll revealed that, although the nation as a whole did not like the AAA, the farmers of the South and Midwest did. As a result, invalidation of the act by the Court did not mean the end of such a policy, but only the beginning of a search to find a new way of accomplishing the same end. Hence there were successive AAA's, whereas, when NRA was declared unconstitutional in 1935, it was dropped, primarily because neither business nor labor, for whose interests it had been organized, found much merit in its approach to their problems.

3 The extent of the intellectual change which the depression measures introduced can be appreciated by a quotation from President Hoover's veto in 1931 of a bill to develop a public power project in what was later to be the TVA area. "I am firmly opposed to the Government entering into any business the major purpose of which is competition with our citizens." Emergency measures of such a character might be tolerated, he said. "But for the Federal government deliberately to go out to build up and expand such an occasion to the major purpose of a power and manufacturing business is to break down the initiative and enterprise of the American people; it is destruction of equality of opportunity amongst our people; it is the negation of the ideals upon which our civilization has been based."

4 Characteristically enough, as his memoirs show, President Hoover had long been interested in both old-age and unemployment insurance, but always such schemes were to be worked out through private insurance companies, or at best with the states — never under the auspices of the federal government. "It required a great depression," he has written somewhat ruefully, "to awaken interest in the idea" of unemployment insurance.

5 It was the misfortune of Herbert Hoover to have been President at a time when his considerable administrative and intellectual gifts were hamstrung by his basic political philosophy, which, instead of being a guide to action, served as an obstacle. Much more of an old-fashioned liberal than a reactionary, and deeply attached to the Jeffersonian dogma of the limited powers of the federal government, Hoover was psychologically and philosophically unable to use the immense powers and resources of his office in attacking unemployment. Back in 1860–61, another President — James Buchanan — had been paralyzed

in the midst of a national crisis by his limited conception of the federal power, but in that instance his inaction was palliated by the fact that his successor was to take office within less than three months. Hoover, however, wrestled with the depression for three years. During that trying period he did a number of things to combat the depression, but he always stoutly held to his rigid intellectual position that federally supplied and administered relief would destroy the foundations of the nation. Never has an American President, including the two Adamses, defied overwhelming popular opinion for so long for the sake of his own ideals as Herbert Hoover did then; and never has a President since Buchanan fallen so quickly into obscurity as Hoover did after March 4, 1933.

6 The providing of work relief instead of the dole did more than fill hungry stomachs; it re-established faith in America and in one's fellow man. "I'm proud of our United States," said one relief recipient. "There ain't no other nation in the world that would have sense enough to think of WPA and all the other A's." The wife of one WPA worker was quoted as saying, "We aren't on relief any more — my man is working for the government."

7 In a postelection survey of the Negro vote, *The New York Times*, November 11, 1956, p. 60, reported that "the party of Lincoln still has a long way to go to regain the politico-racial domination that it held so firmly from post–Civil War days until Franklin D. Roosevelt smashed it twenty years ago." And since the Democratic party under Kennedy and Johnson has made common cause with the Negro, the allegiance of black voters to that party has been almost unanimous. In the election of 1964 some Negro districts voted over 90 per cent for Lyndon Johnson. Even in 1968 Hubert Humphrey won the great majority of Negro votes, North and South.

8 Even before the Wagner Act had won the support of the Supreme Court, Presidential "pressure" and prestige helped the C.I.O. attain some of its most telling victories, like that over General Motors in February of 1937. The sensational exposure of union-busting tactics of employers by Senator Robert La Follette's investigating committee, beginning in 1936, was still another form of governmental assistance to the cause of labor.

9 According to Harold Ickes, Roosevelt was profoundly struck by the adoration which was bestowed upon him by his admirers. During the 1936 campaign, the President told Ickes "that there was something terrible about the crowds that lined the streets along which he passed. He went on to explain what he meant, which was exclamations from individuals in the crowd, such as 'He saved my home,' 'He gave me a job,' 'God bless you, Mr. President,' etc." In May, 1936, Marquis Childs published an article in *Harper's*, entitled "They Hate Roosevelt," in which he described and tried to account for the unreasoning hatred for the President on the part of what Childs called the upper 2 per cent of the population.

10 It is significant that only once during the 1932 campaign, according to Ernest K. Lindley, did Roosevelt call for "a revolution"; and then he promptly qualified it to "the right kind, the only kind of revolution this nation can stand for — a revolution at the ballot box."

11 When an economist suggested to F.D.R. that the depression be permitted to run its course and that then the economic system would soon right itself — as Frances Perkins tells the story — the President's face took on a "gray look of horror" as he told the economist: "People aren't cattle you know!"

12 Social security is an excellent example of how, under the New Deal, reform measures, when they conflicted with recovery, were given priority. In siphoning millions of dollars of social security taxes from the purchasing power of the workers, social security was a deflationary measure, which must have seriously threatened the precariously based new economic recovery. For this reason and others, Abraham Epstein, the foremost authority in America on social security, denounced the act as a "sharing of poverty."

13 The proposition that the New Deal marked a sharp change in attitudes and practices has not been accepted by all historians, to say the least. . . . The two principal schools of criticism are worth setting forth here. On this subject orthodox and New Left historians seem to be in substantial agreement. Arthur Link in his *American Epoch* (New York, 1967), p. 433, sums up the orthodox argument: "The chief significance of the reform legislation of the 1930's was its essentially conservative character and the fact that it stem-

med from half a century or more of discussion and practical experience and from ideas proposed by Republicans as well as by Democrats."

The New Left criticism is vigorously set forth in Barton Bernstein, "The New Deal: The Conservative Achievements of Liberal Reform," in his collection of essays, *Towards a New Past: Dissenting Essays in American History* (New York, 1968), pp. 264–65: "The New Deal failed to solve the problem of depression, it failed to raise the impoverished, it failed to redistribute income, it failed to extend equality and generally countenanced racial discrimination and segregation. It failed generally to make business more responsible to the social welfare or to threaten business's pre-eminent political power. In this sense, the New Deal, despite the shifts in tone and spirit from the earlier decade, was profoundly conservative and continuous with the 1920's."

My reasons for disagreeing with the orthodox view have already been set down above. My disagreement with the New Left historians is a little different. They have set forth a measure of radical change that *no* movement in United States history can fulfill. Such a "consensus" approach to American history may be useful in comparing the United States with other societies, but it ignores the important and noticeable shifts in outlook and practice within the United States that the historian must recognize if he is to avoid making the American past nothing more than a stately, homogenized progression form the seventeenth century to the present. It is in that sense that I speak of the New Deal as a revolution. Certainly the men of the 1930's and 1940's thought an important change in outlook and approach of government toward society was taking place. The historian cannot rely only upon his own criteria for measuring change; he must be sensitive to what contemporaries thought was happening as well.

The Roosevelt Reconstruction: Retrospect, WILLIAM E. LEUCHTENBERG

1 F.D.R. to E. M. House, March 10, 1934, House MSS.

2 Tugwell, "Notes from a New Deal Diary," April 21, 1933. Cf. Aline Chalufour and Suzanne Desternes, "Deux théoriciens de la crise américaine," *Revue des Sciences Politiques*, LVII (1934), 221–235.

3 Douglas to F.D.R., December 30, 1933, FDRL PSF 28; Arthur Schlesinger, Jr., *The Politics of Upheaval* (Boston, 1960), p. 212.

4 F.D.R. to Edward House, April 5, 1933, House MSS.; Blum, *Morgenthau Diaries*, pp. 248–249.

5 Robert Martin, "The Referendum Process in the Agricultural Adjustment Programs of the United States," *Agricultural History*, XXV (1951), 34–47; Ralph Bunche, "The Negro in the Political Life of the United States," *Journal of Negro Education*, X (1941), 577. For another phase of agrarian democracy, see H. C. M. Case, "Farm Debt Adjustment During the Early 1930's," *Agricultural History*, XXXIV (1960), 173–181.

6 *Literary Digest*, CXVII (April 7, 1934), 21; Elizabeth Green, "Indian Minorities under the American New Deal," *Pacific Affairs*, VIII (1935), 420–427; Oliver La Farge, *As Long as the Grass Shall Grow* (New York, 1940), p. 96.

7 Lilienthal, *TVA: Democracy on the March* (New York, 1944); *Congressional Record*, 76th Cong., 3d Sess., p. A4199; Henry Wallace, *New Frontiers* (New York, 1934), p. 200.

8 Grant McConnell, *The Decline of Agrarian Democracy* (Berkeley and Los Angeles, 1953), pp. 72–83; James West, *Plainville, U.S.A.* (New York, 1961), p. 217. In Texas, county agents were instructed that the county AAA committees were to be composed of a banker, a businessman, and a farmer. Henry I. Richards, *Cotton under the Agricultural Adjustment Act* (Washington, 1934), pp. 18–19.

9 *Nature Magazine*, XXXI (1938), 46; Roy Robbins, *Our Landed Heritage* (Princeton, 1942), pp. 421–422; Wesley Calef, *Private Grazing and Public Lands* (Chicago, 1960), pp. 52–77. Cf. Phillip O. Foss, *Politics and Grass* (Seattle, 1960), p. 69. While some conservationists thought of the Taylor Act as a way to save the cattle lands from overgrazing, many stockmen viewed the measure as a way to stabilize their industry by curbing overproduction, a view of "conservation" similar to that held by the oilmen.

[10] Philip Selznick, *TVA and the Grass Roots* (Berkeley and Los Angeles, 1953). Cf. Norman Wengert, *Valley of Tomorrow* (Knoxville, 1952). The TVA even opposed or ignored the programs of New Deal farm agencies — notably the Farm Security Administration and the Soil Conservation Service — that had no such commitments.

[11] R. G. Tugwell and E. C. Banfield, "Grass Roots Democracy — Myth or Reality?" *Public Administration Review*, X (1950), 47–55.

[12] Murray Edelman, "New Deal Sensitivity to Labor Interests," in Milton Derber and Edwin Young (eds.), *Labor and the New Deal* (Madison, Wis., 1957), p. 180; Jonathan Mitchell, "Mr. Roosevelt on Stilts," *New Republic*, LXXVII (1933), 69.

[13] Lippmann, *Good Society*, p. 10; Griswold, *Farming and Democracy* (New York, 1948), pp. 156–157; E. Pendleton Herring, "Second Session of the Seventy-third Congress, January 3, 1934, to June 18, 1934," *American Political Science Review*, XXVIII (1934), 866.

[14] Edelman, "New Deal Sensitivity," p. 167. See Fred Greenbaum, "A 'New Deal' for the United Mine Workers of America," *Social Science*, XXXIII (1958), 154–155; Sidney Fine, "The N.I.R.A. and the Automobile Industry," *Michigan Alumnus Quarterly Review*, LXVI (1960), 249–259.

[15] Persia Campbell, *Consumer Representation in the New Deal* (New York, 1940). When the pure food and drugs bill, first introduced in 1933, was finally passed as the Wheeler-Lea Act of 1938, it was a toothless crone.

[16] Max Lerner, *Ideas for the Ice Age* (New York, 1941), p. 379; Earl Latham, *The Politics of Railroad Coordination, 1933–1936* (Cambridge, 1939); Arthur R. Burns, *The Decline of Competition* (New York, 1936), p. 519.

[17] "Unofficial Observer [John Franklin Carter]," *The New Dealers* (New York, 1934), p. 25. The "broker state" conception of the New Deal is most lucidly developed in John Chamberlain, *The American Stakes* (Philadelphia, 1940), and Burns, *Roosevelt*, pp. 183–202.

[18] Irving Bernstein, *The New Deal Collective Bargaining Policy* (Berkeley and Los Angeles, 1950), p. 101.

[19] *Public Papers*, III, 436. Tugwell recalls that Roosevelt, incensed by the draft he had read of the speech of introduction at the bankers' convention, exploded: "Imagine referring to a representative of the American Bankers Association and the President of the United States as equals! And imagine what national policy would be like if, instead of requiring such groups to conform to the public interest, they were free to bargain about what they would or would not consent or accept. Outrageous!" Tugwell, *Roosevelt*, p. 381.

[20] The Editors of the Economist, *The New Deal* (New York, 1937), p. 149; Representative Robert Luce to Herbert Claiborne Pell, November 14, 1934, Pell MSS., Box 7; Elliott Roosevelt (ed.), *F.D.R.: His Personal Letters, 1928–1945* (2 vols., New York, 1950), I, 723.

[21] Clinton Rossiter, *The American Presidency* (Signet edition, New York, 1956), p. 114.

[22] Felix Frankfurter, "The Young Men Go to Washington," *Fortune*, XIII (1936), 61; E. W. Bakke, *Citizens Without Work* (New Haven, 1940), pp. 52–53.

[23] Richard Neuberger, "They Love Roosevelt," *Forum and Century*, CI (1939), 15; Corwin, *The President*, p. 471; William O. Douglas, *Being an American* (New York, 1948), p. 88.

[24] Josephine Chapin Brown, *Public Relief 1929–1939* (New York, 1940), p. ix; Thomas Paul Jenkin, *Reactions of Major Groups to Positive Government in the United States, 1930–1940* (University of California Publications in Political Science [Berkeley and Los Angeles, 1945]), p. 284.

[25] *Public Papers*, V, 235; J. F. T. O'Connor MS. Diary, June 25, 1933.

[26] Paul Carter has noted the change in the social gospel. The editors of *The Baptist*, he has written, "recognized that the transfer of social privilege involves the use of social coercion, a fact which the Right and Center of the old Social Gospel had not always faced up to." Carter, "The Decline and Revival of the Social Gospel," (unpublished Ph.D. dissertation, Columbia University, 1954).

[27] On the compulsory Potato Act, only six Republicans (and just nine Democrats) voted in opposition.

[28] Wickard *v.* Filburn, 317 U.S. 111 (1942).

[29] Sidney Hyman, *The American President* (New York, 1954), pp. 263–264; Carl Degler,

Out of Our Past (New York, 1959), pp. 391–393. In a few pages, Degler has written the best analysis of the permanent significance of the New Deal.

30 Henry Kariel, *The Decline of American Pluralism* (Stanford, 1961).

31 Henry Wallace, *The Christian Bases of World Order* (New York, 1943), p. 17; Dorothy Dunbar Bromley, "The Future of Eleanor Roosevelt," *Harper's,* CLXXX (1939), 136.

32 *Public Papers,* IX, 545.

New Deal Thought, HOWARD ZINN

1 Moley and Tugwell both insist that the proper name is "brains trust" as originally used by James Kieran, a *New York Times* reporter, although the term became popular as "brain trust."

2 In *The Affluent Society* (Boston: Houghton Mifflin Company, 1958), John Kenneth Galbraith has pointed eloquently to the American economy's emphasis on private rather than public needs. Michael Harrington's *The Other America* (New York: The Macmillan Company, 1963), and Leon Keyserling's *Poverty and Deprivation in the United States* (Washington, D.C.: Conference on Economic Progress, 1962) testify to continuing large blocs of poverty thirty years after the New Deal.

3 David Bazelon, in *The Paper Economy* (New York: Random House, Inc., 1963), and Robert Theobald, in *Free Men and Free Markets* (New York: C. N. Potter, 1963), give trenchant critiques of the American economy in the 1960's.

4 A representative statement is Arthur M. Schlesinger, Jr.'s, in *The Politics of Upheaval* (Boston: Houghton Mifflin Company, 1960), p. 649. "For Roosevelt, the technique of liberal government was pragmatic. . . . Nothing attracted Roosevelt less than rigid intellectual systems."

5 Richard Hofstadter, *The Age of Reform* (New York: Alfred A. Knopf, Inc., 1955), p. 317.

6 Thurman Arnold, *The Symbols of Government* (New Haven: Yale University Press, 1935), pp. 270–271.

7 A notable exception is William E. Leuchtenburg, *Franklin D. Roosevelt and the New Deal* (New York: Harper & Row, 1963), pp. 344–346.

8 *The Symbols of Government,* pp. 16, 110–111, 120. Hofstadter, in *The Age of Reform,* p. 318, analyzes the words that recur frequently in Arnold's books to show his movement away from the Progressivist moralism. Yet even to make this point he finds he must include the word "humanitarian" because it appears so frequently.

9 *The Symbols of Government,* pp. 259–260. Arnold was so reluctant to admit he possessed a set of values that Sidney Hook, reviewing *The Folklore of Capitalism,* took him at his word (or rather at his emphasized words), and described him as one who believed "all standards and ideals are nonsense." *University of Chicago Law Review,* V (April 1938), 341–357.

10 Harry Hopkins, "The Future of Relief," *The New Republic,* XC (1937), 8.

11 James MacGregor Burns, *Roosevelt: The Lion and the Fox* (New York: Harcourt, Brace & World, 1956), p. 376.

12 "Rooseveltian Liberalism," *The Nation,* CXXXVI (June 21, 1933), 702–703.

13 Gabriel Kolko, in *The Triumph of Conservatism* (New York: Free Press, 1963), pp. 302–304, advances his theory of "political capitalism," and distinguishes between "the rhetoric of reform" and its "structural results," and argues that what we call "reform" is really the use by capitalists of "a centralized state power to meet problems they could not solve themselves."

14 Quoted in Joseph Ratner, (ed.), *Intelligence in the Modern World* (New York: Random House, Inc., 1939), p. 100.

15 Reprinted in *Liberalism and Social Action* (New York: Capricorn Books, 1963), p. 54.

16 *Ibid.,* p. 62.

17 *Ibid.,* p. 88.

18 Schlesinger, *The Politics of Upheaval,* pp. 176, 647.

19 "The Myth of the Marxian Dialectic," *Partisan Review*, VI (1939), 66–81.

20 *Reflections on the End of an Era*, quoted in Schlesinger, p. 158.

21 "The Age of Distribution," *The Nation*, CXXXIX (July 25, 1934), 93–96.

22 "The Future of Liberalism," *The Journal of Philosophy*, XXII, No. 9 (1935), 230–247.

23 He won easily in the primary over liberal George Creel, but then, lacking FDR's support, lost to an anti–New Dealer.

24 Upton Sinclair, *The Way Out* (New York: Farrar & Rinehart, 1933), p. 57.

25 Robert MacIver, "Social Philosophy," in *Social Change and the New Deal*, ed. William F. Ogburn (Chicago: The University of Chicago Press, 1934), pp. 107–113.

26 For example, William Z. Foster, for the Communists; Norman Thomas, for the Socialists; and I. F. Stone, as an independent radical.

27 Russell Leffingwell, of J. P. Morgan and Company; Edward Filene, of the Boston mercantile family; Richard Whitney, president of the New York Stock Exchange; and many others.

28 Rexford Guy Tugwell, "The Principle of Planning and the Institution of Laissez-Faire," *American Economic Review*, XXII, Supplement (March 1932), 75–92.

29 Raymond Moley, *After Seven Years* (New York: Harper & Brothers, 1939), pp. 370–371.

30 David Lilienthal, *T.V.A.: Democracy on the March* (New York: Pocket Books, 1944), Chapter 18, "Planning and Planners," pp. 206–213.

31 William O. Douglas, "Protecting the Investor," *The Yale Review*, XXIII (Spring 1934), 521–533.

32 Leuchtenberg, *Franklin D. Roosevelt and the New Deal*, p. 259.

33 Burns, *Roosevelt: The Lion and the Fox*, p. 322.

34 In late 1937, Secretary of the Treasury Henry Morgenthau, Jr., speaking to the American Academy of Political Science, said the 1933 emergency was over; now the budget could be balanced. He suggested cuts in public works, unemployment relief, and farm benefits.

35 Max Lerner, "Propaganda's Golden Age," *The Nation*, CXLIX (November 11, 1939), 523–524.

36 Abraham Epstein, " 'Social Security' Under the New Deal," *The Nation*, CXLI (September 4, 1935), 261–263.

37 Congressman Henry Ellenbogen, of Pennsylvania, *Congressional Record*, August 19, 1935, pp. 13675–13677.

38 Henry E. Sigerist, "Socialized Medicine," *The Yale Review*, XXVII (Spring 1938), 463–481.

The Conservative Achievements of Liberal Reform, BARTON J. BERNSTEIN

1 The outstanding examples are Arthur Schlesinger, Jr., Frank Freidel, Carl Degler, and William Leuchtenburg. Schlesinger, in *The Crisis of the Old Order* (Boston, 1957), emphasized the presence of reform in the twenties but criticized the federal government for its retreat from liberalism and condemned Hoover for his responses to the depression. The next two volumes of his *The Age of Roosevelt*, *The Coming of the New Deal* (Boston, 1958) and *The Politics of Upheaval* (Boston, 1960), praise the New Deal, but also contain information for a more critical appraisal. His research is quite wide and has often guided my own investigations. For his theory that the New Deal was likely even without the depression, see "Sources of the New Deal: Reflections on the Temper of a Time," *Columbia University Forum*, II (Fall 1959), 4–11. Freidel affirmed that the New Deal was a watershed (*American Historical Review*, October 1965, p. 329), but in *The New Deal in Historical Perspective* (Washington, 1959), he has suggested the conservatism of the New Deal as a reform movement. Degler, in *Out of Our Past* (New York, 1959), pp. 379–416, extolled the New Deal as a "Third American Revolution." But also see his "The Ordeal of Herbert Hoover," *Yale Review*, LII (Summer 1963), 565–83. Leuchtenburg, *Franklin D. Roosevelt and the New Deal, 1932–1940* (New York, 1963), offers considerable criticism of

the New Deal, but finds far more to praise in this "half-way revolution." He cites Degler approvingly but moderates Degler's judgment (pp. 336–47). The book represents years of research and has often guided my own investigations.

2 Eric Goldman, *Rendezvous with Destiny* (New York, 1952); Henry Steele Commager, "Twelve Years of Roosevelt," *American Mercury*, LX (April 1945), 391–401; Arthur Link, *American Epoch* (New York, 1955), pp. 377–440. In his essay on "Franklin D. Roosevelt: the Patrician as Opportunist" in *The American Political Tradition* (New York, 1948), pp. 315–52, Richard Hofstadter was critical of the New Deal's lack of ideology but treated it as a part of the larger reform tradition. In *The Age of Reform* (New York, 1955), however, while chiding the New Deal for opportunism, he emphasized the discontinuity of the New Deal with the reform tradition of Populism and Progressivism.

3 Edgar E. Robinson, *The Roosevelt Leadership, 1933–1945* (Philadelphia, 1955), the work of a conservative constitutionalist, does accuse the administration of having objectives approaching the leveling aims of communism (p. 376).

4 Louis Hacker, *American Problems of Today* (New York, 1938).

5 William Appleman Williams, *The Contours of American History* (Chicago, 1966), pp. 372–488; and his review, "Schlesinger: Right Crisis — Wrong Order," *Nation*, CLXXXIV (March 23, 1957), 257–60. Williams' volume has influenced my own thought.

6 Ronald Radosh, "The Corporate Ideology of American Labor Leaders from Gompers to Hillman," *Studies on the Left*, VI (November–December 1966), 66–88.

7 Arthur Link, "What Happened to the Progressive Movement?" *American Historical Review*, LXIV (July 1959), 833–51.

8 James Prothro, *The Dollar Decade* (Baton Rouge, La., 1954).

9 Louis Galambos, *Competition and Cooperation* (Baltimore, 1966), pp. 55–139; Link, "What Happened to the Progressive Movement?"

10 Joseph Brandes, *Herbert Hoover and Economic Diplomacy* (Pittsburgh, 1962); Hofstadter, *American Political Tradition*, pp. 283–99.

11 William S. Myers, ed., *The State Papers and Other Writings of Herbert Hoover* (New York, 1934), I, 84–88 (easier money), 137, 411, 431–33; II, 202 (public works); I, 142–43, 178–79 (lower taxes). The Commodity Stabilization Corporation was created before the crash.

12 Lippmann, "The Permanent New Deal," *Yale Review*, XXIV (June 1935), 651.

13 Myers, ed., *State Papers*, II, 195–201, 214–15, 224–26, 228–33 (on the budget); II, 405, 496–99, 503–5 (on relief).

14 Gerald Nash, "Herbert Hoover and the Origins of the Reconstruction Finance Corporation," *Mississippi Valley Historical Review*, XLVI (December 1959), 455–68.

15 W. S. Myers and W. H. Newton, eds., *The Hoover Administration: A Documentary History* (New York, 1936), p. 119; "Proceedings of a Conference of Progressives," March 11–12, 1931, Hillman Papers, Amalgamated Clothing Workers (New York).

16 *Contours of American History*, p. 428.

17 Lippmann, "The Permanent New Deal," p. 651.

18 For an excellent statement of this thesis, see Howard Zinn's introduction to his *New Deal Thought* (New York, 1966), pp. xv–xxxvi. So far historians have not adequately explored the thesis that F.D.R. frequently acted as a restraining force on his own government, and that bolder reforms were often thwarted by him and his intimates.

19 Bronson Cutting, "Is Private Banking Doomed?" *Liberty*, XI (March 31, 1934), 10; cf. Raymond Moley, *The First New Deal* (New York, 1966), pp. 177–80.

20 Moley, *After Seven Years* (New York, 1939), p. 155; Arthur Ballantine, "When All the Banks Closed," *Harvard Business Review*, XXVI (March 1948), 129–43.

21 William Lemke, later quoted in Lorena Hickok to Harry Hopkins, November 23, 1933, Hopkins Papers, Franklin D. Roosevelt Library (hereafter called FDRL).

22 Baruch to Samuel Gompers, April 19, 1924, Baruch Papers, Princeton University; Schlesinger, *Coming of the New Deal*, pp. 88–89; Gerald Nash, "Experiments in Industrial Mobilization: WIB and NRA," *Mid-America*, XLV (July 1963), 156–75.

23 Gerard Swope, *The Swope Plan* (New York, 1931); Julius H. Barnes, "Government and Business," *Harvard Business Review*, X (July 1932), 411–19; Harriman, "The Stabilization of Business and Employment," *American Economic Review*, XXII (March 1932), 63–75;

House Committee on Education and Labor, 73rd Cong., 1st Sess., *Thirty-Hour Week Bill, Hearings,* pp. 198–99.

24 *Ibid.,* pp. 884–97; Hillman, "Labor Leads Toward Planning," *Survey Graphic,* LXVI (March 1932), 586–88.

25 Irving Bernstein, *The New Deal Collective Bargaining Policy* (Berkeley, Cal., 1950), pp. 57–63.

26 Quotes from Hofstadter, *American Political Tradition,* p. 336. "It is not the function of NRA to organize . . . labor," asserted General Hugh Johnson. "Automobile Code Provides for Thirty-Five Hour Week," *Iron Age,* CXXXII (August 3, 1933), 380.

27 Richard C. Wilcock, "Industrial Management's Policy Toward Unionism," in Milton Derber and Edwin Young, eds., *Labor and the New Deal* (Madison, Wis., 1957), pp. 278–95.

28 Leverett Lyon *et al., The National Recovery Administration* (Washington, 1935).

29 The characterization of Berle, Tugwell, and Moley is from Schlesinger, *Coming of the New Deal,* pp. 181–84, and Johnson's address at the NAM is from NRA press release 2126, December 7, 1933, NRA Records, RG 9, National Archives.

30 "Concert of interests" was used by F.D.R. in a speech of April 18, 1932, in Samuel Rosenman, ed., *The Public Papers and Addresses of Franklin D. Roosevelt* (13 vols.; New York, 1938–52), I, 627–39. (Hereafter referred to as *FDR Papers.*)

31 M. S. Venkataramani, "Norman Thomas, Arkansas Sharecroppers, and the Roosevelt Agricultural Policies," *Mississippi Valley Historical Review,* XLVII (September 1960), 225–46; John Hutson, Columbia Oral History Memoir, pp. 114 ff.; Mordecai Ezekiel, Columbia Oral History Memoir, pp. 74 ff.

32 Quoted from Leuchtenburg, *F.D.R.,* p. 87, and this discussion draws upon pp. 87–90; John Chamberlain, *The American Stakes* (Philadelphia, 1940): James MacGregor Burns, *Roosevelt: The Lion and the Fox* (New York, 1956), pp. 183–202.

33 Quoted from House Committee on Education and Labor, 74th Cong., 1st Sess., *National Labor Relations Board Hearings,* p. 35.

34 For a warning, see Paul Douglas, "Rooseveltian Liberalism," *Nation,* CXXXVI (June 21, 1933), 702–3.

35 Leuchtenburg, *F.D.R.,* p. 88, uses the image of "a parallelogram of pressures."

36 For example see the Columbia Oral Histories of Louis Bean, Hutson, and Ezekiel.

37 *New York Times,* January 30, 1934; House Interstate and Foreign Commerce Committee, 73rd Cong., 2nd Sess., House Report No. 1383, *Securities Exchange Bill of 1934,* p. 3; "SEC," *Fortune,* XXI (June 1940), 91–92, 120 ff.; Ralph DeBedts, *The New Deal's SEC* (New York, 1964), pp. 56–85.

38 Frederick Rudolph, "The American Liberty League, 1934–1940," *American Historical Review,* LVI (October 1950), 19–33; George Wolfskill, *The Revolt of the Conservatives* (Boston, 1962). Emphasizing the Liberty League and focusing upon the rhetoric of business disaffection, historians have often exaggerated the opposition of the business communities. See the correspondence of James Forrestal, PPF 6367, FDRL, and at Princeton; of Russell Leffingwell, PPF 886, FDRL; of Donald Nelson, PPF 8615, FDRL, and at the Huntington Library; and of Thomas Watson, PPF 2489, FDRL. On the steel industry, see *Iron Age,* CXXXV (June 13, 1935), 44. For very early evidence of estrangement, however, see Edgar Mowrer to Frank Knox, November 8, 1933, Knox Papers, Library of Congress.

39 Quoted from Donald McCoy, *Angry Voices: Left of Center Politics in the New Deal Era* (Lawrence, Kan., 1958), p. 55, from *Farmer-Labor Leader,* March 30, 1934.

40 Long, *My First Days in the White House* (Harrisburg, Pa., 1935).

41 Quoted from Sinclair, *The Way Out* (New York, 1933), p. 57. See Sinclair to Roosevelt, October 5 and 18, 1934, OF 1165, FDRL.

42 Nicholas Roosevelt, *The Townsend Plan* (Garden City, N.Y., 1935). Not understanding that the expenditures would increase consumption and probably spur production, critics emphasized that the top 9 percent would have received 50 percent of the income, but they neglected that the top income-tenth had received (before taxes) nearly 40 percent of the national income in 1929. National Industrial Conference Board, *Studies in Enterprise and Social Progress* (New York, 1939), p. 125.

43 Sevareid, *Not So Wild a Dream* (New York, 1946), p. 58.

44 Sidney Lens, *Left, Right and Center* (Hinsdale, Ill., 1949), pp. 280–89.

45 Quoted in Robert Sherwood, *Roosevelt and Hopkins*, rev. ed. (New York, 1950), p. 65.

46 Roosevelt's press conference of June 15, 1934, *FDR Papers*, III, 301; cf., Roosevelt to John L. Lewis, February 25, 1939, Philip Murray Papers, Catholic University.

47 Burns, *The Lion and the Fox*, pp. 217–19; quotation from p. 218.

48 Perkins, Columbia Oral History Memoir, VII, 138, 147, quoted by Leuchtenburg, *F.D.R.*, p. 151.

49 Irving Bernstein, *The New Deal Collective Bargaining Policy*, pp. 100–8; Burns, *The Lion and the Fox*, p. 219.

50 Margaret Grant, *Old Age Security* (Washington, 1939), p. 217. Under social security, payments at sixty-five ranged from $10 a month to $85 a month, depending on earlier earnings.

51 Roosevelt's message to Congress on June 19, 1935, *FDR Papers*, IV, 271.

52 *New York Times*, June 20 and 21, 1935; *Business Week*, June 22, 1935, p. 5.

53 John Morton Blum, *From the Morgenthau Diaries: Years of Crisis, 1928–1938* (Boston, 1959), pp. 302–4.

54 Simon Kuznets, *Shares of Upper Income Groups in Income and Savings*, National Bureau of Economic Research, Occasional Paper 35 (New York, 1950), pp. 32–40.

55 Otis L. Graham, Jr., "Historians and the New Deals: 1944–1960," *Social Studies*, LIV (April 1963), 133–40.

56 *New York Times*, November 19, 1933; May 1, September 30, November 17, December 23, 1934; May 1, 3, 5, 28, 1935; "Chamber to Vote on NIRA," *Nation's Business*, XXII (December 1934), 51; "Business Wants a New NRA," *ibid.*, XXIII (February 1935), 60; "Listening in as Business Speaks," *ibid.*, XXIII (June 1935), 18, 20; William Wilson, "How the Chamber of Commerce Viewed the NRA," *Mid-America*, XLIII (January 1962), 95–108.

57 *New York Times*, May 3, 4, 12, 1935. On the steel industry see L. W. Moffet, "This Week in Washington," *Iron Age*, CXXXV (March 21, 1935), 41; *ibid.* (April 18, 1935), 49; "NRA Future Not Settled by Senate Committee's Action for Extension," *ibid.* (May 9, 1935), 58.

58 Ellis W. Hawley, *The New Deal and the Problem of Monopoly* (Princeton, 1966), pp. 205–86.

59 Freidel, *The New Deal*, pp. 18–19. On Arnold's efforts, see Wendell Berge Diary, 1938–1939, Berge Papers, Library of Congress; and Gene Gressley, "Thurman Arnold, Antitrust, and the New Deal," *Business History Review*, XXXVIII (Summer 1964), 214–31. For characteristic Roosevelt rhetoric emphasizing the effort of his government to subdue "the forces of selfishness and of lust for power," see his campaign address of October 31, 1936, his press conference of January 4, 1938, and his message of April 29, 1938, in *FDR Papers*, V, 568–69 and VII, 11, 305–32.

60 Dewey, *Liberalism and Social Action* (New York, 1935), p. 62.

61 Howard Zinn, in *New Deal Thought*, pp. xxvi–xxxi, discusses this subject and has influenced my thought. Also consider those whom Zinn cites: Edmund Wilson, "The Myth of Marxist Dialectic," *Partisan Review*, VI (Fall 1938), 66–81; William Ernest Hocking, "The Future of Liberalism," *The Journal of Philosophy*, XXXII (April 25, 1935), 230–47; Stuart Chase, "Eating Without Working: A Moral Disquisition," *Nation*, CXXXVII (July 22, 1933), 93–94.

62 See James T. Patterson, "A Conservative Coalition Forms in Congress, 1933–1939," *Journal of American History*, LII (March 1966), 757–72.

63 Hofstadter, *American Political Tradition*, p. 342; cf., Freidel, *The New Deal*, p. 20.

64 Roosevelt's annual message to the Congress on January 4, 1939, *FDR Papers*, VIII, 7.

65 Fiorello LaGuardia to James Byrnes, April 5, 1939, Box 2584, LaGuardia Papers, Municipal Archives, New York City.

66 Hopkins, "The Future of Relief," *New Republic*, XC (February 10, 1937), 8.

67 Tugwell, *The Stricken Land* (Garden City, N.Y., 1947), p. 681.

68 Roosevelt's speech of January 4, 1935, *FDR Papers*, IV, 19.

69 Hopkins, "Federal Emergency Relief," *Vital Speeches,* I (December 31, 1934), 211.

70 Broadus Mitchell, *Depression Decade: From New Era Through New Deal* (New York, 1947), pp. 37–54.

71 Housing and Home Finance Agency, *First Annual Report* (Washington, 1947), pp. 24–25. Timothy McDonnell, *The Wagner Housing Act* (Chicago, 1957), pp. 53, 186–88, concludes that the Wagner bill would have passed earlier if Roosevelt had supported it.

72 Jane Jacobs, *The Life and Death of Great American Cities* (New York, 1963). Racial policy was locally determined. U.S. Housing Authority, *Bulletin No. 18 on Policy and Procedure* (1938), pp. 7–8; Robert C. Weaver, "The Negro in a Program of Public Housing," *Opportunity,* XVI (July 1938), 1–6. Three fifths of all families, reported Weaver, were earning incomes "below the figure necessary to afford respectable living quarters without undue skimping on other necessities" (p. 4).

73 Allen Kifer, "The Negro Under the New Deal, 1933–1941," (unpublished Ph.D. dissertation, University of Wisconsin, 1961), *passim.* The National Youth Agency was an exception, concludes Kifer, p. 139. For Negro protests about New Deal discrimination, John P. Davis, "What Price National Recovery?," *Crisis,* XL (December 1933), 272; Charles Houston and Davis, "TVA: Lily-White Construction," *Crisis,* XLI (October 1934), 291.

74 Robert Vann of the *Pittsburgh Courier,* quoted in Joseph Alsop and William Kintner, "The Guffey," *Saturday Evening Post,* CCX (March 26, 1938), 6. Vann had offered this advice in 1932.

75 See Eleanor Roosevelt to Walter White, May 2, 29, 1934, April 21, 1938, White Papers, Yale University; Frank Freidel, *F.D.R. and the South* (Baton Rouge, La., 1965), pp. 71–102.

76 Quoted from Senate Judiciary Committee, 74th Cong., 1st Sess., *Punishment for the Crime of Lynching, Hearings,* p. 23. Cf. Harold Ickes, "The Negro as a Citizen," June 29, 1936, Oswald Garrison Villard Papers, Harvard University.

77 Roy Wilkins, Columbia Oral History Memoir, p. 98; Lester Granger, Columbia Oral History Memoir, p. 105, complains that Wagner had refused to include in his labor bill a prohibition against unions excluding workers because of race. When Wagner counseled a delay, Negroes felt, according to Granger, that the New Deal "was concerned with covering up, putting a fine cover over what there was, not bothering with the inequities."

78 Ickes, "The Negro as a Citizen." Ickes had said, "since the Civil War."

79 Schlesinger, *Politics of Upheaval,* pp. 362–80; quotation from Tugwell p. 371.

80 Martin Dies, quoted by Burns, *Congress on Trial* (New York, 1949), p. 77.

81 The law raised standards to thirty cents and forty-two hours in 1939 and forty cents and forty hours in 1945. U.S. Department of Labor, BLS, *Labor Information Bulletin* (April 1939), pp. 1–3.

82 Arthur M. Ross, *Trade Union Wage Policy* (Berkeley, Cal., 1948), pp. 113–28.

83 Leuchtenburg, *F.D.R.,* pp. 346–47. The Bankhead-Jones Farm Tenancy Act of 1937 provided some funds for loans to selected tenants who wished to purchase farms. In 1935, there were 2,865,155 tenants (about 42 percent of all farmers), and by 1941, 20,748 had received loans. *Farm Tenancy: Report of the President's Committee* (Washington, February 1937), Table I, p. 89; *Report of the Administrator of the Farm Security Administration, 1941* (Washington, 1941), p. 17.

84 Roosevelt's Inaugural Address of January 20, 1937, *FDR Papers,* VI, 5.

New Deal Historiography: Retrospect and Prospect, OTIS L. GRAHAM, JR.

1 Jerold Auerbach, in an article in *The Journal of Southern History* in 1969, criticized in detail all New Left writing on the New Deal. Without necessarily agreeing with his judgments on individual authors, I am interested here in a more general critique of radical history as a genre. Briefly, however, I regard the writing of Wiley and Cohen as insubstantial, dismiss Gardner's book as not addressed to the domestic New Deal at all, find the essays by Zinn and Bernstein stimulating and important, despite disagreements with their total impact. Zinn is better on New Deal ideology; Bernstein has done more

research and provides a more comprehensive picture. The book by Conkin, *The New Deal,* stands by itself. In places Conkin seems to attribute New Deal failures — in which he is mordantly, mercilessly interested — to political and intellectual ineptitude, usually that of Roosevelt, whom he does not admire. But the book is pervaded by implied labyrinthine barriers, and at one place Conkin concludes: "The plausible alternatives to the New Deal are not easily suggested, particularly if one considers all the confining and limiting circumstances" (p. 106). The strengths of this brilliant little book lie in its too-brief probing of these circumstances. Its weaknesses, to which Auerbach extensively objects, appear when Conkin becomes impatient with the close study of alternatives and moves directly to condemnation.

SUGGESTIONS FOR FURTHER READING

Surveys of the New Deal period are legion, but the indispensable ones are William E. Leuchtenburg, *Franklin D. Roosevelt and the New Deal: 1932–1940* * (New York: 1963); Arthur M. Schlesinger, Jr., *The Crisis of the Old Order* * (Boston: 1957); *The Coming of the New Deal* * (Boston: 1959); *The Politics of Upheaval* (Boston: 1960); Broadus Mitchell, *Depression Decade* (New York: 1947); and the perceptive contemporary report, Ernest K. Lindley, *Half Way with Roosevelt* (New York: 1936). The conservative view is well represented by E. E. Robinson, *The Roosevelt Leadership: 1932–1945* (New York: 1955), and Raymond Moley, *After Seven Years* (New York: 1939). Criticism from the left came from Benjamin Stolberg and Warren J. Vinton, *The Economic Consequences of the New Deal* (New York: 1935), and Mauritz Hallgren, *The Gay Reformer* (New York: 1935). The contemporary New Left is fully cited in appraisals by Jerold Auerbach, "New Deal, Old Deal, or Raw Deal: Some Thoughts on New Left Historiography," *The Journal of Southern History*, 35 (Feb., 1969), and in Irwin Unger, "The 'New Left' and American History: Some Recent Trends in United States Historiography," *American Historical Review*, 72 (July, 1967). Its chief efforts have been by Brad Wiley, *Historians and the New Deal* (n.d.), Jacob Cohen, "Schlesinger and the New Deal," *Dissent*, 8 (Autumn, 1961), Lloyd C. Gardner, *Economic Aspects of New Deal Diplomacy* (Madison, Wisc.: 1964), Howard Zinn, "Introduction" to *New Deal Thought* (Indianapolis: 1966), Barton J. Bernstein, "The New Deal: The Conservative Achievements of Liberal Reform," in Bernstein, ed., *Towards a New Past* * (New York: 1968), and Paul Conkin, *The New Deal* * (New York: 1967). The seminal book for recent criticism from the left is William Appleman Williams, *The Contours of American History* * (Cleveland: 1961). A part of the old conservative position is kept alive, and vigorous, in the writing of the Chicago economist Milton Friedman. His *Capitalism and Freedom* (Chicago: 1962) is a brief and determined criticism of the liberal tradition, and with Anna Schwartz he has written *A Monetary History of the United States, 1867–1960* (Princeton: 1963) to argue, among other things, for a different monetary policy.

On Roosevelt himself, see Frank Freidel's three volumes of a projected six-volume biography, especially *The Triumph* (Boston: 1956), Richard Hofstadter's penetrating sketch in *The American Political Tradition* * (New York: 1948), James M. Burns' *Roosevelt: The Lion and the Fox* * (New York: 1956), and Clarke A. Chambers, "F. D. R., Pragmatist-Idealist: An Essay in Historiography," *Pacific Northwest Quarterly*, 52 (April, 1961). Leading memoirs of the period

* An asterisk following a title indicates that it is available in paperback.

include Moley's critical study, *After Seven Years*, Frances Perkins' *The Roosevelt I Knew* (New York: 1946), Marriner Eccles' *Beckoning Frontiers* (New York: 1951), and Rexford G. Tugwell's uniquely perceptive memoir-histories, *The Democratic Roosevelt* * (New York: 1957) and *The Brains Trust* (New York: 1968). The best biographies of important contemporaries are J. Joseph Huthmacher, *Senator Robert F. Wagner and the Rise of Urban Liberalism* (New York: 1969), T. Harry Williams' *Huey Long* (New York: 1969), Donald McCoy's *Landon of Kansas* (Lincoln, Neb.: 1966), and that combination memoir-biography, John M. Blum's *From the Morgenthau Diaries: Years of Crisis 1928–1938* (New York: 1959).

Many aspects of the New Deal have by now been given monographic treatment. These studies vary considerably in quality. On agricultural policy, the basic study is Edwin Nourse, Joseph Davis, and John D. Black, *Three Years of the Agricultural Adjustment Administration* (Washington, D.C.: 1937); effects of New Deal policies (and the depression) on the poorer farmers are illuminated in David E. Conrad, *The Forgotten Farmers* (Urbana, Ill.: 1966), and the pictorial study by Dorothea Lange and Paul Taylor, *An American Exodus* (New York: 1939); the frustrations of the liberals in AAA as they confronted the Farm Bureau and the southern bloc in Congress are appreciated by reading Conrad, or Sidney Baldwin, *Poverty and Politics: The Rise and Decline of the Farm Security Administration* (Chapel Hill, N.C.: 1968), or Grant McConnell's *The Decline of Agrarian Democracy* * (New York: 1969).

New Deal labor policies are studied by Milton Derber and Edwin Young, eds., *Labor and the New Deal* (Madison, Wisc.: 1957). A sympathetic survey is provided by Irving Bernstein's *Turbulent Years: A History of the American Worker, 1933–1941* (Boston: 1970). Also useful is Philip Taft, *The A.F. of L. from the Death of Gompers to the Merger* (New York: 1959), and Sidney Fine, *Sit-Down: The General Motors Strike of 1936–1937* (Ann Arbor, Mich.: 1969). On the importance of the war in breaking through employer resistance to the Wagner Act, see David Brody, "The Emergence of Mass-Production Unionism," in John Braeman, Robert Bremner, and Everett Walters, eds., *Change and Continuity in Twentieth-Century America* (Columbus: 1964). The literature on the economic impact of unionism is reviewed by Clark Kerr, *Impact of Unions on the Level of Wages* (Berkeley: 1960); a more recent study is H. G. Lewis, *Unionism and Relative Wages in the United States* (Chicago: 1966). On NRA, see Sidney Fine's important monograph, *The Automobile under the Blue Eagle* (Ann Arbor, Mich.: 1963) and Ellis Hawley's indispensable study, *The New Deal and the Problem of Monopoly* (Princeton: 1966). Hawley's book illuminates the relationship of the New Deal and the business community, a much neglected subject. Businessmen's negative reactions are examined by Thomas P. Jenckin, *Reactions of Major Groups to Positive Government in the U.S., 1930–1940* (Berkeley: 1945), and Robert E. Lane, *The Regulation of Businessmen* (New Haven: 1954). But one should also consult case studies of business interest in federal regulation, such as Paul M. Zeis, *American Shipping Policy* (Princeton: 1938), or Harmon Zeigler, *The Politics of Small Business* (Washington, D.C.: 1961).

The background to the Social Security Act is the subject of Roy Lubove,

The Struggle for Social Security: 1900–1935 (Cambridge, Mass.: 1968), and the
passage of the act itself is treated in Dan Nelson, *Unemployment Insurance: The
American Experience, 1915–1935* (Madison, Wisc.: 1969), chap. 9, and in Edwin
E. Witte's memoir, *The Development of the Social Security Act* (Madison, Wisc.:
1963). The regressive financing of the act is given critical treatment in an admirable monograph by Joseph A. Pechman et al., *Social Security: Perspectives for
Reform* (Washington, D.C.: 1968). This recent study reinforces many criticisms
made by Abraham Epstein in his *Insecurity* (New York: 1936, rev.). New Deal relief programs are given extended coverage in the National Resources Planning
Board's *Security, Work and Relief Policies* (Washington, D.C.: 1942), a volume
that conceals within its 640 pages of dull prose and charts a shocking picture of
inadequate public aid. The most imaginative relief programs under the New
Deal, rural rehabilitation and federal aid to the arts, are described in Paul Conkin's *Tomorrow A New World* (Ithaca, N.Y.: 1958) and William F. McDonald's,
Federal Relief Administration and the Arts (Columbus: 1969).

The conservative, bureaucratic outcome of New Deal experiments in the
Tennessee Valley is studied by Philip Selznick, *TVA and the Grass Roots* (Berkeley: 1949). One misses this perspective in traditional studies such as C. Herman
Pritchett, *The Tennessee Valley Authority* (Chapel Hill, N.C.: 1943). Pritchett's
study of the "Constitutional revolution" of the 1930s, *The Roosevelt Court* * (New
York: 1948), is indispensable. The story of the Court Plan is nowhere adequately
told, but an early hint of William E. Leuchtenburg's findings may be found in his
essay "The Constitutional Revolution of 1937," in Victor Hoar, ed., *The Great
Depression* * (Toronto: 1969). New Deal tax policies are surveyed in Randolph
Paul, *Taxation in the United States* (Boston: 1954), and the extent of income
redistribution that occurred over the 1930s and war years is estimated in Herman
P. Miller, *Rich Man, Poor Man* * (New York: 1964), and in Gabriel Kolko,
Wealth and Power in America * (New York: 1962).

On the New Deal and the Negro, see Bernard Sternsher's useful anthology
of essays, *The Negro in Depression and War* * (New York: 1969). There are few
book-length studies of racial issues in the New Deal years, but three indispensable
ones are Richard Sterner's *The Negro's Share* (New York: 1943), Dan T. Carter's
Scottsboro (New York: 1969), and Richard M. Dalfiume's *Desegregation of the U.S.
Armed Forces: Fighting on Two Fronts* (Columbia, Mo.: 1968). Raymond Wolters,
Negroes and the Great Depression: The Problem of Economic Recovery (West-
port, Conn.: 1970) examines the Negro under NRA and AAA, and the responses
of Negro leaders.

New Deal literature on politics is especially voluminous. Although no
good study of the entire Congress in the 1930s has yet been done, much may be
learned from James T. Patterson, *Congressional Conservatism and the New Deal*
(Lexington, Ky.: 1967). The left is the subject of Donald McCoy, *Angry Voices*
(Lawrence, Kan.: 1958), James P. Shenton, "The Coughlin Movement and the
New Deal," *Political Science Quarterly*, 73 (September, 1958), and Charles J.
Tull, *Father Coughlin and the New Deal* (Syracuse, N.Y.: 1965), and a forthcoming
book by Alan Lawson that will presumably bear a title similar to that of his doc-
toral dissertation, "The Failure of Independent Liberalism, 1930–1941" (Uni-

versity of Michigan: 1966). For the conservative opposition, one may consult the
Landon biography by Donald McCoy, Morton M. Keller, *In Defense of Yesterday*
(New York: 1958), a biography of James M. Beck, or a valuable recent contribution
to the study of anti-Roosevelt hysteria, George Wolfskill and John Hudson, *All
but the People* (New York: 1969). Samuel Lubell's *The Future of American Pol-
itics* * (Garden City, N.Y.: 1952) remains an unsurpassed survey of the New
Deal's political effects. Walter D. Burnham's article "The Changing Shape of the
American Political Universe," *American Political Science Review* (March, 1965),
reviews the long-range trends in voting patterns in America and finds that the
New Deal failed to interrupt the trend toward voter apathy and nonvoting. For
the New Deal impact on state and local politics, one must consult Harold Gosnell,
Machine Politics: Chicago Model (Chicago: 1937), and James T. Patterson, *The
New Deal and the States* (Princeton: 1969). There is also much good information
in George B. Tindall, *The Emergence of the New South, 1913–1945* (Baton Rouge:
1969). Case studies of the New Deal in several western states appear in the August,
1969, number of the *Pacific Historical Review*. Otis L. Graham, Jr., *An Encore
for Reform* * (New York: 1967), studies the political ideas and contributions of
surviving progressives in the 1930s.

The literature on the American economy in the 1930s is disappointingly
inconclusive. The results of the Temporary National Economic Committee investigations (1937–1941) are summarized in David Lynch, *The Concentration of Economic Power* (New York: 1946). Monetary policy is analyzed in Friedman and
Schwartz, already cited, and in G. Griffith Johnson, *The Treasury and Monetary
Policy, 1933–1938* (Cambridge, Mass.: 1939); fiscal policy is surveyed in E. Cary
Brown, "Fiscal Policy in the Thirties: A Reappraisal," *American Economic Review,* 46 (December, 1956), Seymour Harris, ed., *Saving American Capitalism*
(New York: 1948), and in H. W. Richardson, "The Basis of Economic Recovery
in the 1930s: A Review and New Interpretation," *Economic History Review,* 15
(December, 1962). Robert Lekachman examines the impact of the ideas of John
Maynard Keynes in *The Age of Keynes* * (New York: 1966), and Daniel R. Fus-
feld looks into Roosevelt's economic understanding in *The Economic Thought
of F. D. R. and the Origins of the New Deal* (New York: 1956). Murray N. Roth-
bard has published one of the few contemporary conservative criticisms of New
Deal economic policy, in *America's Great Depression* (Princeton: 1963); no less
critical, but slightly less ideological, is Herbert Stein, *The Fiscal Revolution in
America, 1931–1962* (Chicago: 1969).

The "broker state" theory and its application in the 1930s is appreciatively
described in John Chamberlain, *The American Stakes* (New York: 1940) and John
Kenneth Galbraith, *American Capitalism* * (Boston: 1952). Recent writers have
been more critical. Henry Kariel, *The Decline of American Pluralism* (Palo Alto,
Calif.: 1961), Grant McConnell, *Private Power and American Democracy* (New
York: 1966), and Theodore Lowi, *The End of Liberalism* * (New York: 1969), all
in varying ways indict modern liberalism for its assumption that the public interest would automatically be forwarded by the interplay of organized groups in
the struggle for federal favors. New Deal efforts to build up the "countervailing
power" (Galbraith's phrase) of unorganized or underorganized groups were of

insignificant effect, and the powerful government erected by well-meaning liberals in the 1930s was captured by strong groups who continued to dominate American economic life as they had since the 1920s and earlier. The economic consequences of the use of political power by corporations are described critically by Walter Adams and Horace Gray in *Monopoly in America: The Government as Promoter* (New York: 1955). A similar criticism of the New Deal for having failed to develop a sufficiently strong, centralized, independent government may be found in an important comparative study, Andrew Shonfield's *Modern Capitalism* * (New York: 1965).

For a more extended discussion of the literature on the New Deal, the reader should consult Frank Freidel, *The New Deal in Historical Perspective* (Washington, D.C.: 1965, rev.), and Richard Kirkendall, "The New Deal as Watershed: The Recent Literature," *Journal of American History*, 54 (March, 1968).